Housing and Poverty in Australia

Housing and Poverty in Australia

M. A. JONES

Research Officer

Department of Labour and National Service

MELBOURNE UNIVERSITY PRESS

First published 1972

Printed in Australia by Wilke and Co. Ltd, Clayton, Victoria 3168 for
Melbourne University Press, Carlton, Victoria 3053
Great Britain and Europe: ISBS Inc., London
USA and Canada: ISBS Inc., Portland, Oregon 97208

Registered in Australia for transmission by post as a book

ISBN 0 522 84022 1
Dewey Decimal Classification Number 301·540994

To

Anne Jones

PREFACE

An adaptation of a doctoral thesis submitted at the Australian National University in April, 1971, this book centres on a study of the State Housing Commissions; but it has more general application to attempts by governments to alleviate poverty. A genuine commitment to helping the poor can be taken for granted in Australia, especially since 1945, as is shown by the large sums allocated by governments at all levels to both direct income grants, in the form of pensions and the like, and to indirect help by such programmes as universal education, job retraining, and public housing. But, as the evidence presented here shows, this general commitment is not enough. The usual answer given by those responsible if programmes do not measure up to expectations is to claim that they are short of money, but here it is argued that with public housing the problem is not lack of funds but inefficient use of existing resources.

Things go wrong for a multitude of reasons. A decision to help the poor immediately raises the question of how, and there is a bewildering variety of possible answers, from encouraging general economic progress in the hope that its benefits will indirectly help the poor, through large-scale education, health, employment and housing schemes, to direct income grants. Public housing has, among these, enjoyed a high priority for a long time. It is clearly visible, tangible evidence of good intentions put into practice; on the surface it seems simple to ensure that the money spent benefits only the poor (where research into education and other programmes suggests that the higher the income of the recipient the higher the benefit gained from the system); it does not rely on the wisdom of the poor household's spending, and thus it prevents such frivolity as spending on alcohol; it is thought that the housing market is hightly imperfect so that the poor cannot obtain adequate housing without government intervention; and most important of all, because poor housing is thought to help cause all sorts of concurrent social evils from crime to bad health, it appears to treat both one of the discomforts of poverty and also the cause of many others.

Unfortunately, the last two of these theories have never before been questioned in Australia. They seemed too obvious. Research elsewhere suggests that they are false. People, it seems, do not become happier and better citizens immediately they are given new houses; and the reason that they cannot find adequate accommodation on their own is not only the fault of an imperfect market. Most of the problems associated with bad housing (above a certain minimal health requirement to keep the rain out) are not problems of housing in itself but of money; they are merely symptoms of low incomes. Yet the whole public housing programme is based on these invalid assumptions of causality. In fact, research also shows that strong and highly supportive social networks are built up in 'slum areas'. Meanwhile the Victorian Housing Commission has been knocking down the slums with great gusto (and expense, especially to the poor who live there) and a feeling of triumph over evil.

Another problem with social welfare programmes is that, in Australia at least, they are formulated and carried out by middle class groups who often lack insight into the needs and aspirations of the people they are dealing with. It is they who decide that the poor must be helped, and, in this particular case, that they must be helped by provision of better housing. Already a huge value judgment is being made by the policy-makers who assume, without reference to those concerned, that housing is a top priority with the poor. Value judgments occur frequently after this point, too, for example in the definition of what constitutes adequate housing. The poor may or may not agree; but, for the moment, the important point is that they are not consulted but have middle class values forced on them, sometimes with disastrous results.

Similarly, who is helped depends largely on the values of administrators. There is great stress in Australian public housing, in both word and deed, on helping those who are poor through no fault of their own and especially those who show themselves willing to help themselves by such virtues as thrift , cleanliness, and hard work. It could easily be argued that the latter group, especially the children involved, will survive by their own efforts whilst 'problem' groups will increase their problems and thus need more help. But this goes against the values of most Australian public institutions, and also denies them the chance of the 'good' results achieved by helping the most responsive clients.

Perhaps one of the basic problems, already hinted at, is the vagueness with which the aims of a welfare programme like public housing are often expressed. A stated objective like helping those 'unable to find adequate private housing within their capacity to pay' leaves open not only how they are to be helped but also the definition of the key variables 'inability', 'adequate housing' and 'capacity to pay'—that is, who is poor? No attempt is made to define the group, and yet poverty groups are so complex, with different needs and attributes, that no simple criterion is applicable and definition is a major task. There are real problems here because if social reformers who mount skilful propaganda campaigns for the adoption of a policy were to use highly qualified academic arguments there would be very little reform indeed. This was very much the case with the reform movement that established the Australian public housing programme. Oswald Barnett, a Melbourne accountant, was the key reformer, and although he showed elsewhere in his writings that he understood the tremendous complexities of the housing problem, his propaganda campaign used most successful, sensationalist techniques. The danger is that the politicians, the programme administrators or even the reformers themselves may come to believe the slogans. There is also the problem of time. Many operational problems in the public housing programme were not apparent when the programme was originally formulated. When families are in need of urgent assistance governments can hardly be expected to wait until the precise policy details are produced. This is no excuse, however, for not reviewing an ongoing programme. Earlier it was mentioned that commitment to alleviating poverty is evident among governments at all levels. Add to these the numerous voluntary agencies concerned, and the sum is a huge quiltwork within which it is very difficult to define functions and responsibilities. Many of the shortcomings of Australian public housing are in the long run the result of buckpassing and disputes within this complex framework, especially between the Commonwealth and state governments. Some of this could probably be avoided by a more rational division of welfare programmes along client, rather than government department, lines. At least some more specific assignment of tasks to organizations is necessary.

Most of the stumbling-blocks listed here could be avoided if the authorities entrusted with social welfare at all levels were more careful in defining their aims, means and client groups. This implies thorough research into each of these aspects. But it cannot be a once-and-for-all operation. Constant checks are necessary. Until public authorities stop seeing research as either an esoteric sideline or a fashionable whim of important pressure groups or a way of putting an intellectual imprimatur on an extant programme, little reform will be achieved. They must be ready to step back frequently and take a long look at what they are doing. They must have many and precise criteria for this appraisal: who gets what, why, and how efficiently in terms of cost, effectiveness, and consumer satisfaction.

Research into public policy is not easy because so many different factors are involved. On the one hand, it takes a knowledge of economics to understand the far-reaching economic effects a welfare programme is to have, a sociological understanding to comprehend the social effects, and so on. On the other hand, tackling isolated aspects of a subject in great detail is not much use to the man who must make policy and carry it out. Research will be useful to him only if it deals with his whole policy, putting it into context, tying all the effects together. This study attempts such a cross-disciplinary approach. There is little theoretical innovation and more stress on applying findings of the various disciplines to the situation studied. The influence of economics is clearest in the overall method of weighing the benefits of a policy against its costs. But when people are concerned the benefits and costs are not purely economic but must be measured in such terms as sociology, town planning, and political ideals, all of which must be informed by some knowledge of the problems of public administration. In a country where academic training is still overwhelmingly organized around the separate disciplines with growing specialization in each, there is a need for more emphasis on the cross-disciplinary approach in the social sciences. It is hoped that this book may show one way in which such an approach can be applied. Those who criticize cross-disciplinary research point out that while poachers often get the fattest rabbits, they sometimes are caught in traps, with drastic results.

The research on which this book is based was carried out between 1968 and 1970. Public policy is best studied at the point of interaction between client and administration, as there is a danger that there will be differences in policy between the upper and lower levels of an organization either through poor internal control or through vague directions. In this respect I was very lucky to be given open access to nearly all the records of the Commissions, who were very ready to face critical study. For this and for the unvaried helpfulness of the Commission officials I express my deepest thanks.

There are no footnotes in the book. Detailed references and justification for all statements of fact can be found in the original thesis, 'The Role of the Australian State Housing Authorities in Low Income Housing', copies of which are available at the Menzies Library, Australian National University, and the Baillieu Library, University of Melbourne. A bibliographical essay is appended as a substitute. The percentages in the tables have been rounded, and this is why, if added, the constituent items in some instances would not total exactly 100.

There remains only to thank all those whose advice and encouragement have helped me with this book, especially Dr Max Neutze of the Urban Research Unit at the Australian National University. Naturally responsibility for errors and omissions remains my own.

ABBREVIATIONS

CBCS	Commonwealth Bureau of Census and Statistics
CBD	Central Business District
CD	Collector's District
CSHA	Commonwealth-State Housing Agreement
NSWHC	New South Wales Housing Commission
QHC	Queensland Housing Commission
SAHT	South Australian Housing Trust
THC	Tasmanian Housing Commission
VHC	Victorian Housing Commission
WAHC	Western Australian Housing Commission

CONTENTS

1 INTRODUCTION

From 1945 to 1970 about 36 per cent of all new houses and flats completed in Australia were directly financed by governments on terms and conditions that made them much cheaper than they could have been obtained in the private market. The programme is so large that, by 1970, about 24 per cent of all existing houses and flats in Australia had been financed with large government subsidies. By 1970 a total of 850,000 subsidized units had been produced, 750,000 since 1945. These units would have a market value in 1970 of at least $8,500 million. Despite this huge expenditure, very little research has been done on the efficiency of the programme. This book attempts such a study. It asks two main questions: what sort of people have obtained the subsidized dwellings, and in particular whether they are the poor; and has the housing been supplied in the most effective manner? The subsidized dwellings have been supplied under a multitude of programmes. The biggest single group has been provided by the State Housing Commissions—they had completed about 360,000 to 1970, 310,000 since 1945 (about 16 per cent of total completions of houses and flats from 1945 to 1970). Although their aims are somewhat confused the vast majority of these dwellings have been provided under a general desire to help the poor obtain adequate housing. These state housing authorities are the prime concern in this book.

The War Service Homes scheme has also been very large, accounting for about 310,000 completions up to 1970, 265,000 since 1945 (about 13 per cent of total completions from 1945 to 1970). For war service homes (and co-operatives, discussed below) the term 'completion' is not strictly true as some of the houses financed from 1945 to 1970 were built before 1945. However, assuming that they are new completions helps to give an accurate view of the scale of the programme. The scheme was begun in 1919 as a reward for those who had fought in World War I. The demand for its services was continued after World War II and the Korean, Malaysian and Vietnam conflicts. In 1969–70 over seven thousand ex-servicemen were financed for home purchase under the plan. Any income group can obtain assistance, for the scheme was to assist the brave, who, of course, are not necessarily poor. The really poor probably do not benefit to any great extent. In 1971 the maximum loan available was $8,000 and almost all borrowers would require at least another $3,000 before they could obtain a dwelling. Second mortgages rarely go to the poor. While the scheme probably does not help the poor it is heavily subsidized; the interest rate in 1971 was 3¾ per cent over 45 years, very favourable conditions indeed. The War Service Homes scheme is not treated any further in this book: either you agree that ex-servicemen should be rewarded for their war service, regardless of objective economic need, or you don't. It is also a value judgment if you agree that most war service homes should be provided (as, in fact, they are) with little or no waiting time, in stark comparison with the very long waiting times for the State Housing Commissions supplying homes to the needy.

Up to 1970 there had also been about 50,000 (about 2 per cent of total completions 1945–70) subsidized dwellings completed under a motley collection of federal programmes: the development of Canberra and the Northern Territory; houses for defence personnel; hostels for migrants and for university students. Nothing further is said about these programmes which are better considered as sections of other policies: Canberra's growth; making the Northern Territory more bearable; rewarding the defence forces; and the immigration programme and university expansion.

In 1956 the Commonwealth government directed that 30 per cent of all funds advanced to the states under the Commonwealth–State Housing Agreement (CSHA) be diverted from the state housing authorities to the co-operative societies or, in states where there were no such organizations, to the permanent building societies and state banks. In fact, most of the funds have gone to the co-operatives. Up to 1970 about 82,000 dwellings had been provided under this scheme (about 4 per cent of total completions from 1945 to 1970). All of them are heavily subsidized. The terminating societies are discussed in chapter 7 but, generally, it is difficult to see how the co-operatives help the poor. They consist of non-profit-making organizations, set up by small groups of people who are often the borrowers. Since they usually need other finance sources in addition to the Commonwealth funds they are generally run by men of substance. Moreover, the lending terms, while having a heavily subsidized interest rate, require relatively heavy deposits and comparatively short repayment terms (about 30 years compared with about 45 years in the State Housing Commissions).

The Commonwealth-financed Aged Persons' Homes scheme has been another source of public housing in Australia. Up to 1970 36,000 units had been completed under the scheme (about 2 per cent of total completions from 1945 to 1970). The scheme was established in 1954 and provides a two-for-one subsidy to private bodies (non-profit) or local governments for the construction of dwellings for aged persons. Although they are so heavily subsidized very little check is kept to see that the units go to the poor. Indeed the basis of the scheme works against it: first of all one-third of the construction costs has to be provided and so it is normally the wealthier voluntary organizations—representing the rich—who supply the bulk of the dwellings. Belonging to a church organization or some voluntary organization is often the key to getting a unit. This scheme is discussed in chapter 4.

In 1966 the federal government introduced the Home Savings Grant scheme to promote the growth of home ownership. It offered a tax-free grant of up to $500 towards the purchase of a house at the rate of one dollar grant for every three saved over a three-year period. Smaller grants are payable on lesser amounts saved. It is payable only on the first marital home. In 1971 the grant would be paid only if the value of the house and land did not exceed $17,500, a sizeable sum, far exceeding the $10,500 for which the State Housing Commissions were able to produce cottages. The home savings grant does not really help the poor. It helps only those able to save the deposit for a home. Up to 1970, 174,470 grants had been paid out, a total expenditure of $75 million. Because of its small size, the home savings grant has not been included in the total public housing completion figures listed above. It is not treated any further in this book.

Rent control, established in all states during World War II, has been of considerable importance in Australia. In 1971, it was in operation in Sydney, Melbourne, Adelaide and Canberra. In Sydney the policy was limited to the rent controls that had been placed on dwellings in World War II. In 1967 there were about 45,000 dwellings rent-controlled in New South Wales, most of them in Sydney. Decontrol has been accelerated in recent years, and since the rate of return allowed on rent-controlled dwellings in Sydney is very low it is probably a major cause of poor dwelling maintenance of the controlled dwellings. Melbourne practises a current rent control policy and in 1971 had about 20,000 dwellings controlled. It is vigorously imposing new controls, and the rent allowed is generally below the free market level, thus encouraging poor dwelling maintenance and discouraging further investment in rental housing. The rent control legislation in Adelaide is pursued with the vigour and sense of mission that generally accompanies rent control but, although used as a method of encouraging rehabilitation of older dwellings, it probably has the classic rent control effects: restriction of the supply of rental housing and poor maintenance of the existing stock. Rent control in Canberra seems to be mainly an ineffective policy. Rent control is discussed in various parts of the book but the numbers of controlled dwellings were not included as part of the total subsidized units listed at the beginning of this chapter. The government does not subsidize rent-controlled houses. The landlord does.

Historical overview

A brief outline history of Australian public housing policy is given here since the general outline of the book is analytical and thematic rather than historical. The first official public enquiry into the housing of the low income group was instigated in 1860 by Henry Parkes. To its dismay, the committee set up found many of the appalling social conditions of the old world duplicated in Sydney. Although the enquiry found poor housing to be an important cause of social problems, it argued that the provision of housing was properly a task for private enterprise. It was not until 1909, in Queensland, that the first state government Act providing subsidized housing to the workers was passed. This marked the first of four main periods into which the history of Australian public housing naturally falls—1909 to 1930; 1931 to 1944; 1945 to 1955; and 1956 to 1969.

Between 1909 and 1919 all Australian states legislated for the provision of public housing, and all except Victoria actually built dwellings. The Commonwealth government also established a scheme for home ownership in 1927. Generally administered through the Commonwealth Bank or state banks, this legislation fell victim to the austerity of the depression from 1930 till 1940, and by 1942 only $2,870,000 had been advanced under the scheme. Up to the depression of the 1930s, then, all governments accepted the principle that some assistance had to be given to enable the worker to obtain adequate housing. But partly out of a desire to help the deserving poor who could afford some deposit and regular repayments, and to avoid the large losses that would result from housing those on the lowest incomes, these schemes were limited to those who could afford home ownership or high rentals.

From 1931 to 1944 a powerful housing reform movement arose. Large-scale unemployment and a drastic fall in the rate of construction of new dwellings helped to create the notorious slums most apparent in Sydney, Melbourne and Adelaide. Strongly motivated by religiously-based indignation at the widespread incidence of poverty, this movement forced the governments of New South Wales, Victoria and South Australia to launch official enquiries into slums. The reports of these enquiries formulated a comprehensive theory of public housing for those on low incomes. Everyone was regarded as having the right to adequate housing within his capacity to pay and this could be achieved only through the provision of housing by governments, a task involving large financial losses. World War II almost halted the production of new housing and added a new element of urgency to the housing problem. As a result of these two factors, public housing authorities were established in New South Wales (1942), in Victoria (1938), in Queensland (1945), and in Western Australia (1947). In addition, the existing authorities in Tasmania and South Australia accepted the emphasis on social welfare.

The Commonwealth Housing Commission was established in 1943 and its recommendations were the basis for the first CSHA, which was signed in 1945. This agreement provided large amounts of funds for the construction of public housing by the states, accepting the principle that this housing should be allocated to those on low incomes, regardless of the losses involved. Up to 1945, then, there were three interrelated conceptions of public housing. The first saw public housing as a reward to the deserving families who could afford home ownership. The second viewed public housing as a long-term programme for the alleviation of poverty, which would be necessary even when the temporary housing 'shortage' was overcome. This idea, at the basis of the reform movement in the 1930s, saw that the main problem was the low incomes of substantial groups in the Australian population. The third conception, probably the dominant one by 1945, was that public housing was largely a temporary necessity to overcome the housing 'shortage' caused by the cumulative effects of the depression and the war on the production of new housing. These three conceptions were to play important roles in the future.

The first CSHA imposed, until 1956, a considerable degree of uniformity on all of the states, except South Australia, which objected to various details of the agreement and did not become an effective partner until 1953, and Tasmania, which withdrew from the agreement in 1953 and did not rejoin until 1956. The terms of the agreement made it difficult for the states to sell dwellings. It also ensured that the available public housing went only to those on the lowest incomes. The states also continued pre-war schemes financed from their own funds.

From 1956 to 1969 many changes were introduced into the CSHA, reflecting largely the differences in political and social philosophy between the Labor Party (especially the federal Labor Party) and the Liberal Party. In 1956 the Liberal government introduced a number of new provisions into the CSHA which came into force in that year. They emphasized home ownership, and the details of the allocation of public housing units were left very much up to the states. As already stated, 30 per cent of all funds allocated under this agreement had to be diverted to the co-operative societies. This latter provision, together with the legislation in 1954 to encourage voluntary agencies to become involved in housing the aged, showed the Liberal Party's emphasis on voluntary organizations rather than state instrumentalities. Disputes developed between the Commonwealth and the states over who should bear responsibility for the losses involved in housing groups such as the aged. In this period from 1956 onwards, increased diversity developed between state policies, with one state—Victoria—placing great emphasis on urban renewal and other states, especially New South Wales and Western Australia, keeping to the spirit of the 1945 CSHA. Most states also continued their pre-war policies in this period.

The justification for public housing

Public housing in Australia can be justified on five main grounds. It is a means of supplying a subsidized good to those on low incomes; of removing the social costs that result from slums (areas of poor housing); of overcoming the inefficiencies caused by the imperfections in the housing market; of promoting the growth of state population by attracting a labour supply and industry; of helping to revive the declining central city (urban renewal); and of economic stabilization.

Public housing as a social service

From the early twentieth century to the present it has become increasingly accepted that Australian governments should provide social services to those unable to attain adequate standards of living without government assistance.

It was shown above that although public housing schemes were established in Australia as early as 1909 it was not until the 1930s that a powerful movement arose that saw public housing as a social service which would involve governments in providing housing to those in need and meeting all the resultant losses. These principles were incorporated into the CSHA in 1945.

Public housing is a favoured method of assisting those on low incomes. Two reasons are the social costs of slums and the so-called imperfections of the housing market, discussed below. But there is some evidence that a large part of the support for public housing comes from what might be called 'paternalistic altruism'. 'Altruism' is defined as the 'practice of unselfish concern for others' and 'paternalism' as the 'system of managing individuals in the manner of a father dealing with his children'. The religious feelings at the basis of the anti-slum movement of the 1930s were an important contribution. The driving force behind the movement in Victoria, Oswald Barnett, was prominent in the Methodist Church and the government Report of 1937, largely written by him, was very similar to his Master of Commerce thesis, University of Melbourne, 1931. In this thesis, entitled 'The Economics of the Slums', Barnett recommended that all babies born in the slums should be taken from their parents and placed in Methodist babies' homes. These religious feelings were reflected in the 1937 Report which claimed that housing conditions in Melbourne were of such magnitude that 'a Christian system cannot be reconciled with a society that continues to tolerate these appalling conditions'. Professions of paternalistic altruism are a constant feature of the literature on Australian public housing.

Public housing was seen not only as a means of redistributing income to the poor but also as a method by which lower-class life styles could be transformed into more acceptable patterns. Professor Irvine, University of Sydney, was sent overseas by the New South Wales government in 1912 to report on public housing in Europe and America. His report frequently condemned lower-class life styles and assumed that improved housing would change these patterns. This and other statements on lower-class life styles are what some term 'corrective', concerned with condemning and reforming the type of life style, rather than 'appreciative', trying to understand the positive, functional aspects of this life. With such views on lower-class life, those managing public housing policy were unlikely to place much importance on making allowances for consumer preferences and aspirations when formulating and implementing policy.

Paternalistic altruism is evident in a number of areas of contemporary public housing policy. The first facet—and possibly the most important—is the distinction between the deserving and the undeserving poor. Sections of the 'undeserving poor', especially 'Skid Row' men and other deviants, are consistently discriminated against in public housing policy. The favourable treatment given to home owners is another illustration of this, since those who can afford the added cost of home ownership are considered more worthy than those who can only afford to rent. Part of the explanation for the distinction between the deserving and the undeserving poor is probably to be found in the two conceptions of public housing referred to above—the short term and the long term. The CSHA in 1945 probably received widespread electoral support because it was not put forward as a solution to the more intractable problems of the slum dweller—the chronically poor who were the subject of the slum clearance movement of the thirties—but rather was directed at the group sometimes referred to as the 'submerged middle class'. This latter group had none of the attributes of a lower working-class life style and were the victims of the rapid social change, much of it causing downward social mobility, that characterized Australian society from 1930 to 1940 and was aggravated by the dislocation of the war. In 1968 the federal Minister for Housing, Dame Annabelle Rankin, said that the objective of public housing policy, and the social service system generally, was '. . . assisting those in most need whilst at the same time not discouraging thrift, self-help, and self-reliance'.

Another probable reason for preferring public housing to alternative methods for redistributing income is that the children in a family may gain more benefit from public housing than from the alternatives. There is some evidence, discussed below, that low income consumers do not spend their income efficiently. The various reports on housing conditions in the 1930s stressed that children were the most deserving of all the poor. As the 1937 Report in Victoria said on the effects of the slums:

> The burden falls most heavily on those least able to bear it. The women, who are unable to escape from their sordid surroundings despite their intense and heroic struggle to maintain a state of cleanliness, and the children, suffer most. These unwholesome conditions sap the physical fitness of the children and develop their mental processes along lines of abnormal quick-wittedness and the lowest ideals. In these areas there are thousands of children who are condemned by the circumstances of their environment to worse than physical death—to slow-warping influences of poverty, to filthy conditions, and to other evils and dangers which it is easier to imagine than enumerate. If slum reclamation by and through the State achieves no more than physical and moral salvation of the children in these areas, it will have more than justified any financial sacrifice involved.

Compared with other aids to the poor, public housing produces 'benefits' that are clearly visible both to the politicians and to those groups who object to the visibility of the slums either because of their conscience, because of their aesthetic values or for other reasons. These factors help to explain why public housing schemes and other aid-in-kind schemes such as medical care are likely to gain more political support than cash grants to the poor.

The social costs of slums

The idea that poor-quality housing causes various social problems, ranging from juvenile delinquency to poor health, has been an important source of inspiration in the initial formulation and continued implementation of Australian public housing policy. The provision of adequate housing under the public housing programme is thought to remove these problems. The Report of the Commonwealth Committee on Social Security produced in 1942 summarized these attitudes when it said:

> Slums are at once recognized as a prime cause of disease, crime and economic wastage and a lowering of personal and civic standards. We can never hope to eradicate tuberculosis while permitting sub-standard houses without proper ventilation and sunlight, and invaded by dampness to remain, or prevent child delinquency while narrow slum streets provide the only playground for children already housed in overcrowded, insanitary and unhygienic dwellings. Nor can we hope to raise the morale and self respect of the slum inhabitants while the slum psychology and environment exists. Only by providing them with healthy housing conditions and adequate living areas can we restore these Australians to proper living standards and wholesome family life . . .

Claims that poor housing causes social problems are usually supported by comparing the physical housing quality of an area with the incidence of various social disorders such as juvenile delinquency and ill health. Since areas of poor housing typically have a high incidence of these problems it is assumed that they are caused by poor housing. This reasoning is open to question since a causal connection cannot be drawn from correlations between two variables without testing for the possible influence of other variables. The most sophisticated attempt to isolate the influence of poor housing from other variables in this area was the Wilner study carried out in Baltimore between 1950 and 1960 (Daniel M. Wilner, *et al.*, *The Housing Environment and Family Life—A Longitudinal Study of the Effects of Housing on Morbidity and Mental Health*, Baltimore, 1962). Two samples were chosen. One was a test group of 300 families who had originally lived in a slum but had subsequently moved to a new housing project. The other was a control sample of 300 families who remained in the slums. Attempts were made to match the two groups on a number of demographic initial health and initial adjustment characteristics. The only variable that would distinguish the two groups was the change in housing conditions. The study showed that improved housing (about 60 per cent improvement) brought a very small (about 5 per cent) improvement in the general level of physical and mental health. Housing, then, did not appear to be an important variable in determining the incidence of various social pathologies.

Research into the causes of juvenile delinquency provides another illustration of the doubtful role of poor housing in causing this condition. A number of reports claim that poor housing causes the large numbers of juvenile delinquents in slum areas. However, studies of the causes of juvenile delinquency that use reliable methods find that it is caused primarily by the large gap between success goals and the means of achieving them in lower class subcultures. Schemes that substantially increase economic opportunity in these groups are likely to have the major impact on reducing the rate of juvenile delinquency.

Recent research in Mexico, Korea and the United States has found very little positive evidence to support the claim that improved housing improves health and labour productivity. This is true even though the groups studied experienced drastic improvements in housing conditions, from desperately inadequate and overcrowded (4.6 persons per room) housing to modern dwellings with many amenities. The studies were similar to the Wilner project in that they included a study of control groups in order to isolate the effects of the change in housing conditions. In contrast to the generally negative findings on the effects of the physical quality of housing, studies of the social environment in low income areas have produced extensive evidence to suggest that the degree of 'social integration' in an area is an important determinant of the residents' welfare. This is discussed in more detail in chapter 5 on slum clearance but mostly in chapter 9 on the social effects of different types of housing developments. Ironically, high-rise flats —a major form of public housing, particularly in Melbourne—may lead to serious health problems. This, too, is discussed in chapter 9.

Although the studies on the effects of poor housing are indeterminate, many people suspect that poor housing does have undesirable effects on health and general welfare. It seems so obvious that this should be so. In present-day Australia the debate has a number of important components. Firstly, in general, there is little desperately inadequate housing in Australia and, as the experience with the Victorian Housing Commission (VHC) shows, much of the argument in Australia on the effects of poor housing is based on much old housing that really is of quite good standard. Secondly, based on the frequent reviews that some of the Housing Commissions make of their waiting lists, the most important effects of inadequate housing on the families they declare in 'need' of assistance are the disproportionate share of income the family has to pay for housing and the degree of overcrowding. Many low income families obtain adequate housing in the private market in terms of physical quality, but it accounts for more than 25 per cent of their incomes, thus making their overall living standards unacceptable to society. Overcrowding is less common even by the very generous standards that dictate that children of different sexes should have separate rooms at quite young ages. If experimental studies have been unable to find clear effects of desperately bad housing they are unlikely to find many undesirable effects from the comparatively good housing standards that exist in Australia. What the strong supporters of public housing often ignore is that critics of the dividends from a public housing programme do not claim that the programme has no positive effects. But the benefits are inefficiently distributed and may be far less than, say, spending the same amount of subsidy on food, clothing, medical care, education, employment retraining, or social work services.

Special features of the housing market

It is often claimed that, because the housing market is imperfect, government intervention is necessary. If the housing market is highly imperfect this means that even families who can afford to pay the true economic costs of housing may not be able to obtain adequate housing. Recent research argues that poor-quality slum housing is largely the result of the low level of demand from low income consumers who cannot afford to pay for housing of adequate quality. According to this view—which has considerable, but by no means conclusive, empirical support—the housing market is very competitive. Although the housing stock, in aggregate, is heterogeneous, it can be analysed as if it is composed of a number of sets of housing units, each containing homogeneous units. Such a set of 'submarkets' may be distinguished by geography, type of dwelling, price range, or a combination of all three. These housing submarkets are sufficiently large to be regarded as fulfilling most of the requirements of a highly competitive market. There are many buyers and sellers of a relatively homogeneous commodity. The major empirical evidence for the competitive theory of the housing market is the extensive work carried out in the United States by Richard Muth. His studies of housing market behaviour over time have shown that the market behaves as one operating under competitive conditions (*Cities and Housing*, Chicago, 1969). Hence the existence of slums is not caused by imperfections on the supply side of the housing market but rather by the low income of slum dwellers. Because of low incomes, slum dwellers demand only a small quantity of housing services and landlords respond by supplying them with a small quantity of such services (poor-quality or overcrowded housing).

In the most thorough study yet of the operations of the private landlord, Sternleib found that private landlords in Newark behaved very much as entrepreneurs in a competitive market. He sees the high rate of return demanded by investors in slum tenements as a compound result of the fear of costly code crackdowns, the basic weakness of the market, both in terms of the possibility of rental increases and of securing full tenancy, the risk of outright loss through the complete abandonment of a parcel, and in substantial part the pejoratives which society heaps upon the 'slum lords'. All of these combine to shape the nature of the market in slum housing. Numerous British studies, while pointing out the imperfections in the private housing market, generally agree that government controls must take a large share of the responsibility for the unwillingness of private investors in Britain to invest in housing to any widespread extent.

On the other hand, those who argue that the housing market is highly imperfect point out that accumulating studies suggest that the low income consumer pays more for identical items than other, higher income, groups. This can be partially explained by irregularities on the supply side of transactions—misleading advertising, hire-purchase complexities and dishonesty by retailers. But there is some evidence that part of the responsibility lies in the peculiar consumer practices of low income families. Caplovitz found evidence of compensatory consumption in low income consumer behaviour. Summarizing the findings of his survey in *The Poor Pay More* (New York, 1963), he says that

> . . . it might be said that the lower class today are apt to engage in compensatory consumption. Appliances, automobiles and the dream of a home of their own can become compensations for blocked social mobility . . . He is trained by society (and his position in it) to want the symbols and appurtenances of the 'good life' at the same time that he lacks the means needed to fulfil these socially induced wants.

The poor are handicapped by a lack of knowledge about prevailing prices, due partly to their low educational levels. The partial validity of the 'poor-pay-more' hypothesis has a number of implications for this study. It may mean that public housing could not be replaced by a system of housing subsidies that operate in the private market. It also has relevance for measuring the amount that the public housing tenant can afford to pay for housing.

Neighbourhood externalities may be another source of imperfection. The housing consumed by a household consists not only of the dwelling itself but also of the surrounding environment, both physical and social. The quality of housing service associated with a particular dwelling depends on the quality of the dwelling and the amount of maintenance applied to it and also on the quality of other dwellings in the neighbourhood and the amount of maintenance devoted to them. For each property in the area, each owner obtains the highest return if his property is undermaintained while all or most others are well maintained. As a result of these factors all properties will tend to be poorly maintained. This situation could be overcome either by voluntary agreements among property holders to co-ordinate their behaviour or by the large private assembly of land in such an area.

It is possible that all the above arguments are complementary to each other rather than in conflict. Muth's empirical work is too highly aggregated to register the specific low income aspects of the housing market discussed—the influence of neighbourhood externalities and the poor-pay-more hypothesis.

Chapter 10 argues that what are often seen as illustrations of the imperfect private market are really symptoms of poor urban planning. The demand for housing is closely connected with the demand for land the supply of which is often very imperfect. The supply of land for residential and commercial purposes is closely connected with the provision of water, sewerage, transport, education and other services, many of which are poorly co-ordinated or in inadequate supply. The Urban Research Unit at the Australian National University is engaged in a research project on the 'Process of Urban Development' that to date has shown that the urban development process in Sydney and in Melbourne is far from perfect. Many commentators point out that the excellent quality of urban planning in Canberra is one of the main forces keeping land prices at reasonable levels compared with other capital cities.

Public housing may be more economical than private development because of economies of scale but there is little support for this claim. In his book *The Dynamics of Large Scale Housebuilding*, J. P. Herzog (Berkeley,

1963) found that any economies of scale ceased at around the 800 units per year level. Many private developers in Australia build more than this number. Hutton argues in his *Building and Construction in Australia* (Melbourne, 1970) that the quality of management seems to be the main variable in comparative efficiency amongst housing producers. Students of large-scale organizations, especially government agencies, stress the diseconomies of large-scale operations rather than the reverse. Moreover, those who argue that government enterprise can attain economies of scale in housing production often confuse it with the economies of planned developments—the coordinated supply and rapid use of water, sewerage and other services compared with the uncontrolled urban sprawl that we hear so much about. There is no reason why the private housing market could not reap the economies of large-scale estates if it were persuaded or compelled to build planned developments. A rational, orderly development plan like that in Canberra must make a developer's life much easier. From the frequent demands for such planning from Australian house builders, especially the larger ones, the government has yet to lead in this way.

Public housing and regional development

At various times in Australia, public housing has been justified on the grounds that it has assisted the development of particular areas: the non-metropolitan areas of the states; the state economy in general; and the inner areas of capital cities.

The development of the non-metropolitan areas of states has been part of an overall policy of decentralization of population away from the capital cities. It is thought that the plentiful supply of public housing in the country areas, compared with the capital cities, will help to retain and increase the population away from the capital cities. Assistance may also be given to the employees of particular industries which are desired in country areas.

The second way in which public housing has been used to promote development is by the provision of public housing to those groups who are declared important in the industrial growth of the state generally, without reference to the non-metropolitan areas of the state. The provision of low-cost housing for these groups is thought to reduce living costs and hence wages, and so to advance industrial growth by attracting desired industries and encouraging labour migration to the favoured regions. The literature on industrial location and migration supports the claim that the cost and availability of housing and the general environmental quality of an area are important factors in explaining development. But it also stresses the importance of the size of the market, transport costs, the availability of raw materials, and power. Area development policies are discussed in chapter 6.

The third type of policy that uses public housing as a form of regional development is urban renewal. Under this policy, areas in the inner suburbs of capital cities are demolished and redeveloped to higher densities. This is because it is thought that these areas are decayed and that it is more economical to develop them than new suburbs on the fringe of the city. This is discussed at some length in chapter 5.

Public housing as a method of economic stabilization

Public housing in Australia has sometimes been used as a method of reviving the depressed building industry and as part of an overall policy of economic stabilization. Full employment without inflation is the major goal. This was particularly popular during the recovery from the depression of the 1930s, when New South Wales, Queensland and Tasmania legislated for the provision of public housing with the dual aims of assisting the poor and boosting the building industry. In 1966 the Commonwealth government advanced funds to the State Housing Commissions to help to revive the building industry which was in a minor recession at the time. Academics have also suggested that slum clearance can be used as a countercyclical tool. No further attention is given to these matters in this book. Since 1945 there has been general full employment in Australia, and governments have a wide range of tools to combat depressions and it is not obvious that public housing is very suitable for these purposes. The gestation period for slum clearance schemes, for example, is so great—usually four years at least from initiation to completion—that it is of doubtful value as a countercyclical device, assuming that urgent stimuli are required.

Implications

Most of the points raised in the foregoing pages will be treated further in various parts of the book, but some of their general implications can be mentioned at this point. Initially it was argued that although public housing is regarded as a social service, it is selective in that it is directed to the deserving poor and, because of the upper income values summarized under the term 'paternalistic altruism', it is unlikely to be replaced by schemes such as cash grants that rely on the discretion of the poor. The feasibility of such cash grants, whether conditional on expenditure on housing or open, will be discussed in the concluding chapter.

The second section of this chapter argued that there is little evidence to support those advocates of public housing who contend that social problems are caused by poor housing. Rather, and this is discussed in greater detail in chapter 9, social integration is more important than the physical environment. This may affect the success of public housing developments that are mainly concerned with improving the physical quality of housing. While the presence of neighbourhood externalities suggests that some form of government intervention is necessary, the general findings that poor housing is largely due to low demand resulting from low incomes have important implications for attempts to raise the quality of housing. The claim that there are certain inefficiencies in low income consumer patterns has implications for rent policy—it affects how much the household can afford to pay—and for the likely effects of housing subsidies used to purchase housing in the private market. On the other hand, however, it could be argued that the prime factors, such as ignorance of market opportunities resulting from poor education, are just as applicable to the public housing programme. The private market probably provides more channels of information on market opportunities—through real estate agents and newspaper advertising—than do public housing authorities, generally not enthusiastic about increasing their already large waiting lists. Lastly, the area development activities of the Housing Commissions may be in conflict with other aims—particularly the aim of housing the poor.

2 STATE DIFFERENCES

In this chapter and in the next four, two main topics are discussed: the socio-economic characteristics of those who gain admittance to public housing under various schemes; and the policies which determine these allocations. The analysis looks at the supply of and demand for public housing, including the kind of public housing supplied, its location, and the allocation of that housing among different groups. This chapter deals with the general characteristics of the total supply of public housing in the various states.

The total supply of public housing in the states: new construction

At the present time, the state housing authorities have in their stock of dwellings few units that were built before 1945. Generally, unless otherwise stated, these pre-1945 units are not included in the figures on the total supply since most of them were sold and very few are available for re-allocation. By 1945 public housing units formed about 0.2 per cent of total houses and flats in New South Wales; 4 per cent in Victoria; 8.8 per cent in Queensland; 13.3 per cent in South Australia; 2.8 per cent in Western Australia and 1.6 per cent in Tasmania. Hence public housing up to 1945 was most important in South Australia and Queensland, and least important in New South Wales and Victoria, the states generally felt at the time to possess the worst housing conditions.

Table 1 shows public housing completions after 1945 as a percentage of

TABLE 1 Public housing units as a percentage of the total stock of occupied dwellings, at the population censuses, 1947, 1954, 1961 and 1966

Year	N.S.W.	Vic.	S.A.	Qld	W.A.	Tas.	Total
	%	%	%	%	%	%	%
1947	1	1	1	1	1	1	1
1954	3	4	9	3	6	4	4
1961	5	5	15	6	10	8	7
1966	7	6	18	8	14	10	8

Source: Public housing completions are taken from the annual reports of the Housing Commissions. The total housing stocks are from the census reports of the Commonwealth Bureau of Census and Statistics (CBCS).

the housing stock at the Census dates: 1947, 1954, 1961 and 1966. The table refers only to those public housing units completed since 1945. It will be seen that South Australia and Western Australia have built higher proportions of the total dwellings than the other states. Table 1 also shows that the two states with the largest populations, New South Wales and Victoria, have the lowest proportion. Other chapters will illustrate that these figures are misleading guides to the relative supply of public housing to low income families in the various states as they conceal wide differences in the socio-economic groups covered by the numerous schemes.

Because population growth rates since 1945 have differed from state to state, Table 1 does not accurately show the role of the Housing Commissions in construction. Table 2 presents the annual completions by the Commissions as a percentage of the total state completions. Public housing completions are generally accounting for a decreasing proportion of total completions, the trend varying among states. Generally, Table 2 repeats the findings of Table 1: South Australia and Western Australia have completed the highest proportion of dwellings and New South Wales and Victoria the lowest.

TABLE 2 *Annual public housing completions as a percentage of the total completions of houses and flats, 1945 to 1970*

Year	N.S.W.	Vic.	S.A.	W.A.	Qld	Tas.	Total
	%	%	%	%	%	%	%
1945–6	24	30	23	28	12	30	23
1946–7	18	20	20	30	10	7	17
1947–8	18	18	29	31	9	14	17
1948–9	19	16	29	32	11	9	18
1949–50	17	16	31	27	11	11	17
1950–1	17	13	27	24	12	16	16
1951–2	16	12	29	17	18	19	16
1952–3	17	15	40	20	22	17	20
1953–4	19	16	45	35	23	18	22
1954–5	18	16	43	32	25	19	22
1955–6	13	17	40	30	23	21	20
1956–7	13	12	41	22	26	19	18
1957–8	14	11	37	22	20	18	17
1958–9	11	10	35	20	20	15	15
1959–60	10	10	33	17	15	16	14
1960–1	9	8	32	21	16	18	13
1961–2	15	10	33	23	20	19	17
1962–3	14	8	28	26	18	20	16
1963–4	13	9	25	23	17	21	15
1964–5	14	9	26	19	13	21	14
1965–6	13	9	27	24	12	22	14
1966–7	12	10	30	15	10	20	13
1967–8	13	6	27	11	11	18	16
1968–9	9	6	21	9	10	20	10
1969–70	10	7	17	11	10	16	10
1945–70	14	11	31	21	15	18	16

Source: Annual reports of the Housing Commissions and CBCS.

A number of reasons can be offered to explain the wide differences in the importance of public housing in the various states. The state governments decide what share of their resources they will devote to expenditure on public housing. The Loan Council, in practice, allocates to each state an overall amount of loan money and, after this allocation, asks each state to designate within its allocation the amount it wishes to use for housing. These designated amounts are advanced by the Commonwealth under the CSHA at a preferential rate of interest: 1 per cent less than the long-term bond rate. A state, once allotted a total, can get more for works only by cutting its designation for housing. Each state uses a different proportion of its total allocations for the CSHA. The available figures reflect the low proportion allocated to public housing by the Western Australian, Queensland and Tasmanian governments and the comparatively high proportion by South Australia. In addition, the more populous states, New South Wales and Victoria, allocate comparatively high proportions of their total available Commonwealth funds to public housing yet they build smaller proportions of total dwellings built than the other states. This is because the Australian federal system favours the states with smaller populations. In 1969–70 New South Wales and Victoria received $115 per head of population from the Commonwealth while Queensland, South Australia, Western Australia and Tasmania obtained progressively larger amounts, Tasmania receiving $261 per head. The average for all states was $152 per head.

Considerable amounts of state funds outside the CSHA are also applied to public housing construction by all states except Tasmania. Victoria provides state funds only to subsidize slum clearance activities, and since this does not result in the construction of actual dwellings it is not discussed here although it is treated further in chapter 5. From 1945 to 1967 the New South Wales Housing Commission (NSWHC) spent $15.5 million of state funds on public housing; the VHC $20.7 million; the Queensland Housing Commission (QHC) $51.5 million; the South Australian Housing Trust (SAHT) $89.8 million; the Western Australian Housing Commission (WAHC) $41.6 million; and the Tasmanian Housing Commission (THC) $27.7 million. The figures for South Australia are somewhat inflated since the SAHT did not use CSHA funds until 1954 and hence the amount shown in the table includes the total funds used from 1945 to 1954. The expenditure of state funds by Tasmania was all during the period from 1950 until 1956 when the THC was not a party to the CSHA. In chapter 7 it is argued that the expenditure by Queensland has benefited mainly middle income groups, and a similar effect has applied in South Australia.

Vacated units

In addition to newly constructed dwellings, vacated public housing units form an important source of supply, but it is difficult to determine the precise importance of vacant units compared with new dwellings. Table 3 shows, however, the number of units vacated during 1968–9 in all states expressed as a percentage of the total allocations during 1968–9 and as a percentage of the total stock of rented units at June 1969. Vacancies formed an important source of public housing allocations in 1968–9 but there were large differences in the vacancy rate in the respective Commissions.

The number of vacant units available for allocation depends on many factors. Of course, once dwellings are sold they rarely become available for reallocation although the Commissions will generally buy back a dwelling where the purchaser wishes to relinquish his purchase contract (the effect of home ownership policies on vacancies is discussed in chapter 7). No Commission forces a household to leave if it improves its economic position while occupying public housing. Rent and home ownership policies discussed in chapters 7 and 8 encourage such families to remain in public housing, although the public housing 'stigma' discussed in chapter 9 may encourage these more affluent households to leave certain types of public housing. The discussion on the problem tenant in chapter 4 documents cases where the Housing Commissions obtain vacated units by the forceful eviction of tenants who do not fulfil certain standards of behaviour. Table 3 shows high vacancy rates for the QHC, the SAHT, the THC and the WAHC. The relatively high vacancy rate in the QHC is possibly directly related to the allocation policies discussed in the next chapter and chapter 8: rental housing is allocated only to those on low incomes and this leads to large concentrations of low income households in one area, a fact that may encourage those who improve their economic position to vacate the public housing unit. The THC sells a higher proportion of its units than any other Commission, rented units going mainly to those households unable to afford home purchase. This may lead to different types of households in THC rental units compared with other states and this may account for the relatively

TABLE 3 Allocations to vacated units as a percentage of the total allocations for 1968–9, and as a percentage of the total completions up to 30 June 1969

State	Vacancies as a percentage of total allocations—1968–9	Vacancies as a percentage of total public housing stock 30 June 1969 (rented units)
	%	%
New South Wales	49	6
Victoria	48	5
South Australia	70	14
Queensland	44	9
Western Australia	57	11
Tasmania	57	23

Note: All of the above figures are net numbers of vacated units, i.e. they exclude units vacated by families who move into another (perhaps larger) unit of public housing.
Source: Annual reports of the Housing Commissions.

high vacancy rate. It could also be that the Tasmanian population is more mobile than the population of other states.

The SAHT constructs a unique type of double-unit, semi-detached dwelling as the main form of rental housing available. These units are deliberately designed to encourage those who are in an improved economic position to vacate the units and find alternative accommodation. These double units, which are not for sale, are probably the basic reason why vacated units accounted for 70 per cent of total allocations in the SAHT in 1968–9, a much higher figure than in other states which typically sell a larger proportion of units than the SAHT. In 1968 the NSWHC conducted a survey on vacancies that showed how comparatively large numbers were forced to vacate because of unsatisfactory behaviour or their inability to care for themselves. The latter group consisted mainly of the aged.

Since an important influence on a household's desire to change its place of residence is the need to adjust the amount of space in accordance with the changes in the family life cycle, public housing authorities can help to determine the vacancies by their transfer policy, that is, the reason for which tenants can transfer from one dwelling to another within the housing stock. This will often increase the total volume of housing space made available. Although all Housing Commissions encourage tenants to exchange dwelling units if they are occupying a dwelling larger than they need, all express difficulty in actually implementing these moves. The problem appeared to be greatest with old people—particularly aged pensioner women, who have initially occupied a large, usually three-bedroom, unit and after the children have grown up and their husbands have died are frequently left alone in the house. A survey in Perth in 1966 found that about 3 per cent of dwellings owned by the public housing authority were underoccupied in this manner. All Commissions use persuasion to induce these people to move to smaller accommodation, but only the VHC withdraws the rental rebate if the person refuses.

Two important conclusions emerge from this chapter. Firstly, there are great differences in the supply of new public housing between the states, and the federal system in Australia is the one important reason for this since it favours the less populous states—South Australia, Tasmania and Western Australia. The special treatment that these states receive under Australian federalism can be severely criticized. There are only small differences between the states in income distribution, and one could well argue that the large metropolitan areas of Sydney and Melbourne have a case for higher revenues necessitated by the peculiar problems of large cities: traffic congestion and spiralling land prices, to name but two. Secondly, vacated units are an important source of supply for public housing and, like new public housing construction, supply proportionately more units in states other than New South Wales and Victoria. The analysis here has used very general statistics. The next four chapters gradually become more specific in determining the particular socio-economic groups who benefit from public housing policy in the different states.

3 MEANS TESTS

Since 1945 the waiting time for public housing units has generally been long, varying from state to state and between the different dwelling types. In the NSWHC it has rarely been less than three years and in the other states it has rarely been less than one year, particularly in the metropolitan area. Hence it is important to determine the groups who are in 'need' so that the available public housing can be allocated to them in accordance with the major objective of the Housing Commissions.

Those in need of public housing—general method

From 1956 onwards policy statements, especially from the Commonwealth government, have attempted to measure the level of housing 'needs' by matching the number of available dwellings with the number of households. From these an overall estimate of the 'housing shortage' is produced. Annual completions are compared with this shortage so that it can be judged whether the annual completion rate is overcoming the housing shortage, allowing for the rate of new household formation. While these methods can illustrate general trends in the housing situation they are open to a number of objections. They are usually highly aggregated, often on a national or a state basis, thus ignoring the geographic limits to any housing market, especially the possible differences between metropolitan and non-metropolitan areas. Nor do they say anything about the price households have to pay for housing or take account of the physical standards of the dwellings.

No attempt is made here to measure the general housing shortage by matching households with the number of dwellings. Rather, emphasis is placed on the capacity-to-pay side, since the inability to obtain adequate housing in the private market is a result of a low level of economic welfare. There are a number of indicators of the level of welfare, economic and non-economic. On the economic side, recent researchers stress the necessity to look at both the income and the outlay of a household's finances. This method takes into account all the various sources of household income: wages, salaries, income from assets and income in kind, including social service programmes such as medical care. It also allows for the differing efficiencies with which households dispose of their incomes. More importantly, perhaps, it considers the differences in budget needs between different households, especially the number of children in a family and the incidence of sickness or important costly events. The important non-economic characteristics include the stage in the family life cycle as a predictor of future income, and behavioural patterns such as the effects of non-western life styles (e.g. aborigines) and the life style of the problem tenant. These non-economic characteristics can also illuminate why certain social groups such as migrants wish to live together in particular areas.

This approach is adopted because it enables consideration to be given to the different housing needs of these groups. Housing needs may range from the highly specialized unit required by the physically handicapped applicant who needs additional services to the married couple with no children who would probably be content with a small flat in an inner area. Different social groups require housing of various sizes (number of bedrooms) and types (flat or cottage). The household's life style is also an important consideration since generally public housing is directed towards the more 'deserving' households without deviant life patterns or at least with a strong willingness to conform to more acceptable levels. In addition to focusing attention on clients' needs, differences between the social groups help to explain why public housing has favoured some more than others. Generally, the households can be divided into three groupings:

(a) those who can afford normal Commission 'economic' rents, do not require 'specialized' services, and are regarded as the deserving poor;
(b) those who cannot afford 'economic' rents, and/or need specialized services but are regarded as the 'deserving poor'; and
(c) those who are regarded as the undeserving poor, with deviant life styles marked by an unwillingness to pay 'economic' rents and a need for specialized reformist services.

The groups considered consist of families with dependent children, husband-and-wife households under 60, migrants, the aged, female heads of households with dependent children, the physically handicapped and those with unstable behavioural patterns (the problem tenants). The evidence about these groups relates to the recent past—1960 to 1970—with more emphasis on the emerging trends.

Information on income, housing costs and current housing conditions, especially the amount of space available and the physical quality of the dwelling and other welfare indicators, is difficult to obtain in Australia. The Commonwealth Census collects no relevant information about the quality of dwellings except the number of shared dwellings and the materials of outer walls. No information is collected in the Census about incomes or housing costs. The approach here is to concentrate on the socio-economic groups that have been shown, in a number of surveys, to be in poverty.

The means tests applied in the states

Each housing authority applies rules to applicants to determine who is eligible and who is not eligible for public housing. The analysis here refers to the low income schemes operated by the Commissions and excludes the home ownership schemes for higher income families operated by the SAHT and the QHC and the small programme of the NSWHC that builds dwellings for those who own their own land. It also largely ignores the criteria for allocation under the generally small 'area development' schemes discussed in chapter 6. Hence it refers to the general rental schemes of the QHC, the general rental and purchase scheme of the NSWHC (although the particular minimum income requirements for eligibility to purchase are discussed in chapter 7), the entire programme, excluding area development, of the WAHC, the low income schemes of the SAHT, all schemes of the THC and all schemes of the VHC (excluding area development).

The Commonwealth government has never stipulated very precisely what groups should receive public housing built under the CSHA. In the 1945 CSHA the Commonwealth required the states to allocate dwellings '. . . amongst persons who are in need of proper housing accommodation'. The 1956 Agreement required that dwellings built under the agreement should be '. . . primarily for families of low or moderate means and may be built in such localities and in accordance with such policy as the State deems fit'.

The NSWHC states that to be eligible for a public housing unit, an applicant must be unable to obtain adequate housing from the private sector within his capacity to pay. Hence, in establishing eligibility it asks income (weekly and over the last six months), family size and age structure, assets, liabilities and occupation. Generally, the Commission determines whether the applicant can afford private rental housing by asking whether or not he could obtain adequate private housing without spending more than 25 per cent of his income on rent. 'Adequate' housing is defined as dwellings that are of a reasonable physical standard in terms of lighting, ventilation, drainage, and other factors. The most frequently cited reason for a housing 'need' is that the household is unable to obtain a large enough amount of housing space within its capacity to pay. Overcrowding is defined as accommodation which does not meet the following minimum standards. One-bedroom accommodation is sufficient for a husband and wife, mother and daughter, father and son; or two sisters or two brothers. Two-bedroom accommodation is necessary for a husband and wife with one child, or two children of the same sex irrespective of age, or a female applicant with two sons and one daughter. Three-bedroom accommodation is necessary for husband and wife with two children of opposite sex or three or more children, and four bedrooms are required for a husband and wife and five children or four children where there is only one child of one sex and three of the opposite sex. For each type of applicant the NSWHC estimates the price of adequate accommodation in the private market and if this amounts to more than 25 per cent of income the applicant is declared eligible for public housing.

The lack of a fixed upper level of income beyond which the applicant is not eligible for public housing provides flexibility. Account can be taken of the size of the family, the long-term family income, as deduced from the occupation of the breadwinner, and the differences in the prices of private rental accommodation in different areas. All enquirers are encouraged to submit applications, and each year the NSWHC rejects about 11 per cent of applicants on the ground that they are able to obtain adequate housing in the private market at a price within their capacity to pay. In 1968–9, 67.3 per cent of applicants received under $50 per week gross income and 6.12 per cent received over $70 per week. Most of the latter are in groups such as country school teachers for whom alternative accommodation is often difficult to find.

After deciding what groups are to be housed, it is necessary to decide in what order these obtain public housing, since the demand for public housing by eligible applicants exceeds the supply and there is a 'waiting period' of about three years between the initial application and actual allocation. Until about 1963 the NSWHC allocated the group of applicants in most urgent need to the emergency housing centres, areas of low-quality housing originally constructed during and soon after World War II. When these centres were closed around 1963 (that is, ceased taking new tenants; they were not completely removed until 1965) the NSWHC established a committee called the Special Allocations Committee, comprising representatives from the Ministry of Housing, the Department of Public Health, the Department of Child and Social Welfare, and the NSWHC itself, to decide on priority allocations, that is, allocation before an applicant's turn was reached on the waiting list. In 1968–9 a total of 185 people in the Sydney metropolitan area received these priority allocations, about 5 per cent of all allocations. The most common reasons for priority allocations were sickness, or some other reason for being unable to work.

Since 1957 the VHC has applied a means test to applicants based on weekly earnings. In 1970 the allowable maximum earnings for eligibility for a VHC dwelling was $70 a week income for families with up to five children and $80 per week for families with more than five children. Only the 'breadwinner's income' is taken into account and although gross wages and salaries are included no account is taken of overtime earnings or income of a working wife. Since the demolition of emergency housing in Melbourne in 1956, the VHC has given priorities only to those home owners whose homes are to be acquired by a government authority for public purposes, families with five or more children, and ex-servicemen. The latter two groups were granted houses in half the normal waiting times. The preference given to ex-servicemen, including those from the Vietnam war, appears to derive from the direction in the 1945 CSHA that 50 per cent of all units were to be allocated to ex-servicemen. The lack of a priority system except for the above groups may be less important because of the comparatively small waiting times for flats in the VHC. In 1969, the waiting time for flats was about ten months for two-bedroom units and eighteen months for three-bedroom units. The waiting time for a two-bedroom house was three years and for a three-bedroom house five years.

The allocation policy of the SAHT reflects the two basic aims pursued by the Trust—the housing of those on low incomes and the housing of those necessary for the growth of industry in South Australia. The second aim, called 'area development', is discussed in detail in chapter 6. It results in preferential allocations to upper income professionals who would not be eligible for public housing in other states. There were 54 of these special allocations in a 12-month period from 1 October 1967 to 30 September 1968. The only data available were on single-unit timber houses in the metropolitan area, the main form of rental housing allocated to 'key personnel'. Out of 208 allocations made during the above year, 54 were to people in the professional category. There is some evidence that these allocations are used by successful applicants only as a form of transitional housing until they obtain higher-quality private housing or middle income SAHT housing.

The SAHT in effect conducts two housing programmes. In one, low-interest money allocated under the CSHA is used to finance rental and rental purchase houses and flats. In the other, higher interest money obtained on the loan market is used for working capital and to provide second mortgages for a sales programme where first mortgages come mainly from banks. The higher interest money is also used for other purposes such as factories and shops. Although the SAHT has no official means test on either form of housing, most of those on higher incomes are diverted to the second programme, where houses at higher prices and of higher quality are available. This was stated in 1962 by Sir Thomas Playford when he said, 'We do not want to make housing more attractive to the detriment of home purchase. Home purchase is what we all strive to foster. If you allow people with big incomes to rent houses at very attractive rents they will never buy'. At the 1970 Housing Ministers' Conference, the general manager of the SAHT expressed similar sentiments when he said that the SAHT made

> . . . the rental houses not unattractive but very modest, and as they are basically in the industrial areas it is usually found that when the family moves up the social scale the attitude is, 'It is about time we moved somewhere else, to be among right-thinking people'. This idea of making sure that these rented properties are not mansions does have that effect. It makes sure that people just do not camp in low-rental houses all their lives when they can well afford to buy something for themselves, and we have found it better as an approach than the family income.

In dealing with the applicants who are not connected with any industrial undertaking, the SAHT relies mainly on the date of application, and about 5 per cent of allocations are out of waiting-time priority. Deserted wives and similar groups have to wait only half the normal waiting time. However, the system is probably more flexible than in other states, since the SAHT keeps waiting lists for separate areas and tends to send urgent cases desiring priority allocation to areas such as Elizabeth, where the waiting time may be quite short in any case.

The SAHT constructs four types of housing. The first type is for those on low incomes and is called the double unit. It consists of low-cost, semi-detached dwellings of standard design which cannot be purchased. The second type is a dwelling of higher quality and cost than a double unit, termed the single-unit rental-purchase. Most of these have been built since 1964 and can be purchased on a low deposit. The third type is the cottage flat, a low-cost flat for the aged, usually pensioners. The fourth type is other flats intended for unmarried persons or married persons without young children. These flats are not intended for those unable to pay economic rents. This latter point is expanded in chapter 4.

Allocation policy in Queensland connects the general means test and the order in which the applicants are housed so closely that they are treated together. The QHC separates all applicants into the categories shown in Table 4 and gives a certain number of 'points' to each group. This table shows that few applicants get the highest number of points while many more receive a small number of points indicating that they are in less need. The column headed 'Applications received 1964–5' shows the classification applied to applications received during that year. The column headed 'Applications on hand at 30 April 1969' shows the stock of applications at that date, classified according to their degree of need. There is no direct income test in the QHC like that in the VHC.

Table 4 shows the channelling effect that this type of allocation system has. Those with more than 60 points get almost immediate entry into public housing while those with less than 60 points have to wait considerably

TABLE 4 Applications to the QHC—degree of need

Priority rating	'Live' applications from families	Applications received 1964–5	Applications on hand at 30 April 1969
		%	%
A '100'	Facing ejectment from present dwelling or homeless	18	3
B '100'	Living in tents, huts or similar accommodation		
C '80'	Living in other premises:		
	(a) condemned by local authority	—	—
	(b) considered by Commission unsuitable for occupation or requiring major repairs	—	1
D '60'	Separated owing to lack of accommodation	6	2
E '40'	Living under overcrowded conditions	40	35
F '40'	Sharing houses with other people		
G 'nil'	Adequately housed and not facing ejectment	36	52
—	Other	—	5
	Total live applications	2,322	5,285

Source: Document entitled *Queensland Housing Commission Rental Applications on Hand Metropolitan 30.4.69 and Country 31.3.69*. The figures for the financial year 1964–5 are from the reply to a question in Parliament, *Queensland Parliamentary Debates*, vol. 241, 1965, p. 171.

longer. In the year 1964–5 the QHC had a total of 932 dwellings available for allocation to rental applicants. Of these, 283 were offered to applicants who had applied before 1964–5, presumably those with 40 points, and the remainder were offered to 1964–5 applicants, those with a high number of points. Table 4 also shows the large number of applicants classed as 'adequately housed', a group who are not likely to be offered public housing.

Since 1956 the WAHC has applied a means test in the form of a maximum income limit. In 1970 the limit for eligibility was $2,799.78 per annum in the metropolitan area, $3,311.89 in the country and $4,378.89 north of the 26th parallel. Each dependent child under 21 in the family raised these income limits by $100. Like the other Commissions, the WAHC takes the gross income of the breadwinner only. In addition to being within these income limits eligible applicants have to prove that they are unable to obtain adequate housing in the private sector, so each applicant is visited by a housing officer. The definitions of adequate housing are the same as those used in the NSWHC described above.

In 1968–9 priority allocations accounted for about 30 per cent of the total WAHC allocations in the Perth metropolitan area. Although there is no formal 'points' system, a general comparison of the different levels of need similar to Queensland's system is used so that preference is given to those living in the worst housing, with the lowest per capita incomes and dependent on social services and/or suffering from illnesses or marital problems such as desertion. The waiting time for these priority cases varied from a few weeks to about half the normal waiting time of around three years.

The THC does not specify any upper income limit for eligibility for its dwellings. The determination of eligibility is similar to the NSWHC's, attention being given to the income, family size, current housing and other such factors. Up to 1968 the THC separated all applicants into A and B categories. Applicants in category A, usually about 50 per cent of the total, were given priority access to public housing, usually after waiting periods from three weeks to six months. Applicants in category B were allocated houses in order of their date of application, making their waiting times about twice those of the category A applicants. Applicants were placed in the A category for similar reasons to those adopted in the QHC—eviction orders, family divided, severe overcrowding, ill health and other factors. In 1968, the policy was changed to place more emphasis on waiting time as a criterion for allocation and only about 10 per cent of allocations are now made out of priority order.

The socio-economic status of public housing areas 1966 Census

This section attempts to measure the socio-economic status of public housing areas and, where possible, to measure the effects of the different allocation policies outlined above. The basic source of information is the

1966 Census. Ideally one would require information on income, assets, life styles and so on, but the Australian Census contains little of this information. Three measures were selected as indicators of socio-economic status: occupation; education; and motor vehicle ownership. Other useful classifications are birthplace, age structure, marital status and type of dwelling.

The smallest geographic area in the Census for which data are available is the Collector's District (CD), usually containing about 300 dwellings. Maps from the housing authorities enabled all CD areas that consisted completely of public housing units to be listed. Since the Commissions generally do not construct large estates outside the metropolitan area, the analysis is limited to metropolitan areas. The WAHC mixes war service homes and private dwellings with its public housing units so that an analysis of WAHC areas using information from CD areas is not possible. In all, the 219 CDs contained a total of 234,318 people (NSWHC, 51,037; VHC, 92,717; SAHT, 55,514; QHC, 19,158; THC, 15,892). Limiting the analysis to public housing areas that were completed CDs does involve some bias. It means that smaller, scattered public housing estates were not included, but this has not led to any important historical bias, since the Commissions generally have built large estates throughout their history.

The CD areas do not contain a perfectly representative sample of public housing completions at the 1966 Census. The main source of distortion is the comparatively high proportion of flats in the Sydney CD public housing areas (29 per cent compared with the NSWHC total of 19 per cent) and the comparatively small proportion of flats in Melbourne CD public housing areas (16 per cent compared with the VHC total of 24 per cent). In various other areas the CD data can be the source of bias. For example, in the QHC, a major, middle income public housing scheme is deliberately scattered throughout the metropolitan area so that none of these units is included in the CD data (they are not built in normal public housing areas). This type of bias is pointed out in the relevant parts of the book.

The other major source of information is that for households who were renting public housing units at the 1966 Census. This information is for the households' heads only and cannot be directly compared with the CD data which are for the total population. The CD data, of course, include many families living in dwellings that are being purchased from the Housing Commissions.

The 1966 Census CD data were available on computer tapes, and with the aid of the computer and manual compilation the information was reduced to manageable proportions. Occupations were available in 72 classifications grouped into these categories from 313 original classifications. They were grouped by the Commonwealth Bureau of Census and Statistics (*Classification and Classified List of Occupations*, Canberra, 1966)

> in accordance with the International Standard Classification, by the general similarity of the characteristics of the work they entail. The most important

feature of each minor group is that the occupations included are more closely related to each other than to occupations outside the minor group as regards the functions involved and the skills, knowledge and abilities required for satisfactory performance. Other factors taken into consideration in forming these groups have been material worked on, work place environment, use of specialized equipment, etc.

For easier interpretation these 72 categories were reduced to seven classifications. This was done by ordering the 72 groups in descending order of socio-economic status using the classifications developed by Broom *et al.*, 'An Occupational Classification of the Australian Workforce', *The Australian and New Zealand Journal of Sociology*, 1965. The only departure from this latter classification was the separation of members of the armed forces into a separate category. This was done because the Commissions supply housing to the armed forces under a special programme and the inclusion of armed forces under another category could have been misleading.

The classifications used for other characteristics are more straightforward except perhaps for marital status and education. For marital status the CD information was for the total population including children who were classified under the 'never married'. This tends to make age composition the main determinant of marital status and hence the marital status information is restricted to those who have at some time been married, that is, the married, the married but permanently separated, the divorced and the widowed. Cross-classification data show that only a very small percentage of public housing household heads are in the never-married category, so this has probably involved little bias. The information on education was also applicable to the total population including children not at school and full-time students. These figures were adjusted by subtracting the number of children not at school from the group listed under 'nil' education, subtracting 30 per cent of the full-time students from the 'attended high school' figure and subtracting 70 per cent of the full-time students from the 'attended primary school' figure. (These were the proportions in New South Wales in 1966.)

This section contains an analysis of the characteristics of the totals of the public housing CDs for each metropolitan area. They include home ownership areas as well as rental, although they do not include the QHC middle income workers' dwellings discussed in chapter 7. People living in these areas are compared with the totals for the metropolitan areas. Information on marital status, age distribution and birthplace for these areas is presented in chapter 4. The objective here is to measure the general socio-economic differentials between Commission and other areas and between Commission areas in different states.

Tables 5, 7 and 9 present the characteristics of the CD areas that consist entirely of public housing developments. Tables 5 and 6 show that public housing areas are of a lower occupational status than the metropolitan averages. Public housing areas have from 12 per cent (NSWHC) to 20 per cent (SAHT) of their workforce in the first two occupational classifications (professional and managerial and self-employed) compared with the metropolitan averages of between 24 per cent and 27 per cent.

The 'professional' category in the occupational classification includes doctors, dentists and lawyers, as well as teachers. Most of the 'professionals' in public housing are teachers and similar lower level professionals. Teachers are not in the highest income groups in Australian society but it is doubtful if they are in the bottom 10 per cent. It has to be kept in mind that, on average, only about 10 per cent of the Australian population are public housing residents so it is very important that public housing be allocated to the bottom 10 per cent of society. Those poor not in the workforce and in need of housing assistance (the aged, female households with dependent children, single men, aborigines, etc.) account for at least 10 per cent of the population, and the two bottom occupational classifications (shop assistants and process workers, and personal, domestic and other service workers and labourers) account for around 30 per cent of the workforce.

Public housing also has a considerable proportion of its workforce population in the third, fourth and fifth occupational classifications. Public

TABLE 5 Occupations of the workforce in metropolitan public housing CD areas (per cent of total), 1966 census

Occupation	Sydney	Melbourne	Adelaide	Brisbane	Hobart
	%	%	%	%	%
Professional	4	4	9	4	4
Managerial, self-employed	8	9	11	9	10
Clerical workers	19	20	18	18	17
Armed forces	2	1	2	3	—
Craftsmen, foremen	18	18	24	18	16
Shop assistants and process workers	30	29	21	28	28
Personal, domestic, service workers and labourers	17	17	14	19	22

Source: Compiled from summary data supplied by the Commonwealth Statistician (Collectors' District data for the total population).

TABLE 6 Occupations of the workforce in metropolitan areas (per cent of total), 1966 census

Occupation	Sydney	Melbourne	Adelaide	Brisbane	Hobart
	%	%	%	%	%
Professional	11	11	12	11	14
Managerial, self-employed	13	13	14	13	13
Clerical workers	23	21	21	24	24
Armed forces	1	1	1	2	—
Craftsmen, foremen	16	15	19	14	14
Shop assistants and process workers	21	22	17	18	17
Personal, domestic, service workers and labourers	14	14	15	16	16

Source: Compiled from summary data supplied by the Commonwealth Statistician (Collectors' District data for the total population).

housing areas have about 4 per cent lower than the average proportion of the workforce in the 'clerical' category and about 3 per cent above average in the craftsmen and foremen group. All Commissions except the SAHT have about 3 per cent above average in the last occupational classification: personal, domestic and other service workers. The most significant difference between the Commissions is the much higher socio-economic status of SAHT areas. These differences are shown very clearly in the tables.

The educational data in Table 7 show that, apart from the SAHT, only about 1 per cent of the occupants of public housing units have attended university or other tertiary institutions, suggesting that those in group one in the occupational classification (professional) are in the lower levels within this group, since many of the upper levels would hold university or other tertiary qualifications. Generally, the educational data verify the occupational information: those in public housing in 1966 were not markedly less well educated than the metropolitan averages. Substantial proportions—ranging from about 50 per cent in the QHC to about 75 per cent in the NSWHC—were high school standard or above, and the public housing tenants were only slightly over-represented in the 'attended primary

TABLE 7 *Education of the population (excluding children not at school and full-time students) in metropolitan public housing CD areas (per cent of total), 1966 census*

	Sydney	Melbourne	Adelaide	Brisbane	Hobart
	%	%	%	%	%
University qualifications	—	—	1	—	—
Other tertiary qualifications	1	1	2	1	1
Matriculation passed	5	8	11	5	9
Intermediate passed	29	16	24	24	23
Attended high school	39	35	32	18	34
Attended primary	23	37	29	50	30
No education	1	1	1	—	1
Not stated	2	2	2	2	2

Source: Compiled from summary data supplied by the Commonwealth Statistician (Collectors' District data for the total population).

TABLE 8 *Education of the population (excluding children not at school and full-time students) in metropolitan areas (per cent of total), 1966 census*

	Sydney	Melbourne	Adelaide	Brisbane	Hobart
	%	%	%	%	%
University qualifications	2	2	2	2	2
Other tertiary qualifications	3	3	3	3	3
Matriculation passed	11	15	12	8	19
Intermediate passed	33	20	21	26	21
Attended high school	26	25	23	18	25
Attended primary	20	32	35	40	25
No education	1	1	1	—	—
Not stated	3	3	3	3	3

Source: Compiled from summary data supplied by the Commonwealth Statistician (Collectors' District data for the total population).

school' classification, when compared with the metropolitan average. The educational data are possibly misleading: there are many differences between Australian state education systems and between educational levels in different historical periods. But it does provide a general indicator.

The educational data in Table 7 are slightly overrated when compared with the metropolitan average. Educational standards have risen dramatically with time, and since the public housing population is substantially younger than the metropolitan average they are likely to be better educated than if they were compared with their particular age group.

Table 9 on motor vehicle ownership in public housing areas shows that

TABLE 9 Motor vehicle ownership in metropolitan public housing CD areas, number of vehicles per occupied private dwelling (per cent of total), 1966 census

No. of vehicles per dwelling	Sydney	Melbourne	Adelaide	Brisbane	Hobart
	%	%	%	%	%
HOUSES					
None	31	26	16	25	26
One	57	53	65	58	58
Two	10	15	16	12	12
Three +	—	3	3	2	3
Not stated	2	2	1	2	1
FLATS					
None	61	57	56	32	71
One	32	34	31	68	24
Two	3	3	6	—	—
Three +	—	—	—	—	—
Not stated	5	6	6	1	5

Source: Compiled from summary data supplied by the Commonwealth Statistician (Collectors' District data for the total population).

TABLE 10 Motor vehicle ownership in metropolitan areas, number of vehicles per occupied private dwelling (per cent of total), 1966 census

No. of vehicles per dwelling	Sydney	Melbourne	Adelaide	Brisbane	Hobart
	%	%	%	%	%
HOUSES					
None	26	24	20	24	22
One	51	51	55	54	54
Two	17	19	19	17	18
Three +	4	4	5	3	4
Not stated	2	2	1	2	2
FLATS					
None	42	39	40	38	38
One	44	47	48	47	47
Two	7	8	7	8	8
Three +	3	1	—	2	—
Not stated	4	5	5	5	6

Source: Compiled from summary data supplied by the Commonwealth Statistician (Collectors' District data for the total population).

although substantial proportions of Housing Commission householders have one motor car, comparatively few have more than one (when compared with the metropolitan averages shown in Table 10). Motor vehicle ownership is only a very indirect indicator of socio-economic status: low income households could spend disproportionate shares of their incomes on car ownership and the data do not tell us the value of the vehicles.

The NSWHC areas in Tables 5, 7 and 9 contained 12,219 dwellings and 51,037 people; 71 per cent of the dwellings were cottages, 29 per cent flats; of the cottages, 55 per cent were sold. The VHC areas (Melbourne) contained 24,877 dwellings and 92,717 people; 84 per cent of the dwellings were cottages and 16 per cent flats; of the cottages 49 per cent were sold. The SAHT areas (Adelaide) contained 13,293 dwellings and 55,514 people; 98 per cent of the dwellings were cottages and 2 per cent flats; of the cottages 45 per cent were sold. The QHC areas (Brisbane) contained 4,170 dwellings and 19,158 people; 98 per cent of the dwellings were cottages and 2 per cent flats; of the cottages 32 per cent were sold. The THC areas (Hobart) contained 3,789 dwellings and 15,892 people; 98 per cent of the dwellings were cottages and 2 per cent flats; of the cottages 47 per cent were sold.

While the CD data provide an interesting analysis of Australian public housing at the 1966 Census, care has to be exercised in explaining why the socio-economic status of the public housing areas is so comparatively high. One explanation is that the various state allocation policies, among them the vague 'means' tests discussed in this chapter, allow a wide range of income groups access to public housing. However, rather than concentrating on the initial entry process, one could emphasize the policies towards the client once he is admitted to public housing. These policies are discussed later but, generally, once a householder has gained entry into public housing he will not be penalized if he improves his socio-economic status. Indeed, chapter 7 shows that very attractive schemes exist enabling the householder to purchase the public housing unit after initially being a tenant—he can purchase regardless of his income—and chapter 8 shows that many tenants of older public housing units are not penalized if their incomes rise and often pay lower rents than more recent tenants.

In chapter 7 there is also a discussion of the degree of upward social mobility in public housing. In the absence of other data, the CD information was analysed to determine the differences between public housing occupied at different times. Exceptions are discussed in chapter 7, but there were very few differences in the socio-economic status of public housing areas built at different times. The reasons for this must remain a matter for speculation although some are suggested elsewhere. Perhaps the comparatively low standard of public housing units encourages those who improve their socio-economic status to vacate and obtain better dwellings. The 'stigma' attached to the occupation of a public housing unit may also play a role here. Possibly there is not much intragenerational social mobility in Australia, particularly among those in public housing.

4 POVERTY GROUPS

The supply of public housing to the socio-economic groups mentioned in the previous chapter is discussed here. Three broad divisions are taken. The first group consists of married couples with dependent children, married couples without dependent children (non-aged), and overseas migrants. These three types of families are able to pay reasonably high rents so that the Commissions can house them without making losses under the financial arrangement described in chapter 8. In addition, many of them would be able to purchase their dwellings, which is also important to the Commissions since sales usually produce profits. Members of this group have no abnormal behavioural characteristics that would classify them as 'problem tenants' and require only services normally available in the neighbourhood: schools, shops and so on.

The second and third groups normally involve the Commissions in heavy losses since they are only able to pay a lower rent than the first group and are virtually unable to purchase units. The second group consists of the aged, the physically handicapped and female householders with dependent children. Both the second and third groups require, in varying degrees, specialized services, ranging from the intricate design of houses for the physically handicapped to the extensive supportive services needed for the aged. Since the Commissions are unable to provide these specialized services in any volume, there are serious problems here.

The distinguishing characteristic of the third group is that they are generally held to be undeserving of assistance, since they often have deviant life styles usually reflected in their failure to pay rent to the Commissions. This group consists of 'problem tenants' in general, two specific cases of whom are single men and aborigines. These social groups, of course, are likely to be overlapping in real life—a migrant family, for example, could also be a problem tenant—but this chapter should illuminate the main issues. Generally two questions are discussed in each section: the important characteristics of the group under discussion, especially their current 'need' for housing assistance; and the extent to which the Commissions have assisted them to date.

The deserving poor able to pay economic rents

The major source of information on poverty in Australia is the survey carried out by the Institute of Applied Economic and Social Research,

University of Melbourne in 1966, the findings of which are summarized in Table 11. Perhaps the most significant finding of the survey is the large numbers of the aged in poverty. Female householders with dependent children and the general (no disability) groups also contribute heavily to the poverty group. The survey did not include those living in lodging houses, thus probably underestimating single men in poverty, and since there are comparatively few aborigines in Melbourne these two groups are among the poor under-represented in Table 11.

TABLE 11 Adult income units classified by disability showing percentage in each adjusted income class. Disabilities defined on a mutually exclusive basis, unknown incomes omitted, Melbourne poverty survey, 1966

Disability	Percentage of total poverty ($0–33) group	Adjusted income ($)				
		0–27 Very poor	27–33 Poor	33–39 Marginal	39 and over Not poor	All classes
	%	%	%	%	%	
Aged male head only	13	10.2	3.5	22.5	63.8	100.0
Female head only	12	5.9	3.3	2.4	88.4	100.0
Fatherless family only	6	18.4	11.3	13.8	56.5	100.0
Large family only	6	1.2	7.2	13.9	77.7	100.0
Recent migrant only	1	1.3	0.3	3.0	95.4	100.0
Sickness or accident only	3	4.9	5.5	8.5	81.1	100.0
Unemployment only	—	9.5	—	—	90.5	100.0
Aged female head only	30	6.9	18.6	13.8	60.7	100.0
Recent migrant, female head only	3	34.7	—	0.6	64.7	100.0
All other disability combinations	6	29.8	3.2	7.9	59.1	100.0
No disability	19	1.7	0.8	1.2	96.3	100.0
Total	100 (59,750)	4.2	3.5	5.2	87.1	100.0

Source: Adapted from R. F. Henderson, Alison Harcourt and R. J. A. Harper, *People in Poverty—A Melbourne Survey*, Cheshire, Melbourne, 1970, p. 41.

Families (married couples with children)

The Melbourne poverty survey did not find that large families (four or more children) were a large proportion of the total poverty group, but the 'no disability' group in Table 11 probably largely refers to 'normal' families with dependent children on low incomes. Children often mean poverty for a number of reasons. The wage system in Australia does not take into account the size of family, single workers being paid the same as workers with children. The social welfare system in general does pay some allowances for children—maternity and child endowment are examples—but these incomes are not enough to keep many large families from being poor. Moreover, the arrival of children in a family often creates a financial crisis with the usual cessation of the wife's income due to confinement and the additional demand on resources, not least of them the demand for additional housing space.

Table 12 shows how the marital status of public housing tenants has undergone considerable changes since 1954. The proportion of married household heads has decreased while the permanently separated, divorced and widowed householders have increased in importance. In 1966 public housing tenants were under-represented in the never-married category, and generally slightly under-represented among widows, most of whom are aged. By 1966 the proportion of 'married' householders in public housing was about the same for that in the total population.

TABLE 12 Marital status of household heads in rented public housing units, total state (per cent total), population censuses, 1954, 1961 and 1966

Total State	Marital status					
	1954 TG	1954 Total	1961 TG	1961 Total	1966 TG	1966 Total
	%	%	%	%	%	%
NEW SOUTH WALES						
Never married	2	7	2	7	2	8
Married	88	78	81	77	75	76
Married, but permanently separated	3	2	5	3	6	3
Divorced	1	1	2	2	3	2
Widowed	6	12	10	12	14	12
VICTORIA						
Never married	1	7	1	7	3	7
Married	92	78	84	80	77	77
Married, but permanently separated	2	2	4	2	6	3
Divorced	1	1	1	1	2	1
Widowed	4	11	9	11	11	11
SOUTH AUSTRALIA						
Never married	2	6	2	6	2	6
Married	93	80	88	80	83	79
Married, but permanently separated	1	1	2	2	3	2
Divorced	1	1	2	1	2	2
Widowed	3	13	6	11	9	11
WESTERN AUSTRALIA						
Never married	3	6	1	6	3	7
Married	90	80	85	80	80	79
Married, but permanently separated	2	2	5	2	5	3
Divorced	1	1	2	2	2	3
Widowed	4	10	7	10	10	10
QUEENSLAND						
Never married	5	8	3	8	3	8
Married	83	79	83	78	81	77
Married, but permanently separated	4	2	5	3	5	3
Divorced	1	1	1	1	1	1
Widowed	6	11	8	11	9	12
TASMANIA						
Never married	2	7	2	7	2	7
Married	93	80	84	80	81	79
Married, but permanently separated	2	2	3	2	4	2
Divorced	—	1	2	1	2	1
Widowed	3	10	9	10	10	11

Note: TG refers to tenant government, i.e. Housing Commission. Total refers to total private dwellings, including owner-occupied dwellings.

Source: Commonwealth Bureau of Census and Statistics (cross-classification data for household heads only).

Table 12 refers only to the household heads in rented public housing units and this increases the number in categories other than 'married', since the former groups are the least likely to be able to afford purchase. Tables 13 and 14 give a more useful picture of the relative numbers of married householders, since they are derived from CD data which include owner-occupied dwellings. They show that the married and the married but permanently separated are over-represented in public housing, while the aged are markedly under-represented. These figures support the general argument in this chapter: that public housing favours the married and the permanently separated, while it tends to neglect the single householder (the never married) and the aged, although the Commissions are gradually accepting responsibility for the non-married groups. Tables 15 and 16 also show that public housing favours families with young children (hence the comparatively high proportion of the population under ten years and also under 30), while it has a comparatively small proportion of the 60 and over group, reflecting in part the comparatively low priority given to the aged programme, discussed below.

The number of public housing units available for families with children will depend largely on the number of three- and four-bedroom dwellings available since, using the standards outlined in chapter 3, a family with two children over five of opposite sexes will require a three-bedroom dwelling and one with more than three children will usually require a four-bedroom unit. In the sense that flats are generally unsuitable for young children (this is discussed in chapter 9) the relative numbers of flats and cottages will also

TABLE 13 *Marital status of the total population (excluding the never married) in metropolitan public housing CD areas (per cent of total population), 1966 census*

Marital status	Sydney	Melbourne	Adelaide	Brisbane	Hobart
	%	%	%	%	%
Married	88	87	93	89	90
Married, but permanently separated	4	4	1	3	3
Divorced	—	1	1	1	2
Widowed	7	7	4	6	6

Source: Compiled from summary data supplied by the Commonwealth Statistician (Collectors' District data for the total population).

TABLE 14 *Marital status of the total population (excluding the never married) in metropolitan areas (per cent of total population), 1966 census*

Marital status	Sydney	Melbourne	Adelaide	Brisbane	Hobart
	%	%	%	%	%
Married	84	86	86	84	85
Married, but permanently separated	3	3	2	3	3
Divorced	2	2	2	2	2
Widowed	11	10	10	11	10

Source: Compiled from summary data supplied by the Commonwealth Statistician (Collectors' District data for the total population).

determine the priority given to families with children even though the flats may have three bedrooms.

This section looks at the different characteristics of occupants of public housing rental flats and cottages. The data derive from cross-classification information for the household heads only and they are presented in three sets: the first set gives the occupation, education, age, birthplace and marital status for public housing metropolitan flats; the second gives similar information for rented public housing metropolitan cottages; and the third gives the averages for the metropolitan area for total private dwellings.

Tables 17 to 31 show the substantial differences between the householders in flats and those in cottages. The occupational data show that the householders in Commission flats are of a generally higher socio-economic status than those in cottages—they have a higher proportion of their household heads in the first two occupational classifications (professional, and managerial and self-employed)—although the flats and cottages are, of course, of generally lower socio-economic status than the metropolitan average. Only in the VHC are public housing flats of lower occupational

TABLE 15 Age structure in metropolitan public housing CD areas (per cent of total), 1966 census

Age group	Sydney	Melbourne	Adelaide	Brisbane	Hobart
	%	%	%	%	%
0–4	14	10	13	14	16
5–9	17	13	15	15	15
10–14	12	14	13	14	13
15–19	8	13	9	11	10
20–29	12	11	12	12	15
30–39	16	12	16	14	13
40–49	10	14	12	11	10
50–59	6	8	6	6	6
60 +	5	6	4	4	4

Source: Compiled from summary data supplied by the Commonwealth Statistician (Collectors' District data for the total population).

TABLE 16 Age structure in metropolitan areas (per cent of total), 1966 census

Age group	Sydney	Melbourne	Adelaide	Brisbane	Hobart
	%	%	%	%	%
0–4	9	9	9	9	10
5–9	9	9	10	9	10
10–14	8	9	10	9	10
15–19	9	9	10	10	10
20–29	15	15	13	13	13
30–39	13	13	12	11	12
40–49	14	13	13	13	12
50–59	11	10	10	11	10
60 +	12	13	13	15	13

Source: Compiled from summary data supplied by the Commonwealth Statistician (Collectors' District data for the total population).

status (in the first two classifications) than Commission cottages. This could be because of the VHC refusal to admit married couples without children to its dwellings (this is discussed below) and the VHC practice of building

TABLE 17 Occupations of household heads in the workforce in metropolitan public housing flats (per cent of total), 1966 census

	Sydney	Melbourne	Adelaide	Brisbane	Perth	Hobart
	%	%	%	%	%	%
Professional	3	2	18	5	8	12
Managerial and self-employed	7	5	14	9	9	7
Clerical workers	16	14	30	13	21	24
Armed forces	6	6	—	1	5	1
Craftsmen and foremen	15	16	11	22	13	10
Shop assistants and process workers	28	30	14	24	17	20
Personal, domestic, other service workers and labourers	25	25	12	24	25	25
% in the workforce	57	57	54	73	42	54

Source: Compiled from summary data supplied by the Commonwealth Statistician (cross-classification data for household heads only).

TABLE 18 Education of household heads in metropolitan public housing flats (per cent of total), 1966 census

	Sydney	Melbourne	Adelaide	Brisbane	Perth	Hobart
	%	%	%	%	%	%
University qualifications	—	—	3	1	1	1
Other tertiary qualifications	1	1	4	1	1	2
Matriculation passed	7	6	10	10	11	9
Intermediate passed	12	20	18	22	18	16
Attended high school	26	32	21	24	39	26
Attended primary	50	36	42	40	27	43
No education	1	1	—	—	—	—
Not stated	3	3	3	2	3	3

Source: Compiled from summary data supplied by the Commonwealth Statistician (cross-classification data for household heads only).

TABLE 19 Age structure of household heads in metropolitan public housing flats (per cent of total), 1966 census

Age group	Sydney	Melbourne	Adelaide	Brisbane	Perth	Hobart
	%	%	%	%	%	%
0–19	—	—	—	—	—	—
20–29	10	10	8	24	8	12
30–39	14	18	8	13	5	11
40–49	17	17	13	20	9	14
50–59	20	16	21	15	15	18
60 +	40	38	51	28	63	44

Source: Compiled from summary data supplied by the Commonwealth Statistician (cross-classification data for household heads only).

large numbers of three-bedroom flats while the other Commissions generally reserve flats for smaller households requiring only one or two bedrooms. The SAHT flats are of very high socio-economic status, well above even the

TABLE 20 *Birthplace of household heads in metropolitan public housing flats (per cent of total), 1966 census*

Birthplace	Sydney	Melbourne	Adelaide	Brisbane	Perth	Hobart
	%	%	%	%	%	%
Australia	78	73	68	62	51	79
New Zealand, England, Wales, Ireland, Scotland	16	18	25	26	39	16
Austria, Czechoslovakia, Germany, Hungary, Yugoslavia	2	2	2	4	2	2
Greece, Italy, Malta	1	2	1	1	—	—
Other	3	5	4	7	7	3

Source: Compiled from summary data supplied by the Commonwealth Statistician (cross-classification data for household heads only).

TABLE 21 *Marital status of household heads in metropolitan public housing flats (per cent of total), 1966 census*

Marital status	Sydney	Melbourne	Adelaide	Brisbane	Perth	Hobart
	%	%	%	%	%	%
Never married	6	6	19	7	7	12
Married	55	55	43	69	53	48
Permanently separated	7	9	4	9	5	5
Divorced	5	4	6	4	5	3
Widowed	26	26	29	12	30	32

Source: Compiled from summary data supplied by the Commonwealth Statistician (cross-classification data for household heads only).

TABLE 22 *Occupations of household heads in the workforce in metropolitan rented public housing cottages (per cent of total), 1966 census*

	Sydney	Melbourne	Adelaide	Brisbane	Perth	Hobart
	%	%	%	%	%	%
Professional	2	3	5	4	3	4
Managerial and self-employed	5	5	6	6	7	5
Clerical workers	9	10	9	9	9	11
Armed forces	3	6	3	8	4	1
Craftsmen and foremen	22	22	27	19	24	20
Shop assistants and process workers	37	33	32	31	31	36
Personal, domestic, other service workers and labourers	23	21	18	23	22	23
% in the workforce	78	84	84	78	80	79

Source: Compiled from summary data supplied by the Commonwealth Statistician (cross-classification data for household heads only).

metropolitan average. This is because the SAHT desires to allocate many of its flats to those on middle incomes (this is also discussed below). Public housing flats generally have fewer blue-collar workers than do public

TABLE 23 Education of household heads in metropolitan rented public housing cottages (per cent of total), 1966 census

	Sydney	Melbourne	Adelaide	Brisbane	Perth	Hobart
	%	%	%	%	%	%
University qualifications	—	—	1	—	—	1
Other tertiary qualifications	—	1	1	1	1	1
Matriculation passed	4	6	6	5	6	6
Intermediate passed	21	13	15	18	18	19
Attended high school	42	31	31	23	54	31
Attended primary	30	45	43	52	19	38
No education	1	—	—	—	—	1
Not stated	2	3	3	2	1	3

Source: Compiled from summary data supplied by the Commonwealth Statistician (cross-classification data for household heads only).

TABLE 24 Age structure of household heads in metropolitan rented public housing cottages (per cent of total), 1966 census

Age group	Sydney	Melbourne	Adelaide	Brisbane	Perth	Hobart
	%	%	%	%	%	%
0–19	—	—	—	—	—	—
20–29	9	7	13	15	13	20
30–39	24	24	25	27	24	27
40–49	33	35	29	27	26	23
50–59	21	22	21	19	21	17
60 +	13	12	12	12	17	13

Source: Compiled from summary data supplied by the Commonwealth Statistician (cross-classification data for household heads only).

TABLE 25 Birthplace of household heads in metropolitan rented public housing cottages (per cent of total), 1966 census

Birthplace	Sydney	Melbourne	Adelaide	Brisbane	Perth	Hobart
	%	%	%	%	%	%
Australia	85	80	65	76	64	88
New Zealand, England, Wales, Ireland, Scotland	11	13	26	17	25	8
Austria, Czechoslovakia, Germany, Hungary, Yugoslavia	1	1	3	1	2	1
Greece, Italy, Malta	1	2	1	1	1	1
Other	2	4	5	5	8	2

Source: Compiled from summary data supplied by the Commonwealth Statistician (cross-classification data for household heads only).

housing cottages (white-collar workers are in occupational groups one to three, inclusive, blue-collar in four to seven, inclusive). The educational data generally follow the same patterns as the occupational information; those in

TABLE 26 *Marital status of household heads in metropolitan rented public housing cottages (per cent of total), 1966 census*

Marital status	Sydney	Melbourne	Adelaide	Brisbane	Perth	Hobart
	%	%	%	%	%	%
Never married	1	1	—	2	2	1
Married	80	84	86	81	79	82
Married, but permanently separated	6	5	3	5	7	4
Divorced	3	1	2	1	3	3
Widowed	10	9	8	10	11	10

Source: Compiled from summary data supplied by the Commonwealth Statistician (cross-classification data for household heads only).

TABLE 27 *Occupations of household heads in the workforce in metropolitan total private dwellings, including Commission units (per cent of total), 1966 census*

Occupation	Sydney	Melbourne	Adelaide	Brisbane	Perth	Hobart
	%	%	%	%	%	%
Professional	11	11	11	10	12	14
Managerial and self-employed	16	16	14	15	11	14
Clerical workers	16	16	15	17	16	18
Armed forces	1	1	—	2	1	—
Craftsmen and foremen	21	21	22	15	22	17
Shop assistants and process workers	22	21	23	24	21	21
Personal, domestic, service workers and labourers	14	14	14	16	16	15
% in the workforce	78	80	78	75	76	79

Source: Compiled from summary data supplied by the Commonwealth Statistician (cross-classification data for household heads only).

TABLE 28 *Education of household heads in metropolitan total private dwellings, including Commission units (per cent of total), 1966 census*

	Sydney	Melbourne	Adelaide	Brisbane	Perth	Hobart
	%	%	%	%	%	%
University qualifications	3	3	3	2	3	4
Other tertiary qualifications	4	5	4	4	5	5
Matriculation passed	10	12	9	6	9	14
Intermediate passed	28	17	18	20	20	17
Attended high school	27	23	26	21	43	25
Attended primary	23	37	38	44	18	32
No education	1	1	—	—	1	1
Not stated	3	2	2	3	2	2

Source: Compiled from summary data supplied by the Commonwealth Statistician (cross-classification data for household heads only).

flats are marginally better educated than those in cottages, with those in the SAHT flats being better educated than those in either SAHT cottages or the metropolitan average.

The age and marital status data reveal the major differences between flats and cottages. The public housing flat programme caters mainly for non-husband-wife households: the never married; the aged; the permanently separated; the divorced; and the widowed. Cottages, on the other hand,

TABLE 29 Age structure of household heads in metropolitan total private dwellings, including Commission units (per cent of total), 1966 census

Age group	Sydney	Melbourne	Adelaide	Brisbane	Perth	Hobart
	%	%	%	%	%	%
0–19	—	—	—	1	—	1
20–29	12	12	12	12	12	14
30–39	19	22	20	18	20	20
40–49	23	23	23	23	22	20
50–59	20	19	20	20	20	20
60 +	25	25	25	26	26	23

Source: Compiled from summary data supplied by the Commonwealth Statistician (cross-classification data for household heads only).

TABLE 30 Birthplace of household heads in metropolitan total private dwellings, including Commission units (per cent of total), 1966 census

Birthplace	Sydney	Melbourne	Adelaide	Brisbane	Perth	Hobart
	%	%	%	%	%	%
Australia	72	68	67	79	63	82
New Zealand, England, Wales, Ireland, Scotland	13	12	16	13	21	9
Austria, Czechoslovakia, Germany, Hungary, Yugoslavia	3	4	4	1	2	2
Greece, Italy, Malta	5	9	7	2	6	2
Other	7	7	6	5	8	5

Source: Compiled from summary data supplied by the Commonwealth Statistician (cross-classification data for household heads only).

TABLE 31 Marital status of household heads in metropolitan total private dwellings, including Commission units (per cent of total), 1966 census

Marital status	Sydney	Melbourne	Adelaide	Brisbane	Perth	Hobart
	%	%	%	%	%	%
Never married	8	8	6	8	6	7
Married	74	76	78	74	77	77
Married, but permanently separated	3	3	2	3	3	3
Divorced	2	2	2	2	2	2
Widowed	13	11	12	13	12	12

Source: Compiled from summary data supplied by the Commonwealth Statistician (cross-classification data for household heads only).

cater primarily for the married, intact households. The data on cottages understate this characteristic, as they refer only to rented cottages which contain a higher proportion of non-husband-wife households than all cottages since married couples under 60 form the bulk of those purchasing dwellings. Public housing flats generally only have about a half of their household heads in the workforce (the exception is the QHC, which has no aged programme), reflecting the concentration on the aged and female householders. On the other hand, Commission cottages have around 80 per cent of their household heads in the workforce, about the same as the metropolitan average.

The overseas born are more heavily represented in public housing flats than in cottages. This could be due to a number of factors: perhaps European migrants are more used to living in flats than are the Australian born; possibly the migrants use public housing flats as 'way stations', the low rent enabling them to save for home purchase in the private sector.

The NSWHC has adjusted its building programme so that families with children gain admission to a public housing unit of their choice (i.e. house or flat) after no longer waiting time than other groups, and in the last five years preference has been given to large families by construction of many four-bedroom dwellings so that the waiting time for these is less than for other units. The NSWHC maintains a balance between cottages and flats by building four types of dwelling in its programme. The first is the aged unit programme, discussed below and shown in Table 32. The second type is flats built in the 'middle suburbs' on non-slum clearance sites. Flats built on slum clearance land form the third type, and the fourth type of construction is cottages. The numbers of these dwellings built since 1959 (when figures are readily available) are shown in Table 32. The figures in this table reveal

TABLE 32 NSWHC completions, Sydney metropolitan area, type of dwelling, 1959–70

Year	Aged units	Slum clearance flats	Other flats	Cottages	Total
1959–60	52	—	456	2,113	2,621
1960–1	241	80	245	1,630	2,196
1961–2	134	390	521	1,952	2,997
1962–3	193	121	538	1,914	2,766
1963–4	208	296	484	1,585	2,573
1964–5	502	—	479	2,184	3,165
1965–6	535	480	497	1,392	2,904
1966–7	208	248	502	1,172	2,130
1967–8	400	148	282	1,667	2,497
1968–9	225	52	616	1,166	2,059
1969–70	212	212	206	1,608	2,238
Total	2,910	2,027	4,826	18,383	28,146

Note: Includes outer metropolitan areas, e.g. Green Valley, Mt Druitt.
Source: Annnal reports of the NSWHC.

a balance between the different forms of construction that is not evident in the VHC programme discussed below.

Up to 1956 the NSWHC provided one-bedroom accommodation in flats but it was always agreed that the tenant would be transferred if his family increased in size. On the completion of high-rise blocks from 1948 onwards the Commission did not allow families with children under seven to occupy flats other than walk-up or ground floor flats. When the first high-rise blocks were completed, no families with children less than nine years old were allowed to occupy them. In 1962 the restrictions on walk-up flats were removed so that families with children of any age could occupy walk-up flats. In 1964 all restrictions on occupation of flats by families with children were removed, although families with young children were given a free choice in the matter with no extra waiting time if they desired a cottage and they were advised by the Commission of the inherent problems associated with flat accommodation. When the family increases in size it is transferred to cottage accommodation, which forms a large proportion of NSWHC completions. In addition, the NSWHC generally does not construct three-bedroom flats so that the only flat accommodation available is up to a maximum of two bedrooms.

In a publication in 1963 the VHC said, 'The major change in policy in 1956 that has affected the Commission's activities most was the decision to get back to slum reclamation work and leave the major provision of single family housing to private enterprise'. In 1967 the Minister for Housing replied to a question in parliament that although any policy change must be gradual '. . . in the metropolitan area, Housing Commission construction

TABLE 33 VHC completions, Melbourne metropolitan area, type of dwelling, 1959–70

Year	Aged units	Inner area flats	Cottages	Total
1959–60	311	290	989	1,590
1960–1	336	261	1,015	1,612
1961–2	54	584	820	1,458
1962–3	240	632	479	1,351
1963–4	167	502	713	1,382
1964–5	428	307	865	1,600
1965–6	370	469	649	1,488
1966–7	597	152	821	1,570
1967–8	—	1,006	279	1,285
1968–9	204	540	369	1,113
1969–70	72	1,057	604	1,733
Total	2,779	5,800	7,603	16,182

Note: The metropolitan area includes Frankston, Broadmeadows, Dandenong. This makes the metropolitan area identical to the area used in the 1966 Census population and produces comparability with the Sydney metropolitan area.
Source: Annual reports of the VHC.

is now practically wholly involved in urban renewal . . .' In addition, all new cottages constructed in the metropolitan area were allocated to those desiring to purchase, and, except for families with five or more children, who were allocated vacated villas, all rental applications were allocated flats. A similar statement was repeated in the publication *State Housing* in 1963:

> Bearing in mind that the Commission policy is to erect 55 per cent of units in metropolitan areas and 45 per cent in country areas in each financial year, and the current growth of Slum Reclamation of inner metropolitan areas combined with the economic necessity to redevelop these areas with flats, tenancy in metropolitan areas is almost entirely limited to flats.

The trend towards flats is indicated in Table 33, which shows also the comparatively small number of cottages built by the VHC. From 1959 to 1970 the VHC supplied 7,603 cottages in the Melbourne area compared with 18,383 by the NSWHC in Sydney. Sydney has a larger population than Melbourne (in 1966 there were 2,447,219 people in Sydney and 2,110,336 in Melbourne) but this does not account for much of the difference. Not only did the NSWHC supply many more cottages during this period, but they also completed many more dwellings overall (28,146) compared with the VHC (16,182). The VHC emphasis on flats is discussed further in chapters 5 and 9.

To compare the relative supplies of houses and flats in the VHC and the NSWHC, the numbers of units vacated have to be taken into account. Vacancies in the VHC amounted to 1,432 flats and 409 villas in the metropolitan area in 1969–70. This compared with vacancies in the metropolitan area of Sydney of 731 flats and 886 cottages (for 1968–9). The reasons for this disparity in numbers of cottages vacated between the VHC and the NSWHC can be explained by the emphasis on flat construction in the VHC, the generally smaller number of completions in the VHC (metropolitan areas) and the VHC policy for the last six or seven years of selling off all new cottages built since 1963, whereas the NSWHC sells only about 50 per cent of its new cottages (this is discussed in chapter 7). The pattern in units vacated therefore intensifies the differences in the availability of cottage accommodation between the VHC and the NSWHC.

While the NSWHC builds no three-bedroom flats, the VHC builds large numbers of them in the metropolitan area, as is shown in Table 34. The waiting times in the VHC strongly favour those desiring two-bedroom flats. In 1971 the waiting time for a two-bedroom flat was ten months, eighteen months for a three-bedroom flat, three years for a two-bedroom house and five years for a three-bedroom house. Many of the occupants of VHC flats would prefer cottages. The Commission conducted a survey in 1965 that showed that as few as 2 to 5 per cent of people on the waiting lists preferred flats. When the Brotherhood of St Laurence, a Melbourne Church of England welfare organization, asked a sample of Commission flat dwellers what their housing aspirations were, 98 per cent of the walk-up flat residents wanted to leave the flats and purchase a villa house, and 63 per cent of the high-rise flat sample wished to do the same. It is possible that the general dislike of flats by families with young children may induce them not to apply for VHC accommodation. This matter is discussed further in chapter 9.

The imbalance between accommodation sizes in the VHC is inherent in high-rise flat projects. Because large numbers of children cause management problems it is unwise to build more than about 55 per cent of three-bedroom flats in any block. Four-bedroom flats are non existent. In contrast the NSWHC can build a six-thousand unit cottage estate with 90 per cent three- or four-bedroom dwellings. This may not provide an ideally mixed social environment but it does provide good housing for big families with young children, the people who were supposed to benefit from the public housing programme rather than the smaller families that benefit from the over supply of smaller sized flats that results from VHC policy. In addition, the 'problem' tenant will be tolerated to a much higher degree of undesirable behaviour if he lives in a cottage rather than a flat where noise, poor cleanliness and other features cause serious annoyance to neighbours.

In 1969 the WAHC decided to change the previous ratio of about 95 per cent cottages and 5 per cent flats to build 50 per cent flats or semi-detached housing. This decision appears to have been derived from a number of circumstances, outlined in its Annual Report for 1967:

(a) The problem of acquiring replacement land in the metropolitan region and the larger country centres at prices within the paying capacity of families of low and moderate means, social cases and elderly pensioner applicants.
(b) The increasing value of land now held and the costs of developing this land.
(c) The need to satisfy an increasing demand for housing, both rental and purchase.
(d) The need to conserve government expenditures on public utility services, schools, hospitals, transport, etc.
(e) The overseas and interstate experience which indicated a change in living habits and the increasing demand for an admixture of residential accommodation such as single houses, duplex, town houses and flats.

TABLE 34 *Bedroom sizes of VHC flats, percentage distribution of the total stock of flats, biennially, 1959–69*

No. of bedrooms	1959	1961	1963	1965	1967	30 June 1969
	%	%	%	%	%	%
1	21	29	27	31	37	33
2	71	59	51	44	40	40
3	9	12	22	25	23	26
Total stock of flats	3,965	5,163	6,673	7,809	9,397	11,147

Source: Annual reports of the VHC.

Another reason for this change to rental accommodation was a radical change in the local political view of public housing. The ruling Liberal Party believed that many of those purchasing WAHC dwellings were en route to higher incomes since Western Australia had become an affluent society. Public housing is seen as essentially a traditional form of housing. Hence the emphasis on rental dwellings (the flats or semi-detached dwellings are not to be sold), which should encourage tenants whose incomes rise to vacate the public housing and obtain housing in the private market, so allowing the housing to be used for the low income applicants on the waiting list. The validity of this view depends on the rate of social mobility amongst WAHC applicants.

Up till the switch towards more high-density dwellings in 1969 the WAHC was able to offer accommodation to all groups eligible after approximately the same waiting time, except that the aged generally waited longer than many rental applicants who gained rapid access because of the short-term allocation system described above. The trend towards more higher-density accommodation may change the relative waiting times.

The SAHT, the QHC and the THC have all built comparatively few flats. Up to 30 June 1969 flats (other than aged units) formed about 3 per cent of total metropolitan completions by the SAHT, about 4 per cent of metropolitan completions in the THC and about 2 per cent in the QHC (for the metropolitan area). Generally these Commissions build very few flats outside the metropolitan area. A representative from the SAHT pointed out in 1968 that flats were provided for young married couples without children and it was hoped that when the family increased through the arrival of children the family would move into cottage accommodation. He said, 'It is far from ideal to have a family in a restricted area. We think it is far better for families to be in more spacious surroundings.' The Annual Report of the QHC expressed similar feelings in 1969: 'The demands on the Commission for housing for families with children, and particularly from large families, is such that preference is given to the construction of dwellings suitable for such families, rather than to flats which provide less accommodation.' In its Annual Report for 1964 the THC said: 'The normal applicant seeking assistance from the Department is, in the main, only interested in single unit accommodation, and does not favour living in multi-unit buildings. This has been the experience of the Department for some years, despite the fact that the flats it has erected are of a high standard. To a considerable extent, flats are regarded by some people as a stop gap for use as a dwelling place pending obtaining permanent accommodation in a single unit dwelling.'

The flats built by these three Commissions generally consist of one- or two-bedroom accommodation. The number of bedrooms in houses built by the QHC was not available but it is most likely similar to the THC where 86 per cent of all homes completed up to 30 June 1969 contained three bedrooms, the remainder consisting of two bedrooms (9 per cent) and one bedroom (5 per cent) (metropolitan area). The THC is probably similar to the SAHT and the WAHC but the emphasis on flats in the VHC and the NSWHC probably increases the proportion of one- and two-bedroom dwellings in these latter Commissions. Generally the Commissions cannot supply precise information on bedroom sizes of their accommodation.

Married couples below 60 with no children

People in this category of households are allocated dwellings in all states except Victoria, where an applicant other than an aged person has to be married and have at least one child. The VHC argues that families with children have a higher priority than households without children. In the other states the priority given to these households depends primarily on the number of flats in the building programme, since they are usually allocated flats. It was seen above that the VHC and the NSWHC have been the major suppliers of flats among the housing authorities, and since the VHC does not allocate flats to this group, the NSWHC probably favours this group more than any other Commission. The NSWHC attempts to ensure that it allocates dwellings only to those families where the husband is on a low income and has a comparatively unskilled occupation, so as to avoid allocating dwellings to married couples who do not intend to have children and who benefit from the earnings of husband and wife. Only the husband's income is taken into consideration.

The NSWHC has found that married couples without children are the most difficult to house in terms of preference for particular areas. From their readiness to refuse offers of accommodation even though it means a longer wait and eventual exclusion from the waiting list, this group would appear to be the least in 'need' of NSWHC applicants. The NSWHC constructs a sizeable proportion of its dwellings in the form of one-bedroom flats, mainly for married couples without children. The number of one-bedroom flats available is partly dependent on the slum clearance programme. From 1963 the NSWHC decided that the waiting time for married couples without children should not be less than that for other categories, a situation that had arisen out of an attempt to avoid placing families with young children in slum clearance flats. The sizeable cluster of household heads in the first two occupational classifications in Table 17 gives some support to the claim that the Commissions house some households not in great need in their flat developments, although the data are only for a single year, 1966, and it could be that households have improved their socio-economic status after entry into public housing.

Migrants

Migrants are defined as those born outside Australia. The NSWHC allowed no migrants into its public housing from 1945 to 1948. In 1948 all British migrants were placed in the same position as native-born Australians after they had served a qualifying period of six months' residence in Australia. This period of residence was increased to twelve months in 1949 and foreign (i.e. non-British migrants) were expressly excluded from public housing allocations even if they were naturalized. By 1953 applications from these latter groups were accepted on naturalization. In 1957 it was decided that all British migrants were eligible to apply for a dwelling after twelve months' residence in Australia. Non-British migrants were eligible for dwellings built after 1956, after twelve months' residence in Australia, but had to be naturalized before they could apply for a 1945 Agreement dwelling. These restrictions were removed in 1962 when all migrants were eligible to apply for public housing on arrival in New South Wales.

VHC policy towards migrants appears to have followed a similar path to that of the NSWHC up to 1953. Until 1963 British migrants were not eligible for accommodation in the metropolitan area or Dandenong, Doveton, Frankston or Geelong, unless they had completed six months' residence in Australia. On completion of this six months they were eligible to join the waiting lists for accommodation. These restrictions on British migrants were removed in 1963. Up to 1963 all non-British migrants were ineligible for VHC housing until they produced a certificate of naturalization, but these restrictions did not apply in country areas where demand for VHC housing was not heavy. From 1963 until 1966 the VHC no longer required non-British migrants to be naturalized but insisted that they be resident in Australia for twelve months before they could apply for accommodation. All restrictions on migrants were removed in 1966.

There is little information on the early policies of the QHC, WAHC and the THC, although there were generally some restrictions on migrants, usually in the form of a waiting period before the migrant could be admitted to public housing. This was eroded by the generous priorities given in these Commissions to needy households, the generally more plentiful supply of public housing in these states and the ambivalent attitudes towards migrants since these states were eager to increase their small populations. By 1963, when accurate information is available, these Commissions had no effective discrimination against migrants. The SAHT has never applied any discrimination against migrant applicants. Indeed, as will be shown in chapter 6, the Trust's desire to promote the growth of South Australia led to favourable policies towards migrants, compared with other applicants. That chapter also shows that all states now give priority to skilled migrants as a method of competing for resources for economic expansion.

Tables 35 and 36 show the birthplaces of the total population in public housing areas and for the metropolitan areas as a whole. There are considerable differences between states. In housing built by the NSWHC, VHC and THC, the Australian-born group are over-represented while in the SAHT and the QHC housing they are under-represented. Generally, migrants from New Zealand, England, Wales, Ireland and Scotland are well represented in public housing, particularly in the QHC and the SAHT. Other migrant groups are generally under-represented in public housing, especially the Greeks and Italians.

These latter groups are generally of very low socio-economic status. Henderson found in the 1966 Melbourne poverty survey that after adjustment for payment of housing an average of 25 per cent of Greek and Italian migrants who arrived between 1960 and 1966 were poor (earning less than $33 per week per income unit). The discrimination against these migrants by the Housing Commissions may partially explain their low representation in public housing but the sociological factors discussed in chapter 9 are probably the major explanation. Briefly, chapter 9 argues that these migrant groups like to live together in older housing in inner areas because of their need to live with groups of their countrymen, which is generally not possible in public housing. A recent, if rather limited, VHC survey suggests that public housing may be becoming more popular with non-British migrants. The survey of 200 VHC high-rise flats tenanted in 1970 showed that 25 per cent of the heads of households were Australian born, 18 per cent were British, 6 per cent Egyptian, 7 per cent Spanish, 9 per cent Italian, 6 per cent Turkish, 5 per cent Yugoslav, 4 per cent Maltese, 6 per cent Greek and the remaining 14 per cent were small numbers of Mauritians, Czechoslovakians, Chinese, Dutch, French, Chilean, Brazilian, Hungarians, Germans and Poles.

TABLE 35 Birthplace of the total population in metropolitan public housing CD areas (per cent of total), 1966 census

Birthplace	Sydney	Melbourne	Adelaide	Brisbane	Hobart
	%	%	%	%	%
Australia	88	83	58	79	93
New Zealand, England, Wales, Ireland, Scotland	8	9	35	15	5
Austria, Czechoslovakia, Germany, Hungary, Yugoslavia	1	1	2	1	1
Greece, Italy, Malta	1	3	1	1	—
Other	2	3	5	4	1

Source: Compiled from summary data supplied by the Commonwealth Statistician (Collectors' District data for the total population).

TABLE 36 Birthplace of the total population in metropolitan areas (per cent of total), 1966 census

Birthplace	Sydney	Melbourne	Adelaide	Brisbane	Hobart
	%	%	%	%	%
Australia	78	74	73	85	88
New Zealand, England, Wales, Ireland, Scotland	9	9	14	9	6
Austria, Czechoslovakia, Germany, Hungary, Yugoslavia	3	3	3	1	1
Greece, Italy, Malta	5	8	6	1	1
Other	5	6	4	4	4

Source: Compiled from summary data supplied by the Commonwealth Statistician (Collectors' District data for the total population).

The deserving poor unable to pay economic rents and/or in need of specialized services in addition to housing

This section discusses three groups, the aged, female household heads with dependent children, and the physically handicapped. All three groups have a very low capacity to pay and therefore mean huge losses to the Housing Commissions. Ironically, female household heads with dependent children have been treated much better than the aged or the physically handicapped.

The aged

Research conducted by the Melbourne Institute of Applied Economic and Social Research from 1966 to 1969 found that the aged were an important part of the poverty group. Table 11 shows that the aged account for 43 per cent of those considered poor ($0–33 a week). Among aged income units in the Melbourne poverty survey, 56.7 per cent owned their own houses free of mortgage debt, and a further 14.8 per cent had rent-free accommodation. Only 6.4 per cent of the aged paid up to $5 a week rent, and it was in the group paying $5 and more per week that the bulk of the aged poor were found. Although they are paid a supplementary allowance of $2 per week, Henderson argues that this amount does not cover the cost of renting adequate accommodation privately. He notes that the supply of adequate housing at a price those fully dependent on the pension can afford is shrinking. In 1969, 79 per cent of those on supplementary assistance (that is, those paying rent and fully dependent on the pension) were women (i.e. not forming a male-female household). The decision in 1969 by the Commonwealth to provide special grants to the states to house single eligible aged pensioners was motivated by the findings of the Melbourne poverty survey on the large numbers of pensioners in need.

This section concentrates on the role of the housing authorities in housing that proportion of the aged able to care for themselves in housing that is not 'specialized' in the sense of having available special nursing care or other facilities. The NSWHC divides the aged population into three categories: aged and infirm incapable of adequately caring for themselves for whom a hospitalization scheme is obviously necessary; elderly people who are able to provide some of their own needs but still need some specialized services; and aged people who are capable of caring for themselves and who desire to continue to live a normal existence in the community. All Australian Housing Commissions have limited their activities to the latter group.

Rosow points out in his book *The Social Integration of the Aged* (New York, 1967) that although the aged population (over 60 years) do suffer from many physical illnesses, only about 9 per cent are housebound and cannot get around alone, and only 14 per cent have a major limitation in activity. In surveys by Rosow, less than 5 per cent of those interviewed express spontaneously any dissatisfaction with their living arrangements (housing), and when they are explicitly asked about housing usually less than

15 per cent express any dissatisfaction. Using these figures as a general guide, the Commissions probably supply housing that would be adequate for about 90 per cent of the aged. The remaining 10 per cent rely on other institutions, usually private organizations assisted by government subsidies and providing intensive nursing care not available in Housing Commission accommodation. Little research has been done on the extent to which the latter group—those needing specialized services—are assisted to an adequate level by non-Housing Commission organizations. Henderson found serious deficiencies in domiciliary care facilities in Melbourne in 1966 (*People in Poverty*, Melbourne, 1970).

The CSHA in 1945 made no specific provision for the housing of the aged, although it was realized that they were an important group in need of public housing. The public housing authorities were theoretically able to construct housing for the aged, even though this would require heavy subsidies. The loss-sharing arrangement in the 1945–56 CSHA was to make this possible. In 1948 the Commonwealth suggested that the states should allocate some definite if small proportion of their output to the aged. The states agreed to this in principle but had to balance the aged building programme against the large families with children and other groups on the waiting list. In addition, the loss-sharing arrangement was dependent on the states' continually adjusting their rents to account for inflation, which they seldom did. From 1945 to June 1956 the NSWHC provided 900 units for the aged, about 2 per cent of the total public housing completions over this period. In this same period the VHC supplied about 542 units to the aged, also about 2 per cent of the total output. The SAHT began the construction of aged housing in 1954–5, completing 190 up to 1956, again about 2 per cent of the total output to that date. The QHC did not build housing for the aged in this period. The Queensland government did, however, introduce a scheme in 1945 that provided for a 50 per cent cash subsidy and the remaining 50 per cent as a loan to any local authority providing homes for the aged. In 1952 the scheme was extended to voluntary bodies, on a dollar for dollar subsidy. The WAHC built 213 aged home units from 1945 to 1956, about 1 per cent of its total completions.

Two events around this time affected the supply of public housing to the aged, the 1954 Commonwealth Aged Persons' Homes Act and the CSHA of 1956. The Commonwealth Aged Persons' Homes Act in 1954 had as its objective to '. . . encourage and assist the provision of suitable homes for aged persons and in particular homes at which aged persons may reside in conditions approaching as nearly as possible normal domestic life, and in the case of married people, with proper regard to the companionship of husband and wife'. The Commonwealth would provide assistance to private, voluntary, non-profit bodies, especially the churches, to build homes for the aged. The intial subsidy was to be $1 for each $1 raised by the organization, but amending legislation soon after extended this subsidy to $2 for each $1 contributed. The legislation was intended to stimulate the voluntary welfare system and grants were not payable to any local authority, State Housing Commission or any other government body. The type of housing supplied under the scheme had to be primarily self-contained and the conditions for grants were designed to prevent housing built under the scheme from becoming nursing homes or hospitals for the aged. In 1969 the Commonwealth scheme was amended to encourage the provision of personal care services in homes for the aged. The resultant form of housing is termed 'hostel' units, midway between nursing homes and non-specialized accommodation.

Up to 1969 a total of 32,617 persons were accommodated in dwellings built under the scheme. Of these dwellings, 55.2 per cent were built by religious bodies, 39.4 per cent by charitable or benevolent institutions, 1.8 per cent by ex-service organizations, and 4.5 per cent by other bodies. Out of the total of 32,617, 16,573 were self-contained, 12,924 were of the hostel type and 3,120 included extensive nursing facilities. The amount of aged housing provided under this scheme differed considerably from state to state. In South Australia, 5.6 per cent of the aged population were supplied with housing under the scheme, Western Australia 3.6 per cent, Tasmania 3 per cent, Victoria 2.4 per cent, Queensland 2.1 per cent and New South Wales 1.9 per cent.

In 1967 the Commonwealth allowed local government authorities to participate in the scheme, but up till 30 June 1969 only five councils had applied, resulting in the housing of 22 aged persons. Possibly because of the low response from local authorities, the Commonwealth granted the state housing authorities a total of $5 million a year for five years from 1969 specifically for housing the aged. This finance was allocated to the states in proportion to the number of aged pensioners receiving supplementary assistance, that is, those paying rent to private landlords and considered most in need.

The Aged Persons' Homes Act did not insist that the dwellings be provided for aged pensioners. All it required was that the males had to be 65 and the women 60. A survey in 1967 found that 35.3 per cent of all units constructed under the scheme had required a capital donation for entry. The size of these donations is not known. The survey also found that 78 per cent of all units were occupied by pensioners, although it does not specify whether this is a complete or partial pension. Hence it is not known how the use of voluntary agencies favours certain groups connected with these organizations.

Aged housing—especially the participation of the State Housing Commissions under the Commonwealth Aged Persons' Homes Act—has been an important factor in Commonwealth-state animosity. After the CSHA in 1956, the states' claim for special subsidies for aged housing was a matter raised at almost all of the annual Housing Ministers' Conferences, frequently at the annual Premiers' Conferences, and often in the press. The nature of this animosity can be seen in the reaction of the Tasmanian government to a letter sent to it by the Commonwealth Minister for Social Services (Mr Wentworth) in 1968. The Premier of Tasmania claimed that, in effect, Wentworth was saying that they would starve pensioners out of their homes if the states did not give aged housing a higher priority in their use of CSHA funds. In the 1969 legislation, to ensure that the poor aged benefited, the Commonwealth placed detailed conditions on the $5 million a year that it advanced to the states for aged housing. In addition, it made clear that these funds were not intended to replace state funds spent on aged housing and stipulated that each state must spend in the 1969–74 period not less than an amount five times the average annual amount spent on aged housing during the period 1966–9.

In the 1956 CSHA the Commonwealth raised the interest rate on CSHA loans and ceased to share losses resulting from rents below costs for such groups as the aged. This made it difficult for the states to build houses for the aged out of CSHA funds unless they were able to raise rents on older houses, so they had to use profits obtained from other activities of the housing authorities, or subsidize aged housing with state funds. In 1956 the NSWHC ceased to use funds advanced under the CSHA for the construction of aged housing. This decision appears to have been based on two main arguments: firstly, the use of CSHA funds would result in large losses that were not recoupable from the Commonwealth and, secondly, the NSWHC appears to hold the belief, shared by the state politicians, that CSHA funds were designed primarily for families of low and moderate means and that this term does not refer to the aged, especially since many of those requiring housing assistance are single.

From 1956 to 1969 the NSWHC built 4,580 aged units, about 17 units per 1,000 aged pensioners in the state in 1969. The NSWHC accepts women as eligible for aged housing when they are 55 years old and men when they are 60. It uses funds obtained from profits from house sales, a special state tax on revenue from poker machines and other non-CSHA funds to construct aged housing.

From 1956 to 1969 the VHC built a total of 3,782 units for the aged. All these units were built from general CSHA funds. At 30 June 1969 there were 183,776 aged pensioners in Victoria. Hence the VHC had built 20.6 units per 1,000 aged pensioners at June 1969 (completions from 1956–69). Women are eligible at 60 years and men at 65 years, but single men were not housed from 1956 to 1969, although it is planned to house them under the Commonwealth grants commenced in 1969. The VHC has obtained much free land from councils in inner areas, which reduces the costs of units. The councils donating the land have the right to nominate the tenants of the units, although they must be pensioners. The VHC has tended to give married pensioners priority over single females. In 1966 the waiting time for a unit for an aged married couple was two years while for a single female it was six years. Generally these waiting times (for single aged) were longer than waiting times for non-aged VHC housing in country areas and for metropolitan housing, although as a result of the slum clearance programme, waiting times for metropolitan cottages have increased to about five to six years.

From 1956 to 1969 the SAHT built 969 units especially for aged pensioners, about 14.6 units per 1,000 aged pensioners in 1969. Women are eligible at 60 and men at 65. The Trust did not use general CSHA funds but rather relied on special state grants or revenue surpluses. In 1966 the Trust claimed that it would concentrate on the provision of units for single women—the main group in need. Because of the priority given to aged units for married couples, the waiting time in 1969 was about twelve months for a married unit, but about six to seven years for a single unit. These waiting times were generally greater than for normal non-aged public housing.

The QHC has not allocated housing to the aged since 1956. At the Premiers' Conference in 1966 the Queensland Premier, Mr Nicklin, said, 'In 1944 a national referendum transferred the responsibility for the provision of social services to the Commonwealth and we feel that since then this is one field in which the Commonwealth has not taken over full responsibility.' The QHC is, however, to construct dwellings for the aged under the 1969 Commonwealth scheme.

The WAHC introduced housing specifically for the aged under its own scheme in 1957–8. By 30 June 1969 a total of 940 units had been built under this scheme, about 18.6 units per 1,000 aged pensioners in Western Australia in 1969. The units are only for pensioners and the Commission has favoured married aged couples over single applicants, the waiting time for married couple units being less than twelve months, while the single unit waiting time is about five years or more. Up to 1964 the State Lotteries Commission provided funds for this housing but since then the WAHC has provided this housing from its general surpluses.

From 1956 to 1969 the THC constructed 260 units for the aged. The total pensioner population of Tasmania in 1969 was 21,029. Until 1963 the THC mainly constructed units for aged couples, but in that year the demand from this group was very small and construction since then has mainly been for single aged. However, by 1969 the waiting times for aged couples was four years. Single men and non-pensioners were not eligible. The THC uses general CSHA funds for this housing. The waiting times for aged housing are generally longer than for other types of housing.

Tables 15 and 16 have already shown that Australian public housing areas in the 1966 Census contained a smaller proportion of the aged than the average for the total population. This was partially due to the fact that most public housing has been built since 1945, thus making the public housing population younger than average. Table 37 gives a better indication of the degree to which public housing has favoured the aged. Unfortunately, the only information available is on aged heads renting public housing units. This means that the data in Table 37 take no account of the aged who have purchased their dwellings. Still, they give a good indication of the numbers of aged allocated Commission dwellings after they have

TABLE 37 Percentage of aged household heads in metropolitan public housing rented dwellings, 1966 census

	Sydney	Melbourne	Adelaide	Brisbane	Perth	Hobart
Aged heads in Commission FLATS as:						
% of all aged renters	9	11	10	2	8	10
% of all aged heads	2	2	2	2	2	2
Aged heads in Commission RENTED HOUSES AND FLATS as:						
% of all aged renters	15	19	34	19	34	33
% of all aged heads	4	4	7	2	7	8

Note: Aged heads are those 60 years of age and over.

Source: Compiled from summary data supplied by the Commonwealth Statistician (cross-classification data for household heads only).

reached 60 years, since this latter group is able only to rent. Of the aged paying rent (those in most need of assistance) Table 37 shows that between 15 per cent and 34 per cent were in Commission dwellings in 1966. The proportion varied widely between states—from 15 per cent in the NSWHC and generally low percentages in the VHC and the QHC (which has had no aged programme since 1956) to about 34 per cent in the less populous states, South Australia, Western Australia and Tasmania. Generally this is due to the favourable treatment that these three states receive under the Australian federal system.

Female household heads with dependent children

Overseas studies have pointed to the high vulnerability of female-headed households with dependent children (deserted wives, permanently separated, divorced and widowed mothers). In the Melbourne poverty survey in 1966, this group was found to have a high proportion in poverty, as is shown in Table 11 on page 34. The group, however, forms only a small proportion of the total poverty group, as is also shown in Table 11.

There is some evidence that the Housing Commissions have given considerable assistance to this group. Table 12 showed that the proportion of this group has been steadily growing when compared with the other households in public housing—the never married and the married. They are eligible for public housing in all states, gaining the benefits of the rebate system. The priority systems in the THC (especially until recently), the QHC, and the WAHC probably benefit this group.

Tables 38 and 39 show female-headed households under 60 years of age to be heavily represented in public housing rental units, especially flats, when compared with the average for the respective metropolitan areas. Since single people under 60 are generally not admitted to public housing, most of the female-headed households below 60 are widows, deserted wives, or divorcees with dependent children. Among female householders in Commission flats from 36 per cent (THC) to 58 per cent (QHC) are aged 30 to 59. The proportions are similar in private flats. When houses and flats are considered, an even higher proportion of female householders in public housing are aged between 30 and 59, a considerably higher proportion than in the average for the metropolitan area.

TABLE 38 *Age of the household heads in female-headed households in metropolitan rental public housing units (per cent of total), 1966 census*

	Sydney	Melbourne	Adelaide	Brisbane	Perth	Hobart
	%	%	%	%	%	%
FLATS						
(a) Age						
up to 29	9	4	2	11	6	4
30–59	37	38	46	58	27	36
60 +	54	59	54	33	67	60
(b) Female householders as a % of total householders	43	43	51	28	44	50
HOUSES AND FLATS						
(a) Age	8	5	6	12	10	8
30–59	56	48	62	67	56	51
60 +	38	47	32	23	33	39
(b) Female householders as a % of total householders	26	25	19	20	25	21

Source: Compiled from summary data supplied by the Commonwealth Statistician (cross-classification data for household heads only).

TABLE 39 *Age of the household heads in female-headed households in metropolitan total private dwellings, Commission and private (per cent of total), 1966 census*

	Sydney	Melbourne	Adelaide	Brisbane	Perth	Hobart
	%	%	%	%	%	%
FLATS						
(a) Age						
up to 29	13	14	12	21	21	18
30–59	41	39	30	43	40	40
60 +	45	46	57	38	41	41
(b) Female householders as a % of total householders	32	32	37	28	35	32
HOUSES AND FLATS						
(a) Age						
up to 29	6	7	7	7	8	7
30–59	44	40	39	42	45	41
60 +	51	54	55	52	48	51
(b) Female householders as a % of total householders	20	19	17	19	20	17

Source: Compiled from summary data supplied by the Commonwealth Statistician (cross-classification data for household heads only).

Perhaps a more revealing figure is the proportion of total public housing rented households headed by a female. A very large percentage of householders in Commission flats are females, from 28 per cent in the QHC (lowest, reflecting the lack of a significant aged housing programme in the QHC) to 51 per cent in the SAHT. For public housing units (the average for houses and flats) the proportion of female householders ranges from 19 per cent in the SAHT to 26 per cent in the NSWHC. This is generally higher than the average for all householders in the population (houses and flats), although in Brisbane and Adelaide the numbers of female-headed households in private housing are close to those in public housing. The social consequences of the concentration of female households in public housing is discussed briefly in chapter 9.

The physically handicapped

The two main categories under this heading are those aged persons in need of regular medical care and the physically handicapped such as spastics. It is difficult to obtain adequate details of the exact numbers of households in Australia falling into the category of low income physically handicapped. In 1960 the Australian Advisory Council for the Physically Handicapped made the claim that there were 50,000 persons in Australia in need of assistance in the form of specialized housing from housing authorities. The SAHT has constructed subsidized housing for the disabled. The programme was begun in 1966 and by 1967 a total of 26 dwellings were available, all with specialized design features such as larger than normal rooms, because of the need for wheel chair manoeuvrability, and special positioning of light switches. The THC constructed three houses for the handicapped in 1968, and the other Commissions generally do minor alterations to dwellings to enable disabled applicants to live in them. The VHC, for example, frequently installs special ramps, but these dwellings are not in the same category as the highly specialized units built by the SAHT and the THC. In 1967 the Commonwealth government legislated for the provision of large subsidies for the construction of specialized housing for the handicapped employed in Commonwealth-managed 'sheltered workshops'. This scheme is operated on the principle of subsidizing private bodies similar to that used in the Aged Persons' Homes Act and, by 1969, 99 disabled persons had been accommodated under this scheme.

The undeserving poor unable to pay economic rents and in need of specialized services in addition to housing

This section looks at the problem tenant in general, and single men and aborigines in particular. The problem tenant raises one of the most important issues in social administration: how to ensure that the available social services reach those in most need even though the most needy are often the most difficult to deal with and often appear ungrateful for the service.

The problem tenant

In all state housing authorities, and in public housing in other countries, there is a small minority of tenants who cause special problems. Almost invariably they come to the attention of the authorities through their failure to pay rent regularly, and this is usually combined with other forms of anti-social behaviour such as fighting with neighbours, damaging the dwelling and generally poor standards of domestic housekeeping. This section is concerned with the characteristics of these tenants and the policies adopted to deal with them.

In defining the 'problem tenant' two classification systems are employed. First are those covered by the traditional definition of poverty, with low incomes and low educational standards as the main criteria. The second definition incorporates style of life indicators as criteria. In an article on 'The American Lower Class' in *Social Research* in 1964, S. M. Miller developed four categories: (a) stable poor, characterized by economic and social stability, although with low incomes and poor education; (b) the strained, with a secure but low income economic pattern and an unstable family pattern (examples are 'wild' younger workers or alcoholic older workers who disturb family functioning); (c) the copers, who manifest economic insecurity but familial security (many of these are likely to be downwardly socially mobile); and (d) the unstable, having neither economic nor personal stability. The problem tenant is likely to be a member of the strained or the unstable group. After reviewing many studies of these groups, Spencer defines multi-problem families (the term 'problem tenant' is used identically here) as those families which are of public concern because of their social and economic cost to the community and are characterized by a pathological family type, shown by inadequate or destructive parent-child relationships by both parents. In addition they are characterized by inadequate social functioning on the part of parents and/or children and extreme emotional immaturity of either or both parents. They are also dependent and/or exploitative towards the community and community agencies, persistently resist efforts to change their behaviour and are often in a state of chronic dependency on the social services. The Brotherhood of St Laurence concentrates on assisting problem families, and its publications document the existence of families with problems identical to those described above.

The numerous reports that were responsible for the eventual establishment of the Housing Commissions made frequent references to the chronically unstable low income households. But the logic of the housing reform movement argued that poor housing was the cause of all the social problems evident in 'slum' areas. The 1937 Report of the Victorian Housing Investigation Board claimed that, in its investigations into Melbourne's slums, it

> . . . found evidence on every hand of men and women heroically endeavouring to maintain a state of cleanliness in hovels in insanitary and vermin infested

areas, of attempts at gardening and other means of making slum houses more tolerable. We found ample evidence to justify the conviction that, given better surroundings and with some measure of home training, a large percentage would respond to and fully appreciate a better home environment. True it is there are a relatively small number of so called 'incorrigibles', 'unregeneratives' and 'unemployables' who might not respond. We believe that in most cases they are the products of the slum environment.

After the completion of the first VHC rehousing schemes around 1941 the VHC was disappointed to find that about 5 per cent of those rehoused from the slums did not respond to their new environment. An 'adequate' response was measured primarily in the standards of house care, especially care of the garden. Of the unregenerate tenants the VHC said in its Annual Report for 1941:

> There are some families whose vicious and slovenly habits are so ingrained that persistent efforts of the Housing Officers to aid their rehabilitation have been fruitless . . . Some are far below the desired standard, and although less than 5% of the total families rehoused, are a very bad influence on the estate . . .

The VHC went on to complain of the impossibility of rehousing many of the unregenerate or incorrigible occupiers of substandard houses and pointed out that as a result of slum clearance activities the 'paradoxical' situation was created whereby the most undeserving tenants were housed since they were in the worst housing while the more deserving tenants kept their old dwellings in reasonable condition and hence were not deemed in need of rehousing. In 1943 an amendment was made to the Housing Act so that rehousing had to be offered to those displaced from slum areas only if they were of good character. There was a change in allocation policy and although some consideration was still given to those occupying substandard housing, '. . . the most careful investigation is made to ensure that . . . the Commission has excluded families [whose] habits are likely to cause trouble.' The VHC expressed its satisfaction that its new allocation policy had resulted in few slum dwellers gaining admission to public housing. These new tenants '. . . were expressing their gratitude for the opportunity to make a home and raise a healthy family by care and good management of the houses, improvement of the surroundings and unfailing rental payments'. The VHC went on to say, 'The problems of the older estates are diminishing probably owing to the eviction of some of the worst families and truancy and delinquency have almost disappeared'. It complained that the tenants of its houses were protected from some forms of eviction by the rent control regulations in operation at the time. By 1949 the policy towards the 'problem tenant' had changed to such an extent that the Minister for Housing in Victoria, Mr A. G. Warner, said in a publication in 1949:

> There have been some complaints to the effect that the selection of tenants should not be based upon cleanliness, past record, etc. The answer to this is that some method of selection has to be used for selecting those persons who

> are entitled to occupy a new home provided with the taxpayers' money. Since we cannot provide reasonable accommodation immediately for everybody it seems sensible to select people according to their merit. Any other system might result in the selection of a dirty family, with a criminal record, receiving accommodation before a returned soldier with a good record and a clean family.

The CSHA in 1945 did not say anything specifically about the 'problem tenant' but it did make an allowance of 5 per cent in its calculation of the economic rent for vacancies and defaults. This was probably in accordance with the recommendation of the 1944 Report of the Commonwealth Housing Commission which argued that no family should be excluded from public housing because of the potential damage they might cause to properties. It also admitted that the housing of families in need of social re-education would cause many difficulties to the management, and the measure of success in this area should be the steady improvement in the attitude of these tenants towards the property and increased sense of responsibility in paying rent.

From 1945 to the present time all Housing Commissions in Australia have adopted similar policies towards the 'problem tenant'. All applicants have to undergo an 'investigation' before they are admitted to public housing. This investigation concentrates on their responsibility in paying rent regularly, and in having adequate standards of personal hygiene and social behaviour. The tenant generally has to produce references from landlords to show that he is a good rent payer. The dwelling occupied by the applicant when he applies for public housing is visited by a Housing Commission officer who reports on the standards of domestic hygiene and other relevant factors. The applicant is not told of the reason for these visits, so he can be observed in his normal life style. Below are two extracts from these reports from the NSWHC for tenants excluded from entry to public housing on the grounds of unsatisfactory domestic standards:

> *Case 1*: wife with ten children, eight under 14 years. 'The applicant appears to have acted without restraint for many years and without regard to the security of the family she was bringing into the world.'
> *Case 2*: 82-year-old woman. 'Applicant was of unkempt and dirty appearance, the interior of the house contains a lot of rubbish and the natural housekeeping standards are far below those required of NSWHC tenants.'

From extensive examination of about fifty cases, including tenants refused initial entry into public housing and others evicted after initial entry, a general pattern emerges. In cases where the inability to pay rent or poor domestic standards was obviously caused by such forces outside the applicants' control as sickness, the NSWHC was extremely lenient towards the client. But where the poor rental history or poor domestic standard was not due to any apparent outside factor, then the blame for the condition was attached to the client and he was likely to be declared an unsuitable tenant and denied the right to obtain or continue occupancy of public housing.

This is an example of the common distinction in welfare administration between the deserving and the undeserving poor. The exclusion of these tenants for such substandard behaviour appears to all Commissions all the more justified when it is realized that generally there are long waiting lists for public housing and there are likely to be many on the waiting lists who are similar in income to the families excluded but appear more deserving because they are likely to pay the rent on time and have acceptable standards of domestic behaviour. The NSWHC, and probably all the Commissions, sees the proper course of the problem tenant as was described by the NSWHC in 1955. Discussing the beneficial effects of improved housing, the Commission said:

> Proof of this is evidenced in cases where the first decent accommodation some 'problem families' had known was that obtained from the Commission. With assistance and encouragement they have reacted favourably to their new environment, developing house pride as tenants and eventually proceeding towards home ownership.

In its Annual Report for 1965–6 the Commission refers to the problem tenants as the

> . . . small percentage who will not accept normal community responsibilities and conform to a proper standard of social conduct . . . these irresponsible few forfeit their rights and entitlements . . . if they are allowed to remain, estates could deteriorate into uncontrolled and unsavory communities which decent people would wish to shun.

In its Annual Report for 1954 the SAHT complained of the 'substandard tenant'—'. . . one who is below a reasonable level of cleanliness, likely to be a menace to neighbours, or, without excuse, has avoided financial obligations in the past.'

In 1969 the WAHC explained its attitude towards 'problem tenants' when the Minister for Housing, Mr O'Neil, said in parliament

> It has been the Commission's policy since its inception to require applicants to have a reasonable paying history—unless adequate reasons are advanced—reasonable domestic and garden standards and acceptable social behaviour. The WAHC is not the sole provider of housing and it is considered that there is a greater obligation to house those applicants who comply with the Commission's requirements than to assist those who do not . . . The policy is not contrary to government policy. The Commission is required to repay principal and interest on loan moneys provided for its housing programmes. It could not meet its obligations if its tenants were not required to meet theirs.

There are few data on the exact numbers of such tenants who are either evicted from public housing or not allowed initial entry. In the NSWHC for 1968–9, a total of 132 tenants were either evicted or left under threat of eviction and another 214 were prevented from initial entry because of poor household standards or a bad rental record, together representing about 0.63 per cent of the total number of rental accounts at June 1969. No other reliable figures were available. There could possibly be others for whom public housing is noted for its attempts to change life styles and who may therefore feel discouraged from making an initial application.

The tenant with poor social behaviour such as annoyance of neighbours and poor care of the dwelling is usually also a poor rent payer, so the initial contact between the Commission and the problem tenant will be over rental arrears. If a tenant has no rental arrears and takes reasonable care of the property he will generally never have any contact with the Commission's officers except to pay his rent. Research in Britain has shown that rental arrears are almost invariably a symptom of what has been referred to above as unstable behaviour. Where arrears are due to unavoidable factors such as sickness very considerable latitude is given to the tenant. But when the arrears appear to be caused by the tenant's irresponsibility he will be pressured to pay the outstanding arrears and eventually threatened with eviction. Since the rent policy in the Commissions is generally based on the belief that the lowest rents charged are within the capacity of all tenants to pay, the failure to pay these rents leads to prompt action from the Commission. The VHC stated its policy towards arrears in 1958, and as it constitutes the one case where the policy pursued has been published in detail it is quoted here. The Commissioner of the VHC said at the Housing Ministers' Conference in 1958:

> We in Victoria emphasise that we mean business and the method works very effectively. The Commission's policy on eviction is: Final notice is sent when the tenant is two weeks in arrears. This gives seven days to pay in full. Notice to Quit is served when the tenant is three weeks in arrears.

By 1958 the VHC had written off only $2,286 since its inception in 1937, and it employs a debt collector to collect long-term debts. Rent policy is discussed further in chapter 8.

Single men and women

Up to 1969 Australian public housing authorities did not generally provide accommodation for single men or women under the age limits for aged persons' housing. The WAHC introduced a small scheme of ten flats for 'single working women' in 1967. These flats, however, were not available to unemployed women and they were not part of a continuous programme but were rather intended to encourage women's organizations to provide similar accommodation from their own resources. The SAHT does provide flats but they are restricted to those who can afford to pay an economic rent (this was discussed above). All Commissions except the THC evict single men when they become the sole occupant of a dwelling after the departure—by death or otherwise—of the other occupants of the house.

While the single person in regular employment can probably afford private market rentals for adequate accommodation, there is evidence that many single people cannot do so. An indirect guide is the number of invalid pensioners under 65 years of age (the general eligibility age for Commission aged housing). At 30 June 1969, invalid pensions were paid to 121,744 persons, all except 1,500 being under 65 years of age. Of these invalid pensioners (including those over 65) 38.2 per cent were paying rent in the private market. About 45,000 of these persons were in receipt of supplementary assistance for the payment of rent, which implies that they were generally in receipt of very low incomes. Of those on invalid pensions, 80 per cent were single, making the number on invalid pensions and paying rent about 36,000 single people. The level of invalid pensions is virtually the same as that for the aged, and it was amongst the aged pensioners paying rent that Henderson found widespread poverty.

Because information on the condition of single women in this category is lacking, attention here is focused on the low-income single male. The male population who do not live in family groups may be divided into three subgroups: adolescents or young adults who have left home either to assert their independence or to be near educational facilities or jobs; men from 25 to 60 in low-paid unskilled employment who are able to afford only poor-quality accommodation in the private market; the 'Skid Row' males distinguished by (i) their spatial concentration in inner city areas; (ii) a limited development of unique subcultural characteristics; and (iii) low-paid, unstable work patterns and chronic material dependence on welfare agencies. Jordan has estimated that the latter population is about 2,500 men in Melbourne, with a constant turnover of about twice this population annually. After extensive research, Jordan concludes that since 'homeless men have low and irregular incomes, their status is low, and their tastes are somewhat peculiar . . . much of their accommodation is of very poor quality. The whole inner city population of men should be housed better than at present'. He documents the current types of housing occupied by these low income single males:

> . . . The most chronic type of accommodation for this group is in lanes, deserted houses, sheds, railway carriages and under bridges; the next type is a bed in a large dormitory with communal facilities for eating. Storage and laundry and recreation facilities are generally absent. Included in this latter category are the jails and certain private welfare organizations; the latter type of accommodation consists of single rooms with shared facilities. The first two categories are the most common type of accommodation available in Melbourne for homeless men.

Jordan claims that the type of self-contained accommodation provided under the public housing schemes for the aged would be suitable for single men on low incomes. It could range from independent accommodation, hostel units with single rooms with communal housekeeping and eating facilities to hostels with intensive supervision for such groups as alcoholics.

Aborigines

The information about the housing of aborigines is very sparse, but an attempt is made to describe some of the general aspects. At the 1966 Census there were a total of 80,207 persons who described themselves as being 50 per cent or more aboriginal. Out of this total only 5,339 lived in metropolitan areas, 16,557 lived in other urban areas and the remaining 58,311 lived in rural areas. In 1966, 74 per cent of aborigines were resident in Queensland, Western Australia and the Northern Territory, compared with only 21.3 per cent of the total population.

From evidence available it appears that the aboriginal people of Australia are generally living in housing of poor quality. Poor housing is but one part of the overall problem of a non-western group whose native culture is gradually being eroded and who are able to obtain only low-paid, low-status jobs. With extremely low educational levels the Australian aboriginal population is inadequately educated for an agricultural economy of the late nineteenth century, much less an industrial economy of the late twentieth century. C. D. Rowley, an authority on the Australian aborigines, summarizes the position in New South Wales in 1965. The quotation is from his paper in the Duke of Edinburgh's *Third Commonwealth Study Conference*, published by Sun Books in 1965.

> With about 53 per cent of the total Aboriginal population under fifteen years of age, housing is in such a critical state that the special welfare authorities have attempted to develop their own housing schemes and standards, often with unfortunate results. Referring again to the non-metropolitan areas of the State of New South Wales, where conditions may be about average for the southern regions, and are certainly far better than in the north and centre of the continent, some 9 per cent of Aboriginal homes were legally owned by the occupiers or in process of being purchased as against 67 per cent for all homes in these areas of the State. Over one home in three, in 1965, was a shack; and a high proportion of these were built from industrial scrap and materials from town rubbish tips. Australia, perhaps partly as a result of the emphasis on large-scale investment and on immigration from Europe, has been faced for two decades with a serious housing shortage. For the nation as a whole, just over one person in every hundred lived in what is returned as 'shed, hut, etc.,' in the census. The figure for non-metropolitan New South Wales Aboriginals indicated in this survey was over 36 per cent. Aboriginal houses averaged under four rooms, *including all* inner sub-divisions as rooms, with nearly seven persons per dwelling. The average for all Australia was over five rooms, *excluding* bathrooms, and occupied by an average of well under four persons.
>
> Location of Aboriginal housing on the fringe of a town, where this happens, means that it is often on public land, so that the occupier has no control of the site. As occupation may be illegal, municipal services may be limited and the house subject to demolition. These are the sites most liable to flooding; and with poor construction they seem to offer special health hazards.

Generally each state has an authority that does provide housing for aborigines, but this housing is usually below normal Housing Commission standard and, as Rowley points out above, tends to be segregated from the white population—usually on the fringe of country towns. All State Housing

Commissions have always allowed aboriginal tenants access to public housing provided they fulfil the normal requirements for payment of rental, care of grounds and general satisfactory behaviour described above in the section on the 'problem tenant'.

A University of Queensland study by F. J. Schonell *et al.* (*School Attainments and Home Backgrounds of Aboriginal Children*, Brisbane, 1960) found that, out of a sample of aboriginal households visited, in a majority:

> Not only were the homes dirty but yards were littered with rubbish and no attempt had been made to grow lawns or gardens. There was an obvious need for instruction, advice and example to the aborigine community in regard to this aspect of living. In addition the households had poor standards of domestic economy, wasting money on non-essentials, strong drink and gambling.

At the Housing Ministers' Conference in 1964 a representative from the WAHC complained that the aboriginal tenants '. . . are lamentably poor payers . . . only 40 to 50 per cent of them pay their rent'. Referring to the Victorian scheme, Mr Gaskin, the VHC chairman, said at the 1964 Conference:

> Up to date we have had no problems with them other than the ordinary aboriginal problems. They do not think they should pay rent . . . Under the scheme the Commission has housed only 8 or ten families . . . We investigate these families carefully to see whether they will become suitable tenants and will be able to live among the white population. If they do not come up to requirements we do not accept them . . . We feel that by careful selection and close supervision accepted aborigines can become suitable tenants.

The situation is similar in the NSWHC, the QHC, the THC and the WAHC. The Commissions accept the more assimilated families while the others are either accommodated by other government organizations or find their own, often inferior, housing.

In her study printed in Ronald Taft *et al. Attitudes and Conditions (The Australian Aborigines)*, Canberra, 1970, Pamela Beasley found that although the aborigines there were considerably more assimilated than those in the country, few of them were eligible for Housing Commission dwellings, partly because they wished to place more than one family in a dwelling, a practice generally not allowed in Commission housing. Although the collection of numerous related individuals under one roof was partly an effort to cover the cost of high rents it was also the result of the obligations of kin to provide hospitality and a desire to be with relatives and friends from one's own rural area.

In 1968 the Commonwealth government allocated funds for the provision of housing for aborigines in need of assistance. Although not always administered by the Housing Commissions, this scheme does generally plan to provide housing of normal Housing Commission standards, integrated into white suburbs. In 1968–9, the first year of the scheme, the Commonwealth advanced $2,400,000, in 1969–70, $3,715,000 and in 1970–1, $4,800,000. The number of dwellings built was unavailable. Since the aboriginal population is growing at a much more rapid rate than the overall population, this programme may not be sufficient to overcome the backlog of poor aboriginal housing and provide for the additional growth. Lovejoy argues that to overcome the backlog in aboriginal housing in twenty years, about $18 million a year would have to be allocated ('Costing the Aboriginal Housing Problem', *Australian Quarterly*, March 1971).

Strategies for assisting the problem tenant and the aborigines

One possible strategy for dealing with problem tenants is the provision of low-quality dwellings. From 1945 to around the mid-1950s all states (except New South Wales and South Australia where it continued until about 1964) had an adequate supply of poor-quality dwellings for problem tenants. These were termed 'emergency dwellings' and were converted war-time buildings to deal with the severe housing shortage after World War II. Generally they were of poor quality and were rented cheaply. These dwellings provided temporary housing for various groups but they acted as a type of 'filter' for problem families. Generally only those families with adequate housekeeping and rental paying habits were allocated to permanent dwellings so that after a period the emergency housing areas became concentrations of problem tenants. They were typically the subject of much unfavourable publicity, and the removal of these temporary dwellings probably meant that a larger number of problem tenants were not allowed into public housing. It is the normal practice in the United Kingdom to establish special housing areas for the treatment of problem tenants. The dwellings provided are of the normal public housing standard but the families are grouped together and are under constant supervision. When they improve their behaviour they are allocated a normal unsupervised dwelling. Some concentration of these tenants enables detailed supervision by social workers and other specialists. This approach has also been used in Sweden.

One possible objection to this emphasis on social rehabilitation of problem families is that it may be an attempt to force people to change their life styles against their will. Some recent research into poverty has suggested that some sections of the poor have a separate culture where the types of behaviour that are generally considered pathological (crime, desertion, delinquency, lack of tidiness) are actually distinctive features of a particular life style. Much discussion of the problem family may, in fact, reflect the attitude of middle class groups when confronted by the lower class subculture. Ideas of responsibility, child rearing in certain ways, housekeeping standards, and social morality all involve value judgments. There is much controversy on this matter and no definite conclusions can be given. However, the most recent research suggests that there is not a definite 'culture of poverty' and lower-class life styles are usually an adaptation to low incomes and a highly insecure life style. The question of whether or not to concentrate problem tenants in comparatively large numbers is discussed in chapter 9.

Although the Commissions generally admit that they have some responsibility for the supply of services in addition to housing, financial constraints prevent them from providing additional social services. The estate officers employed by the Commissions have as their tasks the inspection and maintenance of properties, and usually the collection of rent. These officers usually have many dwellings to supervise (in the VHC the ratio in the metropolitan area was one estate officer to 700 VHC dwellings). The only social service function that the estate officer can attempt to fulfil is that of referring the tenant to the various social welfare agencies, both private and government. In 1969 none of the state housing authorities employed qualified social workers. The only major attempt by an Australian housing authority to use intensive casework methods for the rehabilitation of problem tenants was the VHC from 1940 to 1945. The VHC also co-operated with the Brotherhood of St Laurence in the attempt to rehabilitate problem families in Melbourne, but this project was small and did not lead to additional projects. The Brotherhood of St Laurence continues casework with problem tenants as part of its normal welfare programme. A worker at the Brotherhood said in 1966:

> . . . in our own agency there are many people who have already been evicted from the Commission (VHC) home that they waited years to get, because they are not fit tenants. Much of our casework with so called problem families is aimed at getting them to a certain standard so they will be acceptable to the Commission, and once they are granted a dwelling, constant supervision and support is often needed to keep them there.

This form of assistance to problem tenants is dependent on the voluntary welfare network and obviously may be piecemeal and unco-ordinated.

Before we can have much confidence in rehabilitation casework, social workers must prove that intensive counselling has positive effects. To date two research projects which appear to be soundly based have tested casework effectiveness and come to very pessimistic conclusions. They are Henry Meyer, *Girls at Vocational High* (New York, 1965) and Gordon Brown (ed.), *The Multi-Problem Dilemma* (New Jersey, 1968). Where there is some role for social workers—in form filling and routine claim verification and some mild community participation planning—American experience has shown that non-professional indigenes are much more efficient than highly qualified, middle class social workers. Many social workers do very routine office work that could be done by much cheaper personnel, and the use of non-professionals in community planning avoids the difficulties of social class differences between traditional social workers and the poor. These arguments are verified in Frank Riessman, *New Careers for the Poor* (New York, 1965) and S. M. Miller, *Social Class and Social Policy* (New York, 1968), especially chapter five, 'The Credential Trap'.

The situation with the problem tenant reflects one of the key problems in welfare administration: the relative advantages of supplying services by function (for example, housing or medical care) or by client group (for example, to specific groups such as the problem tenants, deserted wives, and so on). If public housing was organized by clients, the Commissions would build and maintain the dwellings—which presumably is their specialization—but the administration of what might be called the specialized groups such as the aborigines, deserted wives, single men and the problem tenant generally, would be given to organizations who were concerned with supplying co-ordinated services to them. Something along these lines has been developed in Victoria to deal with aboriginal tenants in the VHC. The specialized organization in charge of aborigines (the Aboriginal Welfare Board) guarantees rental income and other charges to the Commission which in effect transfers responsibility for the tenant to this Board. At the Housing Ministers' Conference in 1968 the various Commissions argued for some arrangement that provided for the acceptance of rent defaulters by other authorities. This would remove the tenants from the possibility of eviction and would tend to supply specialized services to those tenants in need of assistance. This would eliminate the problem tenant from the Commissions' point of view except for the problems caused by poor standards of domestic behaviour.

Studies of other bureaucracies suggest that little will be done to assist the problem tenant. Bureaucracies generally direct their resources to those who respond readily to the service—the deserving poor—and neglect the problem cases who require a disproportionate share of available resources and with whom obvious success may never be realized. On the other hand, the poor may not be suited to dealing with bureaucracies and the complicated procedures involved in applying for public housing may elude them.

Conclusion

This chapter has been made difficult by the lack of data on many questions, especially on exactly who are in 'need'. Generally, however, Australian public housing appears to have favoured the 'normal' intact family with dependent children. The only exception to this is the recent VHC high-rise flat programme and possibly the WAHC trend towards high-density developments. The VHC emphasis on high-rise flats is further discussed in chapter 5 and chapter 9. Married couples without children and in employment appear to benefit from the flat programme in all states except Victoria where they are not eligible for public housing. Generally, migrants benefit from access to public housing, the notable exceptions being Greeks and Italians.

Public housing is less favourable towards those who cannot afford 'economic rents' and/or need costly specialized services in addition to housing. The one exception to this is the female householder with dependent children who has been very favourably treated in all states. The aged have suffered from constant disputes between Commonwealth and state governments over who should pay for their housing, which requires a very large degree of subsidy. The 1969 legislation may alleviate the aged housing situation although, as for virtually all groups, there is little accurate information on future 'needs'. The physically handicapped receive little assistance.

The third group—the undeserving poor with a low capacity to pay and in need of specialized services—fare the wost of all in their access to public housing. Attempts to 'reform' the life styles of these groups may meet with hostility and it may be more efficient for social policy to concentrate on improving the educational and employment opportunities rather than on housing which is probably not a dynamic agent for change in life styles. In the short term, housing subsidies may assist this group more efficiently than public housing. This is discussed in chapter 10.

5 SLUM CLEARANCE

In chapter 1 it was pointed out that public housing in Australia was partly the response to public indignation at the presence of large areas of slums in the capital cities. These slums were thought to cause social problems and their removal was to be one of the important tasks of the newly created Housing Commissions. By 1970 the NSWHC and the VHC were the only two Commissions to become involved in slum clearance and had cleared about 5,200 slum dwellings in block clearance schemes, replacing these dwellings mainly with about 12,000 public housing units. Thus only about 4 per cent of all public housing completions (in the six State Housing Commissions) are units built on slum clearance sites. But the discussions in this chapter are important despite the comparatively small role that slum clearance schemes have played up to the present time. The VHC desires to vastly expand its role in urban renewal in Melbourne, and the possibility of the supply of Commonwealth funds for this purpose becomes more likely as the Commonwealth becomes more involved in urban development. Much of the discussion here is centred on the VHC and particularly on the appraisal of future VHC policy.

Slum clearance and urban renewal policies in Australia have derived from four main objectives. First is the replacement of slums—inner suburban areas of poor housing—with modern dwellings, usually public housing units. The second aim is to achieve economies by the use of the surplus capacity in inner area services and at the same time alleviate the suburban sprawl. Third, there is the wish to arrest the decline in central city population by boosting residential population densities in inner areas. Last, it is hoped by these policies to implement general land use planning ideas, especially the elimination of non-conforming land uses, the improvement in the street planning and other aspects of 'comprehensiveness' in city planning. A discussion of these four objectives forms the basis of this chapter.

Urban renewal has had support from a wide variety of groups. Architects, social workers and town planners have contended that urban sprawl leads to such probems as social isolation. In addition, many of the decayed inner suburbs whose demolition was recommended were regarded as aesthetically offensive. Central city interests saw a chance to boost city government revenues and increase population in inner areas to help revive a declining central business district (CBD). They were joined in this by members of the intellectual elite who deplored the supposed cultural barrenness of suburbia and saw in urban renewal an opportunity to revive or create the cosmopolitan life of the central city. The building industry applauded the increase in building construction that would accompany renewal. Socialists endorsed such large-scale government intervention in the property market. Most debate on urban renewal is centred on the problem of finance, especially the 'need' for the Commonwealth to assist the states. It is generally assumed that 'urban renewal' in its current block clearance form is a worthwhile policy.

Table 40 summarizes the volume of redevelopment carried out by the VHC and the NSWHC. It can be seen that a much greater volume of land has been cleared by the VHC than by the NSWHC and that the building of public housing units on the cleared sites has more than doubled the number of dwelling units formerly on the land.

Between 1966 and 1970 the VHC has become increasingly involved in urban renewal. In 1966 it wanted to change its name to the Housing and Urban Development Commission, and in 1970 the Minister for Housing was attempting to pass legislation that would greatly increase the role of the VHC in urban renewal in Melbourne. On the other hand, the NSWHC has halted its already small urban renewal programme.

TABLE 40 Block clearance schemes in the NSWHC and the VHC up to 1958 and 1970

	New South Wales		Victoria	
	to 1958	to 1970	to 1958	to 1970
Total area cleared (acres)	31	74	47	275
Number of houses demolished in areas cleared in block clearance	720	1,430	568	3,788
Total number of public housing units built on cleared sites since 1945	1,411	3,472	1,371	8,635
Public housing completions in cleared areas as a percentage of the total metropolitan public housing completions since 1945	5	6	6	23
Public housing completions in cleared areas as a percentage of total metropolitan public housing completions for 1957–8 and 1969–70	(1957–8) 2	(1969–70) 9	(1957–8) 18	(1969–70) 75
Percentage of total area cleared used for private redevelopment	0	0	0	13

Note: The area cleared in Victoria includes about 30 acres of vacant land donated by councils, which have been used for flat building, and at one time were 'slum' areas. The figures for the number of houses demolished up to 1958 are estimates since the exact figures were not available. All figures refer to the position at 30 June for each year.
Source: Internal records of the Housing Commissions.

Removing poor housing

This section concentrates on four questions: first, whether the Commissions have developed reliable criteria for classifying the quality of housing; second, how much substandard housing still remains; third, whether the worst housing has been concentrated in areas subjected to block clearance, or scattered throughout the suburbs; and, fourth, whether the Commissions have developed effective policies for the rehabilitation of old housing. Each of these questions is relevant both to past activities and to future plans.

The definitions of substandard housing used in policy statements in the VHC have varied considerably over time. Table 41 summarizes the main estimates and is meant as a general guide. The first major investigation into the extent of 'substandard' housing in Melbourne was in 1937. In that year the report of the Housing Investigation and Slum Abolition Board was published. This report developed complex criteria to define a 'substandard' house. Firstly, the Board conducted external examination of the 85,779 dwellings within a five-mile radius of the centre of Melbourne. Of those that looked poor from the outside, 7,330 were selected for internal inspection.

TABLE 41 Estimates of the number of substandard houses in Melbourne, 1937–70

	Condition	
	Requires demolition	Repairable
1937 Report	3,046	3,138
1956 Annual Report of the VHC	12,000	
Shaw-Davey Report 1960	10,000	
VHC Housing Standards section (total in Melbourne—December 1968)	1,450	1,938
VHC Housing Standards section (maximum number in Shaw-Davey areas (above)—December 1968)	986	1,095
Number cleared in VHC slum clearance areas to 30 June 1970	1,822	1,966*

* Includes 407 houses demolished but not classed as substandard. The sources and relevance of these figures are given in the text.

Access was gained to 6,390 and they were classified according to the following characteristics:

brick, wood or stone
height of land in relation to kerb
external condition
estimate of age
state of drainage
construction and state of roof, whether any skillion roof
height of walls at lowest point
level of floor above ground
size of back yard
material in walls, condition of walls and party walls

distance from adjoining buildings
whether adjoining factories or stables
width of streets, whether through or blind streets
width of right of way
condition of natural lighting
condition of ventilation
number of rooms, sizes of rooms
internal condition of building
whether provided with bathroom, toilet, wash-house, kitchen sink, cooking facilities
whether subject to flooding

Out of these 6,390 dwellings, 3,046 were found to be unfit for human habitation and incapable of being made so. Another 3,138 houses were found to be temporarily unfit for habitation, but capable of being made so with adequate repairs. The remainder (206) were found to be fit for habitation. Many of the houses inspected internally had poor domestic facilities: 32 per cent had no bathrooms, 51 per cent had no kitchen sinks, and 27 per cent had no electricity connected.

The VHC Annual Report for 1956–7 claimed that there were 12,000 houses in Melbourne in need of demolition, but there is no indication of how this figure was reached. The Shaw-Davey Report in 1960 claimed that there were at least 1,000 acres of housing in Melbourne '. . . so substandard in nature that economic repair was out of the question'. This would amount to about 10,000 dwellings. The survey was conducted by two officers of the Commission driving around Melbourne in a car, and classifying areas in 'need' of redevelopment according to the external appearance of the house and the fences. The areas were assessed by streets and blocks rather than by individual houses. Referring to the findings on this survey, the Minister for Housing described these thousand acres of slums as wretched, sordid and verminous. The VHC has often quoted this figure of a thousand acres of slums. It was, for example, the basis for a major policy statement in 1966 entitled 'The Enemy Within Our Gates'. It was also used as evidence of the extent of slums in Melbourne during the controversy over the demolition of an area in Carlton in 1969.

The Shaw-Davey Report listed the areas it had found in need of reclamation in rough order of priority within each suburb but made no attempt to put all areas in a priority order. From 1960 to 1969 the Shaw-Davey Report was the basis for VHC slum clearance areas although the VHC did clear some areas in Kensington and Brunswick not recommended for clearance in the report. The VHC departed from the report in 1964 when it declared a 400-acre 'comprehensive development area' in Carlton where the Shaw-Davey Report had recommended only about 120 acres for clearance. In 1969 the VHC declared its intention to begin clearance of part of this area. In 1969 it also placed an immediate redevelopment order on an area in Richmond that was not included in the Shaw-Davey Report. The VHC, like the NSWHC, has very broad powers and can resume almost any area. The section of the Housing Act under which the VHC declares areas for reclamation states that the VHC may reclaim an area:

> Where in any area there are any houses which—
> (a) are unfit for human habitation; or
> (b) are in the opinion of the Commission in any respect insanitary or unhealthy by reason of the excessive number of buildings within the area or the bad arrangement of such buildings or the bad arrangement or narrowness of streets or the insanitary condition of the area for human habitation *or for any other reason* [my emphasis]
>
> and the Commission considers that housing conditions within the area cannot be satisfactorily dealt with unless the area is dealt with . . . as a reclamation area.

A Housing Standards section of the VHC, established in 1937, administers the housing standards regulations and decides what houses are in need of demolition and what dwellings are capable of repair. The standards used are similar to those defined in the 1937 Report outlined above and are based on detailed internal inspections. The section learns of substandard dwellings by reports from its own officers who inspect dwellings that appear to be dilapidated, from outside appearance, from information from the local councils and from various other channels including anonymous information. The section applies three standards of dilapidation to dwellings. The first classification is for a dwelling held to be fit for demolition. The second is a compliance order, which means that the dwelling can be repaired to bring it into compliance with the housing regulations. The third denotes a mild state of disrepair. At 30 December 1968, there were demolition orders on 1,450 houses in the metropolitan area, and a total of 1,938 houses in the metropolitan area with compliance or state of disrepair orders, making a total of 3,388 'substandard' houses in Melbourne. In country areas there were orders on 1,617 houses, 1,092 of them in the demolition category. Although the Housing Standards section is a part of the VHC its data have not been used to justify policy.

The NSWHC slum clearance areas in Redfern and Waterloo were the subject of numerous governmental reports from 1936 onwards, using methods similar to those used in the 1937 enquiry in Victoria. In 1965–6 the NSWHC carried out an extensive survey of potential sites for future redevelopment. Using data on property values, a reasonable guide to housing condition, the Commission found that out of a total of 278 acres of potential redevelopment sites in inner areas, only 3.63 per cent were considered to be 'ripe for demolition'. An indefinite proportion of houses considered 'substandard' were in areas with a sizeable amount of industrial and commercial land uses which could not be dealt with in block clearance proposals. In 1965 the Commission also noted that:

> It was apparent during the investigations that the constant deterioration which was a feature of the slum clearance areas at Waterloo, Redfern and the Glebe, has been partially arrested. Due no doubt to the sales of a considerable number of the dwellings in these suburbs, the physical appearance has been improved, and often quite substantial improvements carried out. Further, the forlorn atmosphere which was associated with slum areas, engendered by an obviously low standard of civic pride and community hygiene, was generally absent. This was so noticeable that in general it could almost be said that what were formerly looked upon as slum clearance areas would be better regarded as rehabilitation areas.

The NSWHC does not collect information on dwelling condition in a manner comparable with the Housing Standards section in the VHC, this task being left to the local councils, who appear to apply it only very haphazardly.

The VHC beliefs on the volume of slum housing in Melbourne are a classic case of failing to keep abreast of changing conditions. In 1937 when Melbourne was still suffering from the effects of the depression, a very thorough survey found that there were about 3,000 houses in need of demolition and 3,000 in need of repairs in the Melbourne area. From 1937 to 1970 much has happened. The inner suburbs have changed from rental housing to owner occupation, a key factor in rehabilitation. Incomes have risen enormously and migrants have moved into the inner suburbs. The economy is healthy and there is very little unemployment. Every possible indication suggests that the volume of slums in Melbourne is decreasing rather than increasing as the VHC suggests. Moreover, the VHC has demolished over 3,000 dwellings since 1937 as part of its clearance programmes and countless others have been demolished in other areas as a result of its housing standards legislation. In addition many poor houses have been removed by the expansion of industry into much inner urban housing areas and also the very large private flat building programme which is naturally attracted to areas of poor housing, especially the small pockets. It is a pity that the VHC does not read the 1937 Report more carefully. Oswald Barnett was a very intelligent man and while he very skilfully played on people's emotions to establish a public housing programme he knew that the problem of the slums was overwhelmingly the problem of poverty. He also knew, and his survey had shown, that the most important feature of poor housing in Melbourne was its scattered nature. He recommended small, pocket redevelopment and rehabilitation, rather than block clearance on the VHC scale.

Quality of housing demolished in block clearance

Since 1937 the VHC has cleared 275 acres of 'slums', containing a total of 3,788 dwellings of which 1,822 were deemed fit only for demolition under the standard of habitation regulations. Another 1,559 were declared to have been repairable and 407 were not in any way substandard. Figures provided by the Housing Standards section in the VHC suggest that a maximum of about 12 per cent of the houses in the Shaw-Davey areas planned for future clearance are suitable only for demolition. Many of the houses with demolition orders may not be in these clearance areas, partly because the Commission does not consider that clearance in areas of industrial development is a feasible proposition, given the high cost of acquisition. The Shaw-Davey Report in 1960 admitted that it had taken no account of the industrial zones in Melbourne: '. . . some of which contained the worst houses in the most advanced stages of deterioration'. Except for a minor project at Sale, block clearance has been a metropolitan policy and has done nothing to remove 'substandard' housing in country areas. The effect of block clearance on the removal of housing fit for demolition had been further complicated by the tendency of the Commission to clear areas that were not deemed fit for clearance in the Shaw-Davey Report.

By June 1970 the NSWHC had virtually ceased the clearance and redevelopment of the areas commonly known as 'slums'. It had demolished a total of 1,130 dwellings in clearance areas. All available indicators suggest that these houses were generally of poor quality. Table 40 showed that the areas cleared in New South Wales were of much greater density before clearance than in Victoria. A case study of the area cleared by the Commission in Redfern showed that, with a few exceptions, the houses in the areas cleared were of lower average value than in non-clearance areas nearby.

Rehabilitation policies

Except for a small scheme in the WAHC to assist aged pensioners to maintain their dwellings and a brief period during which the VHC retained sound dwellings and built terrace houses between them, no state housing authority does anything positive to assist dwelling rehabilitation, although there is provision for this in the Housing Acts in most states. The Commissions could usually provide subsidies for this from profits which are discussed in chapter 8. Britain and the United States supply loans and grants for the rehabilitation of old dwellings as an integral part of housing policy.

It was pointed out in chapter 1 that, because of the presence of neighbourhood externalities, some government intervention would be necessary to rehabilitate slum areas. Government-controlled zoning or code enforcement legislation may attain co-ordinated maintenance. The VHC and the SAHT operate extensive code enforcement schemes where dwellings are threatened with 'unfit for human habitation' orders unless the owners improve them. Studies in the United States have found that punitive action against owners of substandard housing without assistance through subsidies results in the accelerated abandonment of the units or their conversion to non-residential functions. A number of studies have also shown that rent control can lead to low levels of maintenance and that owner-occupancy is associated with a higher standard of maintenance than other forms of occupancy. Hence policies that relax rent control and increase owner-occupancy are likely to improve the quality of dwellings.

Rehabilitation has not had a very happy career in the United States and Britain. Indeed in both countries there has been much bitter opposition to rehabilitation programmes from people in the areas to be 'improved'. The reason for this has already been mentioned in this chapter: poor housing is a symptom of low incomes and anything that improves the quality of housing will raise its price and so, unless the poor are given the capacity to pay for improved housing, in the long run they will have to leave the improved housing for cheaper housing of lower quality. Thus, in some ways the effects of rehabilitation are not very different in principle from those of block clearance—it simply still displaces the poor. Even if rehabilitation costs are completely subsidized the problem remains: the housing still passes into a higher income group if the initial low income household vacates for some reason. In Australia urban renewal is such a powerful movement that, in Melbourne at least, the suggestion that rehabilitation is really not a very desirable alternative to clearance is treated with accusations of heresy. It is better to support it than the even more destructive block clearance. Perhaps when economists or sociologists obtain more influence in the planning profession they will shift the focus of attention to the basic problems—the low incomes that cause poor housing and the likely high preference for apparently poor-quality housing by substantial sectors of the population—rather than simple aesthetic preferences by professional groups. Or at least the real objectives should be stated and the rhetoric of urban renewal not be couched in terms of general good, or worse still the good of those living in the areas to be treated.

The effects of redevelopment on those displaced from areas cleared

Virtually all past clearance activities by the VHC and the NSWHC have involved the displacement of groups of residents from the areas to be cleared. All these schemes have as one of their main objectives the improvement in the housing conditions of these groups. In the preface to the Shaw-Davey Report in 1960, the Victorian Minister for Housing wrote that '. . . the thousands of families living here in Melbourne under wretched, sordid, verminous conditions in the city's 1,000 acres of suburban slums . . . must be given the opportunity of moving into decent modern houses and flats'.

The only detailed relocation study was undertaken by the VHC in 1945. It disclosed that in North Melbourne:

> . . . the majority of the residents had no desire to leave the locality with its advantages of cheap transport, shopping, and markets, schools and churches, and amusements at convenient distances. Their rents ranged from 8s to 25s per week (probably averaging 16s per week), while those of the Commission's new houses on the outer estates were in the vicinity of 35s to which must be added the considerably higher cost of fares. The cost of the new flats to be built on the area presented a further problem as they indicated that the rents

> are likely to be over £2 for the three-bedroom unit and only slightly under for the two-bedroom flat. Even with the operation of the rental rebate provisions under which houses are let by the Commission, these rents are likely to impose a heavy burden on the average family to be rehoused. Coupled with rental difficulties are problems arising from the diversity of family groups which range from single occupiers to families with several children, while over half the houses contain families of varying numbers of young children. There are several owner occupiers who are reluctant to sell until they can obtain alternative accommodation. Some own houses elsewhere but cannot obtain vacant possession. One owner will not accept the purchase money insisting that the Commission should buy her another home and others have adopted a completely resistant attitude and eventually will have to be forced to vacate. Some owners and tenants are conducting backyard businesses, one a carrier with stabling accommodation for lorry and horses, and another a trainer of dogs. Some houses contain two and three families, others elderly pensioner couples and even single persons living alone whose most cherished possession probably is the privacy and independence of the small houses they inhabit. Mentally deficient persons, incorrigibles, and undesirables add to the complexities of the social problems inherent to extensive reclamation of inner suburbs.

This statement is from the VHC Annual Report for 1947. An examination of VHC Annual Reports around this time reveals a dramatic change in tone. If their content is a reliable indicator then the effective control of the VHC passed from people like Oswald Barnett and the author of the above report on clearance in North Melbourne to engineers, builders, architects and general administrators. Under the old regime the Annual Report was concerned with subtle human problems, especially the adjustment of individual families to rehousing. Under the new one the concern was with the buildings themselves, the visual quality of the site plan, a preoccupation that persists to the present. When the Park Towers project was opened in 1969 the VHC produced a booklet that is sought after by engineering and architectural students. It was the saga of Park Towers without the human element. The Commission was proud of the fact that Park Towers was given an award judged by the architectural profession. The residents' opinions were not sought.

An increasing proportion of households displaced from successive slum clearance areas by the two Commissions have been owner-occupiers and/or continental European migrants, especially Greeks and Italians. Furthermore, what limited evidence is available suggests that these two groups do not find public housing attractive when they are forced to vacate their houses. By June 1968 the NSWHC had cleared a total of 74 acres of 'slum' areas containing 1,430 dwelling units occupied by 1,829 families. That a higher proportion of owner-occupants has been encountered in the more recent projects is shown in Table 42. The proportion of the displaced population born overseas has also increased in more recent projects. In 1947 only 3 per cent of the population in the Redfern municipality were born outside Australia. Before clearance, about 20 per cent of the population in the area in Waterloo

TABLE 42 Percentage of householders who were owner-occupiers in the areas acquired by the NSWHC, 1947–65, before clearance

Date cleared	Percentage owner-occupied	Number of households
1947–9	1	583
1950–7	6	99
1960–5	51	849
Average	36	1,531

Source: Information supplied by the NSWHC.
'Households' includes a number of subtenants.

TABLE 43 Percentage of owner-occupied houses and flats in areas acquired by the VHC, 1950–67, before clearance

Date cleared	Percentage owner-occupied
1950–5	28
1956–8	54
1959–61	54
1962–4	59
1965–7	53
Average	53

Source: Information supplied by the VHC. These figures for Victoria do not include subtenants and hence are not exactly comparable with those for New South Wales. However, they do point to the main differences.

TABLE 44 Percentage of owner-occupied houses and flats in projected clearance areas in Melbourne, 1966 census

Clearance area	Percentage owner-occupied
Carlton	60
Collingwood	76
Fitzroy	59
Prahran	66
Richmond	73
Average	67

Note: The above table was compiled by matching Census Collectors' District boundaries with the areas defined for clearance in the Shaw-Davey Report in 1960.
Source: Compiled from summary data supplied by the Commonwealth Statistician (Collectors' District data for the total population).

demolished by the Commission since 1960 were born in Greece, Italy or Malta.

In comparison with New South Wales, the clearance areas in Victoria have contained, before demolition, larger proportions of owner-occupiers, as shown in Tables 43 and 44. Table 44 suggests that the proportion is likely to increase in the areas designated for clearance in the future. Before clearance, the areas acquired by the VHC have contained an increasing proportion of the overseas born, especially continental European migrants. This is shown in Tables 45 and 46.

Both the NSWHC and the VHC offer the displaced households public housing of similar tenure to that occupied by them in the 'slum' area. For example, a household who had previously rented a house would be offered a rental flat, or, if the family size warranted it, a cottage. If the household had previously owned a dwelling it would be offered a public housing unit for purchase. Neither the New South Wales nor the Victorian Commissions offer rehousing to single men under 65 or to single women under 60 displaced in slum clearance schemes, although they sometimes make exceptions in the case of women. There is evidence (given in chapter 4) that many single men

TABLE 45 *Birthplace of the foreign-born population in areas cleared between 1961 and 1966 (per cent of total) 1966 census*

Clearance area	Greece	Italy	United Kingdom	Total foreign-born
	%	%	%	%
Carlton	2	26	3	46
Prahran	13	9	6	43
Richmond	10	7	6	30
Average	7	14	5	38

Source: Compiled from summary data supplied by the Commonwealth Statistician (Collectors' District data for the total population).

TABLE 46 *Birthplace of the foreign-born population in projected clearance areas in Melbourne (per cent of total) 1966 census*

Clearance area	Greece	Italy	United Kingdom	Total foreign-born
	%	%	%	%
Carlton	7	25	4	49
Collingwood	30	8	2	50
Fitzroy	28	11	3	57
Prahran	21	2	9	44
Richmond	21	9	5	43
Average	28	10	4	50

Source: Compiled from summary data supplied by the Commonwealth Statistician (Collectors' District data for the total population).

are in 'need' of some type of housing assistance. The NSWHC has, since 1964, refused rehousing to those owner-occupiers in clearance areas who received comparatively large amounts in compensation. Although precise figures are not available, this has probably involved few families. The VHC does not refuse rehousing to such displaced home owners. It was shown in chapter 4 that the VHC and the other Commissions evict problem tenants from public housing. These evictions make it difficult for the Commissions to achieve the rehabilitation of social deviates which was an important motivation for the public housing movement in its early days. Presumably, many of these social deviates are displaced in slum clearance schemes. Apart from those households that the Commissions do not house even if they are displaced from clearance areas, the Commissions do not apply the normal 'means tests' described in chapter 3. Nor do those displaced have to wait for access to public housing after displacement; they are allocated immediate public housing.

The NSWHC has always been able to offer a wide range of housing to those displaced in slum clearance schemes. This is because it has concentrated on the construction of a balanced mixture of inner area flats, middle suburb flats and outer area cottages so that the waiting time for these three forms of housing is approximately equal. This was shown in Table 32 in chapter 4. The relatively wide range of rehousing offered to those displaced by the 'slum' clearance schemes is one explanation for the comparatively high proportion of them who accept the housing offered in New South Wales. An alternative explanation is the smaller percentage of home owners and continental European migrants displaced by the NSWHC than the VHC. This is partially verified by the recent decline in the proportion of displaced who accept rehousing by the NSWHC. This decline is correlated closely with the movement into clearance areas where the proportion of continental European migrants, particularly home owners, is comparatively high. For example, up to 1952 only 94 families out of a total of 755 displaced declined the public housing offered. In the clearance area in Waterloo cleared in the period from 1965 to 1968, 221 out of 689 declined the public housing offered.

Up to 1968 about 55 per cent of those displaced in VHC slum clearance schemes relocated in public housing. It would appear that, as in Sydney, it is displaced home owners and/or continental European migrants who find the public housing offered unacceptable. In July 1970, the VHC conducted a survey of its files on an area in Richmond, Melbourne, cleared in 1967–70. The area contained 127 owner-occupied houses (67 per cent) and 63 tenanted dwellings (33 per cent). Out of the total of 190 households, 72 relocated in public housing. Out of the 127 owner-occupiers in the area, only one purchased a VHC house in an outer area, 22 purchased VHC dwellings in middle range suburbs and 14 accepted a VHC flat, leaving 90 households to obtain their dwellings without resort to public housing. Of the households who had occupied tenanted houses in the area (63 in number) two accepted a rental VHC house and 33 a rental VHC flat, leaving 28 to find their own housing. These figures suggest a number of points. The overall proportion of displaced households who did not accept public housing (62 per cent) is higher than the VHC average given above. That 44 per cent of those renting in the cleared area did not accept VHC housing compared with 71 per cent of the home owners suggests that the home owners did not find the VHC housing attractive. The VHC did not compile any data on the birthplaces of the heads of these displaced households but an analysis of 1966 Census data for these areas showed that 21 per cent of the population was born in Greece, 9 per cent in Italy and 13 per cent in other European countries. This suggests that the arguments advanced later in chapter 9 are relevant here. These migrants wish to live in concentrations of their countrymen for sociological reasons: the social network in these areas helps to cushion the dislocative effects of migration.

The effect of relocation on the displaced home owner will be partly determined by the amount paid in compensation by the housing authority. In May 1970 considerable publicity was given to the amount of compensation paid to a household displaced by a VHC reclamation plan in Richmond. The Richmond Association claimed that in this particular case the VHC paid about 14 per cent less than the householder had paid three years before and that it was the normal practice for the VHC to do this in the area in Richmond. The VHC takes the average of two valuations made by local valuers. These valuations are claimed to represent the market value of the dwelling at the point of resumption. The chairman of the VHC (Mr Gaskin) suggested that the woman involved had paid too much for the dwelling in the first place, and the Minister for Housing (Mr Meagher) argued that the taxpayer should not have to pay for profits that householders in reclamation areas want to make.

The prices the NSWHC pays for properties in slum clearance areas are determined by the Valuer-General's Department. The basis for these values is the average of recent sales in the area. Apart from a $30 removal allowance paid by the VHC, neither Commission makes explicit allowance for the costs of moving, including such expenses as legal fees and stamp duties involved in a change in home ownership. The determination of the market value of a property in a slum area is a difficult process. Since the character and availability of finance is a prime determinant of market value in slum areas, prices of slum properties may be inflated to offset the high risk of lending and increase the effective interest rate. The lenders of high-interest finance may also require payment of almost all the interest on the loan even if the loan is paid out before the period of the loan has expired. This could happen quite frequently in slum clearance areas. Hence it is possible that compensation based on full market value may be insufficient to pay out the mortgage, let alone compensate the householder for his equity in the dwelling.

In 1971 the VHC had to pay about $180,000 per acre for its slum clearance land while the cheapest block the NSWHC could find, with the worst housing in Sydney, would cost $400,000 an acre to acquire. One would expect the opposite since the NSWHC has cleared only about 74 acres of slums compared with the VHC's 275 acres. Part of this difference is undoubtedly due to the general differences in land values in Sydney and Melbourne. But it is possible that the VHC has a large part to play in the depression of inner urban land values. Any real estate agent in Carlton will confirm that the VHC interest in the area is a major factor in keeping down land values. Moreover, the VHC slum clearance activity is much more widespread and unpredictable than the limited predictable NSWHC clearance concentrated in particular areas. The valuation procedure in Melbourne is open to criticism. There is no expert central Valuer-General's Department as there is in Sydney, and, given the absurdity of a free market in a slum clearance area, it is impossible to prove in a court that a VHC valuation is unfair. The VHC should not do its own valuing, because the vested interest is too great, and especially because the VHC believes that the 'slums' are overpriced owing to people's gullibility and rapacious landlords. Using a local valuer is also no guarantee, since he can hardly determine market values in such an area. If the VHC were really interested in helping those displaced obtain better housing they would replace the market value system with the more expensive but much better social welfare practice used by the University of Sydney when it took over large areas of Darlington. It tried to find the people housing at least as good as that from which they were displaced, and the people decided their preferences, within the low cost limits of course.

One important effect of clearance is the dispersal of such group-dependent people as migrant communities without the provision of satisfactory rehousing. Extensive research overseas suggests that it has a complex but generally damaging effect on migrant welfare. It is argued in chapter 9 that many so-called 'slum areas' perform valuable positive supportive functions in the lives of some low income groups.

The effects of VHC high-density redevelopment on the supply of public housing

In this section two questions are examined: whether inner area high-rise flats constructed by the VHC have been more expensive than lower density flats in middle suburbs or cottages on the fringe; and, if they have been, whether building them rather than the alternative housing types has reduced the supply of public housing in the Melbourne metropolitan area.

It has already been shown that flats have recently been the main form of public housing built in Melbourne. Since 1961 the VHC has constructed high-rise flats in slum clearance areas, and in 1968 all flats constructed were of 12 storeys or more. Such figures as are available suggest a wide disparity between costs of cottage estates and costs of high-rise blocks built by the VHC on slum clearance sites. There also appears to be a large difference between the cost of the VHC high-rise flats and the NSWHC flats built on non-slum clearance land in intermediate suburbs.

According to the official VHC statistics for the Horace Petty Estate completed in 1967 the flats in the estate cost about $12,780 per unit without land and $16,470 if the cost of the land is included. The estate consists of 614 flats (416 three-bedroom, 96 two-bedroom and 102 one-bedroom). Another estate for which figures are available is the Park Towers project, a 30-storey block in South Melbourne. The costs per unit without land were: three-bedroom flat $17,216, two-bedroom $14,348 and one-bedroom $10,465. This project was completed in 1969. Land costs increase these figures by about $2,000 per flat.

The VHC has its own factory which produces pre-cast concrete wall units for flat construction. The chairman of the Commission, Mr Gaskin, said in 1967 that past attempts by the Commission to build cottages in pre-cast concrete had not been very successful. Brick-veneer and timber-framed dwellings had been cheaper to construct and the public took a dislike to the design of concrete houses and showed a marked preference for the normal conventional home. The emphasis on flat construction by the VHC may be influenced by the need to keep the factory in production. The factory employed 798 in 1968, while other sections of the VHC employed 799.

Evidence from the NSWHC suggests that high-rise flats are inherently expensive. The Commission invited world-wide tenders for the construction of 16-storey blocks in Waterloo in 1969–70, and the successful tender was for flats costing $13,500 (per two-bedroom flat) excluding land costs and about $14,600 per flat including land costs. These costs are lower than those quoted for the VHC Park Towers project but are much higher than the NSWHC's costs for either cottages or middle area, low-rise flats. The cost of underground or multi-storied car parks is also peculiar to high-rise construction. They have to be provided or else open space is taken up mainly with car parking. Not only are high-rise flats more expensive to build but they are more expensive to maintain. Compared with cottages, flats contain large common areas that have to be maintained. Cleaners, caretakers, in VHC estates, numerous security guards to prevent vandalism, and lifts are some of the costly services, which, if involved at all in cottages, are done usually quite happily by residents.

In 1971 Commissioner Burkitt disclosed that the VHC was currently able to get land quite close to Melbourne, and much closer than, say, Mt Druitt is to Sydney, at around $2,000 per acre. Development costs for roads, water and sewerage were about $1,200 per block, bringing the cost of a fully costed building block for cottages to around $2,200. Good-quality, brick-veneer cottages cost the VHC around $8,000, so they could sell the cottages for around $10,500. Paradoxically, the VHC seems much more fortunate in cottage construction costs than the NSWHC where costs are rapidly escalating due to poor urban planning generally.

The NSWHC averaged its development costs for 8,200 lots at Mt Druitt, developed between 1966 and 1969: the average cost of water, sewerage and roads (including kerbing and guttering) was $1,773 per block and of raw land per block, $426—bringing the total cost per block, complete with services, to $2,199. Since the average cost of a cottage built for the NSWHC was about $7,000, the Commission was able to sell the houses at around $9,000 although in 1970 costs for a three-bedroom unit had risen to $9,500–$10,500. The NSWHC builds large numbers of flats in 'middle' suburbs in Sydney. These are not sites cleared of 'slums'. The capital costs of these flats ranged (in 1969) from $7,000 to $9,500 per two-bedroom unit, including all land costs, although by mid-1970 these costs had risen to $10,500–$11,000.

The high-rise flats built in Melbourne have been costly compared with walk-up flats in middle suburbs in Sydney built by the NSWHC. Hence, to obtain a given number of public housing units the VHC would have to use more finance than if it built cottages or flats. The VHC has refused to release the details of how it costs the flat production in its concrete housing factory. It has invested considerable funds in the last ten years and it could well be that the amortization rate for this investment is quite unrealistic and that the costs of VHC flats are heavily underestimated.

In 1968–9 the NSWHC spent about $35 million on dwelling construction (including land costs) and produced 4,277 dwellings. In the same period the VHC spent about $27 million and produced 2,131 dwellings. Hence the NSWHC dwellings were produced at an average cost of $8,400 per unit while the VHC cost per unit was about $12,000. These figures are highly aggregated and do not take account of quality differences between the two Commissions but they do point to the broad forces at work—the NSWHC concentrating on cottages and middle area flats and the VHC emphasizing high-rise flats.

The NSWHC receives grants from the state government to compensate for the additional cost of high-rise flats built in slum clearance areas compared with flats in the middle suburbs (walk-up flats). Because of this the NSWHC does not build fewer new units because of its slum clearance schemes than it would build had it constructed only cottages and walk-up flats. In comparison, the VHC is compensated by the state government only for the cost of acquisition of slum areas, and the entire cost of construction of high-rise flats (such as Park Towers mentioned above) comes from general CSHA advances, with a small proportion, similar to that in the NSWHC, coming from profits from house sales.

The effects of private redevelopment on the supply of low income housing

Up to 1968 the VHC had cleared, or was clearing, a total of 37 acres for redevelopment by private enterprise or other government departments. This policy has been justified on a number of grounds. The VHC argues that it will provide housing for the higher wage earners who wish to reside close to the city, thus alleviating the tendency for VHC estates in these areas to become low income ghettos, and that it will also help boost the declining central business district and lessen suburban sprawl—two aims of the redevelopment programme in general. Probably its most important justification is the belief that only the large-scale entry of private enterprise into the redevelopment process will enable the VHC to remove the slums at an acceptable rate, given the restrictions on the amount of public finance available. In April 1970, the VHC said that the 'redevelopment of the greater part of the cleared areas [i.e. slum clearance areas] in the future will need to be carried out by private developers'. Up to 1970 only about 13 per cent of the total area cleared by the VHC had been used for private redevelopment. That area previously contained 553 houses, most of them occupied by low income households. The new construction on this land is a mixture of private home units and office developments. This replacement housing is not intended to cater for the low income group, although the land was sold to the private developers at a price well below the cost of its acquisition. Overall, this subsidy has amounted to 56 per cent of the cost of the land. Table 47 shows that, if anything, the level is increasing.

The sale of slum clearance sites to private developers at a large loss tells many things about the VHC. It persistently maintains that this is not a subsidy to those living in the newly constructed accommodation. It fails to realize that there is at least a three-fold subsidy. Firstly, there is the subsidy caused by the use of compulsory acquisition powers and the dubious methods the VHC uses for paying the 'market' price for compensation purposes. In effect the householders displaced bear some of the loss. Secondly, there is the subsidy that is the difference that private developers are willing to pay for the land—and that is heavily influenced by the costs of alternative land—and the cost of acquisition. As the figures above showed, this was very substantial indeed. Thirdly, the finance for these units built on the cleared sites

TABLE 47 Land cleared by the VHC and sold to private developers, acquisition costs, sale prices and dates of sale

Approx. date of sale		Cost of reclamation	Sale price	Sale price as % of cost of acquisition
		$	$	
1959	O'Shannassy St, Nth Melb.	164,134	95,000	58
1961	Harris St, Nth Melb.	576,216	264,000	46
1963	Hanover St, Fitzroy	346,561	184,650	53
1965	DeMurka St, Windsor	245,514	95,000	39
1965	Lee St, Carlton	444,376	213,100	48
1967	Cross St, Carlton	480,268	199,000	41
1967	Wood St, Nth Melb.	605,090	208,800	35
	Total	2,862,159	1,259,550	44

Source: *The Real Estate and Stock Journal*, January 1970.

by private developers is supplied by the Home Finance Trust, a government organization, and is very favourable indeed: in 1970 it was at 5 per cent interest over 30 years, but the deposit was around $3,000, making it unsuitable for those on low incomes. Surveys of these estates have shown that they rarely do much to increase residential densities since they are mainly small flats occupied by childless couples who use the spare bedroom as a study. Many academics and other professional people with either small families or none at all think of the programme as a gift from heaven.

In May 1971 Commissioner Burkitt of the VHC gave a paper at an urban renewal seminar on a benefit-cost study of the programme. It gave excellent insights into VHC thinking. It has an engineer's perspective: it dealt with the demands on the services nearby and the additional revenues to the servicing authorities. There were small increases in revenue to the servicing authorities after the additional dwellings were constructed but this is not an argument for the programme. The essence of the benefit-cost analysis is the consideration of alternatives. And if the block of old housing had not been cleared in the first place and the money that was spent on both acquiring the land and constructing the new dwellings had been spent on housing in other parts of the metropolitan area and on rehabilitation to the existing authorities' houses then the return to the servicing authorities and to the taxpayer generally would have been much higher than under the block clearance arrangement. There is continual private redevelopment of older areas without any subsidy and the money that was spent on the subsidized additional units could have been spent on inner area public home units, with the same small amount needed for service amplification. When confronted with these arguments the VHC retreated to the claim that some income mixing was necessary and justified the subsidy to prevent the high-rise estates from becoming ghettos. Stopping the block clearance programme seems a much better way of avoiding the whole problem.

The surplus capacity in inner area services

In a publication in 1965 the Victorian Minister for Housing, Mr Lindsay Thompson, said that '. . . building up the population of inner areas along the sensible lines of modern town planning acts as an antidote to the suburban sprawl and . . . helps to ensure that the existing facilities in the way of roads, electricity, gas, hospitals and schools are used to full capacity'.

This section makes three points. Firstly, it argues that although there is often surplus capacity in inner area water and sewerage services there is rarely excess capacity in the inner suburban schools. In the case of schools the high cost of sites in inner areas probably makes servicing more expensive than in outer areas. Secondly, the capital cost of VHC high-rise flats is of such magnitude that it may exceed the cost of cottages on the fringe, even allowing for the cost of new servicing. Thirdly, there may be a surplus of services in the middle suburbs.

Inner area redevelopment generally needs no amplification in the water and sewerage network. Since public housing flats cater primarily for families with young children, schools, child care centres, kindergartens, hospitals and other similar facilities are likely to be important in inner areas. Although there is little comprehensive evidence on the effects of redevelopment on these services it is possible to study the effect of VHC high-rise redevelopment in Fitzroy, Melbourne. The population displaced from the area consisted of 351 children and 206 adults. The population of the newly constructed VHC flats was 1,568 children and 1,456 adults. Thus the total population increased from 557 to 3,024. About 86 per cent of the children in the redeveloped area would be 16 years or under, 46 per cent five years or under. There was no surplus capacity in the existing schools in the area so that additional schools would have to be built to house the estimated increased school population of 1.5 pupils per new VHC flat (the original school population has been deducted from this figure). Commissioner Burkitt of the VHC stated at a seminar in Melbourne in November 1969 that the per pupil cost of school construction in inner areas was $1,300 compared with $400 in outer suburban areas. He obtained these figures from the Victorian Education Department. Hence the probable additional school construction cost per flat in the new VHC development is about $1,350. This is because the schools in inner areas have to be built on expensive 'slum clearance' land and have to employ expensive multi-storey constructions to conserve space.

Even if it were assumed that there were no servicing costs for high-rise VHC flat developments, the high capital costs of the flats exceed the costs of cottage developments, including servicing costs. These figures were given above. The costs of three-bedroom flats, including land but excluding servicing costs, was over $19,000, compared with under $10,000 for a cottage, and around $10,500 for a NSWHC middle area flat, including land and servicing costs in both cases. NSWHC experience suggests that the one area where the surplus in services argument is of some validity is in the middle suburbs. The NSWHC has built many flats in these areas since 1945. Generally they are in small developments (under 100 flats), are of low capital costs (currently around $10,000 per two-bedroom unit, including land) and rarely require any amplification in the schools and other services in the area. The VHC does not currently build flats in these areas. Much more research would be necessary before definite conclusions could be reached on this matter. The costs of roads, hospitals, and other services would have to be compared.

The argument that since the VHC and the NSWHC account for only about 6 to 10 per cent of metropolitan completions of houses and flats, their policies, in isolation, can have only small effects on the alleviation of urban sprawl would also have to be considered. It could also be argued that since the Housing Commissions typically build well-planned estates on the fringe of the city—well planned in the sense that they usually consist of a large number of dwellings in a compact area, are occupied quickly and usually have basic services such as water and sewerage—they do not promote urban sprawl. Sprawl usually refers to the unplanned and scattered expansion on the suburban fringe.

Effects of redevelopment on the 'declining' central city

The current Minister for Housing, Mr Meagher, said at a conference in 1968 that '. . . we anticipate that by the year 2000 A.D. . . . in the inner areas of Melbourne there will be a need to accommodate an additional 700,000 people. They will be accommodated in areas generally run down and in urgent need of redevelopment'. Table 40 in this chapter showed how redevelopment by the VHC and the NSWHC has more than doubled dwelling densities in clearance areas. This has meant more rate revenues for inner area councils and, depending on where the VHC residents shop, more income for inner area retail establishments.

It can be shown that VHC policy has had only a relatively small effect on the loss of population from the central part of the metropolitan area. From 1947 to 1966 the inner suburbs of Melbourne (Melbourne, Fitzroy, Collingwood, Richmond, Brunswick, Prahran and South Melbourne) would have lost about 80,498 residents—if there had been no VHC redevelopment. This figure was obtained by adding the net population changes in VHC reclamation areas to the actual population loss from these areas in the 1947–66 period. The VHC redevelopment in this period reduced by about 19 per cent the total population loss from these areas. Muth has recently cast doubt on the assumed causes of this population loss from inner areas in American cities. It is part of urban renewal beliefs that this population loss is due to the decay of the inner suburbs—caused basically by the increase in the areas of slums. While much more research is needed on this matter there is some evidence that the loss in population is due to the increase in housing standards in these areas—especially the reduction in overcrowding—and the demolition of houses or their conversion to non-residential uses such as offices. There is no evidence to verify the 'increasing slums' hypothesis mentioned above.

Comprehensiveness

From policy statements and documents on urban renewal in Australia it is clear that the original aim of assisting those on low incomes—the slum dwellers—has become secondary to what can be termed 'urban planning objectives'. Two of these, the use of the surplus in inner area services and the revival of the CBD, have been referred to in the preceding sections. But since about 1960 two Housing Commissions—the NSWHC and the VHC—have become concerned with what is generally termed 'comprehensiveness'. This is partly the reaction of the Commissions to the constant criticisms of their original urban renewal efforts which were almost entirely limited to the removal and replacement of dwelling units. The movement towards comprehensive planning of a large area includes the provision of amenities such as open space, schools and hospitals. It was this type of planning that formed the basis of the VHC's 1964 plan to redevelop in Carlton an area involving 270 acres 'comprehensively'. Although the NSWHC admits that there is little substandard housing in Sydney that would justify block clearance from the viewpoint of housing condition alone, its planning officer stated in 1965 that future redevelopment in Sydney '. . . must be more than the replacement of substandard dwellings—it must aim to improve the total environment of predetermined areas and as such include action to improve street patterns and open space provisions, to remove incompatible land uses and to deal with the conservation of the better types of buildings'.

In Australia the trend towards comprehensiveness has been largely limited to physical planning considerations in contrast to the United States where recent programmes have moved much more in a social direction. The U.S. policy attacks the social problems of people in an area—the low incomes, low educational levels, poor job opportunities and so on. Because it incorporates social considerations, this movement in America—the basis of the model cities legislation—is based on the rehabilitation of areas of old housing. This is mainly because of the desire to avoid the effects of block clearance mentioned above. There are indications that pursuing the comprehensiveness objective in the VHC urban renewal policy will mean a continuation of block clearance and replacement with mainly high-rise flats. NSWHC policy also seems to follow this trend. Hence the movement towards comprehensiveness will not necessarily remove the difficulties raised above: the high cost of high-rise flats; the concentration on high-rise flats; the inefficiency of block clearance in dealing with poor housing; the effects of block clearance on those displaced; the doubtful surplus in inner area services; the conflict between assisting the growth of the CBD and assisting the poor; and finally the dubious benefits of so-called improved housing in alleviating social problems.

In May 1971, the VHC announced that it was phasing out high-rise development, without being precise. It also stated that it would place more emphasis on rehabilitation of older dwellings. In many ways it is just acknowledging the political facts. Since 1968 a highly organized protest movement—with the same strange bedfellows as the original supporters—has made it virtually impossible for the VHC to clear areas with the speed it needs to keep up with the output from its concrete housing factory. The building unions placed complete black bans on the clearance of areas for rebuilding by private enterprise. They also black banned areas for high-rise flat development, but released this ban in 1970 when it became obvious that many of their members in the concrete housing factory might soon be unemployed. The inner area councils almost all turned hostile towards the VHC; but the most important factor in effective resistance was the attitude of people living in the 'slums' to be cleared.

Despite great hardships—living under the threat of a bulldozer is not a pleasant experience, nor is the feeling when houses around are being vandalized or demolished—people in the areas have overwhelmingly resisted the VHC. In most areas the VHC had acquired only about half the houses two or three years after the initial order had been placed. Unless the VHC resorted to physical eviction methods—with the resultant publicity—clearing an area was very hard indeed. This had a shock effect on VHC psychology: it had really believed what it so often said, that residents actually looked forward to the clearance of an area and their removal from the slums. Most of the protest had been blamed on professional agitators, manipulating helpless people. The cynics argue that the supposed VHC repentance is a mere token: the VHC will establish decoy rehabilitation programmes and construct some four-storey terrace housing (a glorified name for walk-up flats?) but basically keep on with its block clearance and high-rise policy. The critics point to the fact that the VHC has not released its strangleholds on quite large areas of inner area real estate, in Carlton, Prahran, Fitzroy and Richmond. They also point out that the VHC is still talking of its 'comprehensiveness' despite achievements to the contrary. Moreover, the VHC is still convinced that the slums of Melbourne are not only still of huge magnitude but are spreading at a rapid rate. And private redevelopment of cleared sites is still thought to be a brilliant idea. As with most policies, time will tell whether it is best to watch the VHC's mouth or its feet.

Conclusion

The above analysis raises some important questions about the Housing Commissions' future in urban renewal schemes. If the Commissions are attempting to fulfil the original objective—to improve the housing conditions and hence the general welfare of the slum dweller—they are not likely to do so by a continuation of block clearance, especially in the direction of 'comprehensive redevelopment'. The Commissions have failed to assist the slum dweller adequately. The VHC has not developed reliable criteria for classifying slum housing, and block clearance is a wasteful method of removing the ever-decreasing amount of such housing. The relocation facilities for those displaced from slum areas may not ensure that the 'slum' dweller obtains improved housing. In this chapter, in chapter 1 and in chapter 9 it is argued that slum clearance is based on very doubtful assumptions. There is no evidence that poor-quality housing causes social problems, and if the quality of the social environment in a so-called 'slum' area is considered it may be that it is a much more supportive area than the types of environments sometimes associated with public housing, particularly high-rise flats. Slum clearance policies are inseparably linked with the supply of public housing since the cleared areas are almost entirely used for the construction of public housing units, usually flats and, increasingly, high-rise flats. In addition to making the inner area flats the major form of public housing available in Melbourne the high cost of VHC high-rise flats means that the overall supply of public housing is much less than the volume produced by other methods. Block clearance policies further reduce the supply of low income housing by removing older but mainly habitable dwellings from the housing stock. The VHC policy of selling cleared land to private developers at a large subsidy does not assist the low income household in any way, and although this policy has been only on a small scale to date the VHC plans to expand it vastly in the future. This latter policy, the aim to assist the central business district and the move towards 'comprehensive redevelopment' are clear examples of the tendency for the VHC to expand its operations beyond the housing of those on low incomes and towards wider urban planning objectives.

It is doubtful if redevelopment of the inner suburbs could raise inner suburban population densities. Public housing high-rise developments are usually able to double residential densities in redeveloped areas but this gives a false impression of the possibilities. The older inner suburban areas being redeveloped contain much higher overall densities than is likely under a total high-rise development pattern. This is because they were built when there was little demand for non-housing services. Today there are highly vocal demands for open space, schools, child care centres, car parks, libraries, shopping centres, swimming pools, hospitals and so on. Because of the need for these services the total redevelopment of an area may well reduce overall population densities. Public housing high-rise redevelopment has been able to raise densities in these areas only because of its essentially parasitical nature: it rarely provides any additional services even though serious strains often result from the redevelopment. It can survive only if done on a relatively small basis, the excess demand on the services being within accepted limits of political tolerance.

The next chapter shows how the SAHT has pursued two aims, industrial growth and low income housing, with little conflict because it has concentrated on expanding the total supply of housing as well as being very generous towards the low income group. It has managed to separate its urban planning aim from its low income schemes to a much greater extent than the VHC. The VHC emphasis on urban planning objectives is in serious conflict with housing the greatest possible number of low income households in housing that satisfies consumers' preferences.

6 AREA DEVELOPMENT

The argument behind the provision of public housing for area development is that easy access to such housing will attract or retain population, which forms a labour supply which helps to attract secondary industry. Industry is also attracted by the lowering of production costs implicit in the lowering of housing costs and hence of wages. In this way country areas are developed and the states compete for the location of industry.

Public housing and industrial development

The CSHA in 1945 resulted in the large-scale provision of public housing in Australia. The prime objective of the agreement was to '. . . provide a plan for housing . . . families of the lower income group, adequately, effectively and hygienically on a scale in advance of all our past performances'. Considerable attention was given to rent policy in the agreement with the intention that every family would have access to public housing within its capacity to pay. The Labor government under Chifley also envisaged that housing policy would serve other aims. The 1945 Agreement provided that up to 50 per cent of the houses built under the agreement would be allocated to ex-servicemen, the dependants of servicemen still serving, and members of the merchant navy. An unspecified percentage of the remaining houses were to be allocated to applicants who were 'essential' workers and were having difficulties in obtaining suitable accommodation near their place of employment. The Commonwealth may desire to populate certain areas for defence purposes, and for the same reason it may desire that the population be decentralized as far as practicable, so Dedman made another important provision: the allocation of dwellings between metropolitan and country areas was to be agreed to from time to time between the Commonwealth and the states.

The Premiers' Conference in August 1946 recommended that '. . . an appropriate number of houses should be erected under the Commonwealth and State Housing Agreement in such areas as may be approved by both Commonwealth and State governments in pursuit of the already endorsed policy of decentralization of industry'. The impetus for this policy appears to have come from the Commonwealth. The immediate proposal was to develop a satellite town at St Mary's, an outer Sydney suburb. In 1946 a conference organized by the Secondary Industries Division of the Commonwealth Department of Labour and Industry declared that there were three different types of 'decentralization'. The first was called long-distance decentralization which concerned country centres outside a radius of 150 miles from Sydney. Important centres were Lismore, Grafton, Tamworth, Wagga Wagga and Albury. Middle-distance decentralization involved places outside the metropolitan area but within 150 miles of Sydney. This zone included Goulburn and Wollongong. Short-distance decentralization referred to the building up of 'satellite' industrial centres in townships near Sydney, such as Liverpool and St Mary's. Housing policy was given a vital role in these plans for decentralizing industries.

The next important statement of Commonwealth policy was a circular sent to state housing authorities by the Labor Prime Minister, J. B. Chifley, expressing concern over the shortage of building materials which was interfering with housing policy. The Commonwealth Employment Service was to ascertain those places in which the provision of extra housing would benefit the production of building materials. Chifley asked the states to consider the Commonwealth's proposal that a special programme of housing expansion be embarked upon in specific areas and that priority in the allocation of dwellings be given to persons who were prepared to work in designated industries particularly important to the housing programme. Finance would come from the Commonwealth. The next innovation in Commonwealth policy was the enactment of a bill in 1950 which provided for the import of houses for allocation to essential workers. These imported houses were to be placed primarily in areas producing coal or steel or where other activities essential for national development were carried on. They were to be allotted first to workers engaged in essential industries and would attract workers to those basic industries on which the whole economy depended, namely coal, steel, transport, power and water conservation. Housing would encourage the workers to live in the areas in need of labour. It is difficult to establish the number of these special allocations between 1950 and 1956.

With the passing of the CSHA in 1956, the Commonwealth formally relinquished any power over the use of housing policy to promote the development of particular areas. The dwellings could be built in such localities and in accordance with such policy as the state deemed fit. The Commonwealth did stipulate, however, that 5 per cent of all funds advanced under the agreement should go to providing houses for serving members of the defence forces, and this provision has continued to date. At a meeting of housing officials in 1967, the state representatives unanimously rejected a tentative suggestion that the Commonwealth might stipulate that, say, 3 per cent of the advances under the CSHA be used for the housing of migrants. The states argued that there were already inadequate funds available for the provision of housing to low income earners. There is no evidence available to ascertain the Commonwealth's attitude towards the extensive use of housing funds in state policies of area development since 1956.

In the period from 1945 to 1950 it was agreed that housing policy in

New South Wales should promote the decentralization of industry. The subsidy conditions of the States Grants Imported Houses Act of 1950 provided that, in the selection of areas in which imported houses were to be erected, prime consideration was to be given to areas where coal and iron were produced and these houses allocated to workers engaged in these industries. By June 1954 the number of allocations under this system of preference was 2,839. The Commission had built a total of 30,525 dwellings in New South Wales to 30 June 1954. About 15 per cent of these special allocations were at St Mary's, just outside Sydney, 40 per cent were at Wollongong, Newcastle and Port Kembla and the rest were in other country areas. While it is impossible to ascertain the precise socio-economic status of the groups given these special allocations, the Commission did stipulate that these individuals be eligible under the normal eligibility requirements. As a result, these allocations were to members of the low income group, although they were given preference to others on the waiting list.

By 1954 these preferential allocations had virtually ceased. There had been numerous and widespread criticisms of them. Often these protests included a claim that the preference should be extended to additional categories of employees and interests. Prominent among them were requests from the various classes of public servants. Criticism became so powerful that on 6 July 1953 Clive Evatt, the Minister for Housing in a Labor government, decided that all preferential allocations were to be terminated immediately and claimed that the federal government had no power in the matter.

As shown above, the 1956 CSHA provided considerable latitude in the use of funds for 'area development' housing. Since 1956 various schemes have been introduced in New South Wales to allow the government to provide subsidized housing for groups ranging from government employees in country areas to migrant tradesmen in the metropolitan area. By 30 June 1968, of a total of 89,851 homes built by the Commission, 2,031 were allocated under these various schemes.

The link between housing policy and decentralization had been established in Victoria before the passing of the CSHA in 1945. The Dunstan (Country Party) government, in power from 1935 to 1943, initiated the use of housing as a key factor in decentralization and the principles were followed by the Cain (Labor) government which was in power, with some short periods in opposition, until 1947. From 1945 to 1948 about 400 homes were allocated to key personnel of decentralized industries, in preference to normal low income applicants. There was a change of policy in 1948 when a Liberal government came to office and A. G. Warner, the Minister for Housing, did not agree that public housing should be allocated in any way other than those in 'need'. The criteria that Warner used for the allocation of houses were designed to house only the lowest end of the socio-economic spectrum and he rejected a 'tremendous number' of applications for admission to the waiting list and for preference within that list. The

Liberal government was replaced by a Country Party government in June 1950, and there was a return to a policy favouring country areas.

This policy has continued to date. At June 1968 there were '. . . well over 2,000 houses regarded as tied', divided between various government departments and private industry. The most recent policy statement on this matter was in 1965 when Mr Lindsay Thompson, the Minister for Housing in a Liberal government, said that one goal of the Housing Commission in Victoria was to: '. . . foster the growth of carefully selected country towns on a sound economic basis. This will ensure not only that the pressure on living accommodation will be relieved but also that a growing proportion of our population enjoys the benefits of healthier, less crowded conditions in rural and semi-rural areas.' This was from *Victorian Housing—Today and Tomorrow*, a VHC publication.

South Australia has always regarded housing policy as an important factor in the economic growth of the state. In introducing the bill that established the South Australian Housing Trust in 1936 the Premier, R. L. Butler, stressed that the primary motive in the legislation was the promotion of the economic growth of the state. Fundamental to any policy of fostering secondary industry was the necessity to ensure that the cost of living in South Australia was lower than elsewhere in Australia. The provision of housing by the government was one means of lowering living costs. The policy had other aims which were summed up in the first Annual Report of the Trust in 1937: 'The provision of accomodation necessary for decent living at low rentals for persons coming within the low income group is vital to the maintenance and expansion of the industrial life of this State. Further, the health, morals and general tone of the community are closely involved in the matter.'

The primacy of the development aim continued even after the passing of the CSHA in 1945 and has received support from all political parties in South Australia. The original Act was introduced by H. C. Hogben, an Independent, and was accepted in principle by all parties, debates on the bill being concerned with details of implementation rather than the principles behind it. The Liberal government under Playford was in power from 1938 to 1965 and fully endorsed the activities of the Trust in using housing policy to assist the economic development of South Australia, as did the Labor government led by Walsh and Dunstan (1965–8) and the Liberal-Country Party coalition, in office 1968–70.

A general statement of these aims was given by A. M. Ramsay, the general manager of the Trust, in an article in *The Australian* in March 1969.

> All through its history the Trust has provided land, perhaps factory buildings, and certainly an in-built labour supply for most of the industrial development of the State. Whether it be the expansion of steel making and ship building at Whyalla—where the Trust provides almost all the houses and therefore, indirectly, the labour supply—or the location of most of the major industries since the war, like the oil refinery at Port Stanvac or the Chrysler plants at

Tonsley or Lonsdale, the Trust has provided the land. South Australian costs are lower than other States' and productivity generally higher and I believe the main reason for this is the merging of industrial development and housing in attempt to balance, in any area, job opportunities with the labour supply. Lower costs of housing naturally contribute, and South Australia prides itself on having the lowest such costs in Australia. Unique among the housing authorities of Australia, the Trust, for example, has the powers to build and lease factories and it has several million dollars invested this way. One of the Trust's activities has been to plan a development programme and supply a labour supply for an industry anywhere. Apart from Whyalla there was a power station at Port Augusta, a softwood paper mill at Millicent, a fish canning factory at Port Lincoln, and any number of small and large industrial developments where, with proper planning, the Trust has taken a labour supply to the four corners of the State.

The Trust has assisted in housing migrants by establishing an office in London in 1958, sponsoring migrants with sufficient capital and employment potential and offering them Trust houses within seven days of their arrival in South Australia. Particular emphasis was placed on the attraction of migrants with necessary skills in particular industries, especially those connected with the motor, printing, and metal trades and the building industry. From 1958 to 1966, the Trust housed an average of 650 to 700 of these migrants per year. The number of houses required by migrants under all schemes is shown in Table 48. Also shown is the total number of completions by the Trust. Migrants account for a considerable proportion of allocations. Tables 35 and 36 in chapter 4 and Table 100 in chapter 9 show that SAHT areas have a very high proportion of migrants, especially from Britain.

TABLE 48 Number of housing units allocated to migrants by the SAHT, 1960–7

Year	Number SAHT units allocated to migrants	Total SAHT completions	Vacations plus completions
1960	2,712	3,174	5,151
1961	2,448	3,314	6,095
1962	2,448	3,258	6,483
1963	3,984	2,882	5,946
1964	4,068	2,858	6,018
1965	4,668	3,317	6,637
1966	4,488	3,250	6,722
1967	2,680	3,228	6,833
Total	27,496	25,281	49,885

Note: The figures for the number of migrants are given in calendar years and the figures on SAHT completions and vacations are for financial years, June to June. Hence the completion and vacation figures are for 1959–60 to 1966–7. The above table, however, should point out something of the general magnitude of the migrant allocations.
Source: Annual report of the SAHT 1967–8 and information from the SAHT.

The most important single development by the Trust is at Elizabeth, a 'satellite' town about 19 miles from Adelaide. The Trust developed extensive industrial areas in Elizabeth which are either leased or sold to clients, usually manufacturers. By 30 June 1968, Elizabeth contained 47,000 people, with about 98 per cent housed by the Trust. In addition to the development at Elizabeth, the Trust has assisted the growth of industry in more than thirty country towns. The most extensive project was at Whyalla where, by 1968, 4,449 houses had been provided. The Trust also provides mobile homes for temporary housing for the period between when it first receives a request for assistance from a firm and when it is able to complete the construction—a period of about 12–18 months. The fast building rates in all these areas of industrial development are the result of close liaison between the companies involved and the Trust.

Up to 1955 the QHC had not become involved in allocating houses to 'key personnel' to any significant extent. Gradually this policy changed and by 1968 a total of 1,364 houses were tied in that they were allocated to applicants such as public servants and employees of private industry on a preferential basis. Total construction to 30 June 1968 was 36,605 dwellings. A Labor government was in power from 1932 to 1957. From 1957 to the present a Country-Liberal Party coalition government has been in office. It would appear that this policy had reached its peak by 1968. A 1967 statement referred to a policy change whereby industries were required to make greater contributions to the housing of their employees by building two houses for every one built by the Commission in the area being developed. Like some other states, Queensland introduced a scheme for migrant tradesmen in 1966. Overseas skilled migrants were given absolute priority for housing, and in 1967 a figure of 120 houses a year was given by the Minister for Housing as a likely number of houses to be used in this manner.

The first instance of the use of housing policy to assist industry in the country areas of Tasmania was in 1949 when the Commission listed a number of areas where it had allocated houses to industry in accordance with the expressed policy of the state and federal governments. The policy resulted in the diversion of resources to places of industrial expansion like Georgetown, where 250 dwellings were built to house the workers employed by Comalco. The two policies of giving priority to key personnel in country areas and building extensively in areas of industrial growth have continued to date. In 1965 a scheme was introduced to give skilled overseas migrants absolute priority in access to public housing in Tasmania. This was deemed necessary because of the shortage of some types of skilled labour urgently required to enable Tasmanian industrial enterprises to expand production. Up to 30 June 1969 a total of 300 families had been housed under this scheme, 178 in Hobart, 81 in Launceston and 41 elsewhere in Tasmania. In 1968–9 these allocations to skilled migrant tradesmen accounted for about 8 per cent of total THC houses available. The Minister for Housing in the Labor government, S. V. Ward, claimed in 1967 that the need to attract industry overcame his Socialist principles. He justified giving priority to migrants:

> . . . perhaps they [the migrant tradesmen] are at an advantage over the normal applicant but we think that if we are to make progress in Tasmania it is necessary for these tradesmen to come to our State to make our industries flourish in order that Mr Average Worker might have an opportunity to continue to work and be able to purchase his own home.

During the period 1950 to 1957 the WAHC gave priority to tradesmen employed in the building industry. About 400 units were involved and these homes were financed from general Commonwealth-state loan funds. To 30 June 1969 the Housing Commission had built a total of 910 homes for industry. This was about 3 per cent of total WAHC completions from 1945 to 1969 (excluding war service homes). Although general loan funds were used for most of this housing they were not advanced under the CSHA. It appears that this policy of assisting industry has reached its peak, and industry is now persuaded to accept the provision of housing as part of the establishment costs which should be paid for by the company involved. Mr O'Neil, the Minister for Housing in a Liberal government, went on to say that in his government's view the use of CSHA funds for this type of 'area development' housing was against the spirit of the 1945 Agreement and was not the purpose for which these funds should be spent. He claimed that this money was intended to help the low and moderate income groups, whom he saw as different from the groups benefiting from area development.

All state housing authorities provide for the housing of government employees in country areas, and the SAHT provides for government employees in the metropolitan area. Under these schemes a number of dwellings are made available to such groups as country school teachers, police, railway workers and others.

Decentralization—the general priority given to country areas in public housing policy

This section looks at the normal low income public housing programme and how it is divided between metropolitan and non-metropolitan areas. Hence it does not refer to the comparatively small proportion of the country programme concerned with supplying housing to specific industries and government employees although these dwellings are included in the figures used here. All Commissions have favoured non-metropolitan areas in that they generally build a larger proportion of the public housing units in these areas than is warranted by the demand for them. Hence the waiting time is generally shorter in country than in metropolitan areas. The following section, which attempts to measure this preference, is subject to a number of qualifications. It is assumed that the number of eligible applications is a reasonably accurate guide to the number in need of public housing. Some favouring of country areas may be justified on the grounds that private enterprise provides very little rental housing in these areas compared with large cities and the elasticity of the supply in the building industry in country areas may be appreciably less than that in the city. Hence the Housing Commissions often have considerable difficulty in obtaining tenders for cottage construction in country areas, and building costs tend to be higher than in metropolitan areas since the contracts in rural areas are typically small and transport costs high; but the low cost of land in these areas tends to offset the higher cottage construction costs.

Table 49 suggests that housing costs are considerably lower outside the

TABLE 49 *Rent per room, dollars per week unfurnished, in tenant, public housing and private, metropolitan, other urban, and rural, 1966 census*

1966 Census	Tenanted Houses		Tenanted Flats	
	Commission	Private	Commission	Private
NEW SOUTH WALES				
Metropolitan	1.56	2.00	2.11	3.41
Other urban	1.59	1.48	1.86	2.68
Rural	1.39	1.06	1.14	1.70
Average	1.57	1.65	2.07	3.27
VICTORIA				
Metropolitan	1.73	2.57	2.00	4.07
Other urban	1.69	1.55	1.80	2.64
Rural	1.62	1.12	1.55	1.82
Average	1.71	2.02	1.99	3.92
SOUTH AUSTRALIA				
Metropolitan	1.34	1.88	2.41	2.83
Other urban	1.42	1.14	1.49	1.81
Rural	1.22	0.82	1.65	1.18
Average	1.36	1.37	2.36	2.68
QUEENSLAND				
Metropolitan	1.66	1.98	2.73	3.08
Other urban	1.65	1.61	2.17	2.24
Rural	1.74	0.96	1.19	1.67
Average	1.66	1.55	2.52	2.64
WESTERN AUSTRALIA				
Metropolitan	1.49	2.03	2.14	3.40
Other urban	1.61	1.40	1.72	2.19
Rural	1.47	0.94	1.47	1.47
Average	1.52	1.58	2.02	3.19
TASMANIA				
Metropolitan	1.81	1.87	2.53	2.74
Other urban	1.70	1.53	2.65	2.46
Rural	1.25	0.78	1.73	1.21
Average	1.73	1.26	2.55	2.53

Source: 1966 census of population.

metropolitan area, being lowest of all in country areas, and that the rent levels in public housing units are very similar in all parts of the state. In Table 49 'metropolitan' refers to the capital city (e.g. Sydney, Melbourne, etc.), 'other urban' refers to all other urban centres (that is, those areas with a minimum density of 500 persons per square mile in population clusters of at least 1,000 people), and 'rural' refers to all other areas.

Table 50 shows the varying importance of public housing in the metropolitan, non-metropolitan urban, and rural areas of the states at the 1966 Census. It can give only a very general indication since it is a stock figure and refers only to rented public housing units. The low percentage of public housing units in the rural areas could mean that there has been very little demand from these areas, that is, the population growth rate is low.

The NSWHC has favoured country areas in the normal low income programme, although this has varied over time. From 1945 to 1955 it was official government policy to make the waiting times for public housing in country areas shorter than for the metropolitan area, but in May 1955 the Minister for Housing claimed that the previous government had been too favourable to country areas and that more emphasis would be placed on metropolitan housing. As well, from 1956 to 1963 there was a policy of selling 80 per cent of all new homes built under the 1956 CSHA and no rental rebates were allowed on new dwellings. Since non-metropolitan applicants prefer renting more than metropolitan applicants, this decision tended to favour the metropolitan area. From 1963 to 1969, country areas have been favoured. This was made clear by the Minister for Housing in 1962 when he said, 'From a cursory glance at the demand in some of the towns I think we might squeeze a bit more for them on the basis that it is a good policy to keep people in the country and we must help to that end'. Since 1963 the NSWHC has built more dwellings in country areas than would be warranted by the proportion of non-metropolitan applications. Each year the total number of applications for country and metropolitan areas is listed and the country building programme is 'loaded' so that waiting times are generally about half as long as in the metropolitan area. This policy was verified by a detailed examination of the relevant files. The extent to which the non-metropolitan areas in New South Wales have been favoured is indicated in Table 51.

TABLE 50 Dwelling units rented from state authorities as a percentage of total dwellings, metropolitan, other urban, and rural, 1966 census

	N.S.W.	Vic.	S.A.	Qld	W.A.	Tas.	Total
	%	%	%	%	%	%	%
Metropolitan	5	4	10	6	8	8	5
Other urban	6	7	14	2	13	6	6
Rural	2	—	2	2	4	1	1
Average	4	4	9	3	8	5	5

Source: 1966 census of population.

Table 51 may not register regional shifts in population outside the metropolitan area. It is possible that population was decreasing in one area in the country while rapidly increasing in another area and since housing is generally immobile, this could lead to severe housing shortages in some areas that would not be shown here.

The VHC has always had a general policy of giving preferences to the non-metropolitan areas of the state by making the waiting times there lower than in the metropolitan area. The VHC has been required to build at least 45 per cent of its output in country areas, although the percentage of applications from these areas has generally been less than this. Up to 1963 the VHC lessened the effect of this rule by including outer Melbourne suburbs such as Frankston and Dandenong in its definition of 'country' areas, a practice severely criticized by the 1963 Committee on the Distribution of Population in Victoria. Dandenong and Frankston have been major areas of VHC construction since about 1960, and the continued inclusion of Frankston as part of the non-metropolitan area helps to offset some of the effects of the 45 per cent rule. (Dandenong was changed from country to metropolitan in 1964.)

Waiting times in the country areas are generally lower than in the metropolitan area although the slum clearance activities have tended to make comparisons between these areas difficult. While the main form of public housing available in country areas is cottages, the major type available in Melbourne is flats. The waiting time for flats in Melbourne in 1969 was about the same as the waiting time for cottages in the country (less in many cases), but the waiting time for cottages in the metropolitan areas was at least twice as long as in country areas. The latest project is the plan for construction at Churchill, a satellite town in the Latrobe Valley. By June

TABLE 51 *NSWHC completions per thousand of population increase, 1947–66, metropolitan and non-metropolitan areas*

Period	Metropolitan	Non-metropolitan
1947–54	37	a
1954–61	47	128
1961–6	67	104

[a] There was a net decrease in population in non-metropolitan areas of 6,196 and the NSWHC built 2,108 dwellings in these areas.

Note: The boundaries for the metropolitan areas for Tables 51 to 56 were those used in the 1966 census of population. For these boundaries see *Field Count Statement No. 4—Population: Principal Urban Centres of Australia, Census of the Commonwealth, 30 June 1966, Appendix A.* These metropolitan areas include the outlying metropolitan suburbs.

Source: Annual reports of the NSWHC and censuses of population.

1968, 551 houses had been built but as there was little demand for housing, waiting times were very short. There was a possibility of surplus houses despite the removal of the restrictive 'means' test that applies in other areas of Victoria. The general favouring of country areas is shown in Table 52.

The SAHT generally favoured country areas but, as was pointed out above, particularly those centres experiencing a growth of industry. Table 53 shows the completions in the metropolitan and non-metropolitan areas compared with the growth in population. Waiting times for SAHT units were generally considerably lower in non-metropolitan areas, although Table 53 suggests that the Trust did not build a great deal of housing in non-metropolitan areas from 1947 to 1954. This was possibly due to the difficulty, often mentioned in the Trust's Annual Reports for this period, of obtaining building materials in non-metropolitan areas.

As shown in Table 54, the QHC strongly favoured country areas from 1954 to 1961, but from 1961 to 1966 relative completions have been about equal.

The WAHC favours the growth of country areas. Details of waiting times were not available but it was stated that waiting times were about half the comparable times in the metropolitan area, and this situation has existed since the early 1950s. There has always been a difference between the maximum income for eligibility in the metropolitan area and the country areas, particularly the isolated northern parts of the state. The income limits

TABLE 52 *VHC completions per thousand of population increase, 1947–66, metropolitan and non-metropolitan areas*

Period	Metropolitan	Non-metropolitan
1947–54	37	88
1954–61	30	389
1961–6	30	105

Note: The boundaries used for metropolitan (Melbourne) population and completions are those used in the 1966 census of population.
Source: Annual reports of the VHC and censuses of population.

TABLE 53 *SAHT completions per thousand of population increase, 1947–66, metropolitan and non-metropolitan areas*

Period	Metropolitan	Non-metropolitan
1947–54	103	56
1954–61	98	1,251
1961–6	95	417

Source: Annual reports of the SAHT and censuses of population.

as at 30 June 1970 were given in chapter 3. Table 55 shows that the WAHC has favoured country areas especially since 1954. Like the SAHT, the WAHC favoured the metropolitan area from 1947 to 1954, probably for reasons similar to the SAHT's.

Waiting times in rural Tasmanian areas in April 1969 were all under twelve months, about 80 per cent of applicants being housed in six months or less. These were fairly typical of waiting times during the 1950–69 period. There has always been a shorter waiting time in country areas than in Hobart. Table 56 shows that the THC has favoured the metropolitan area from 1947 to 1954 and from 1961 to 1966. The shorter waiting times in the

TABLE 54 QHC completions per thousand of population increase, 1954–66, metropolitan and non-metropolitan areas

Period	Metropolitan	Non-metropolitan
1954–61	45	362
1961–6	61	66

Note: Completion figures were unavailable for 1947–54.
Source: Annual reports of the QHC and censuses of population.

TABLE 55 WAHC completions per thousand of population increase, 1947–66, metropolitan and non-metropolitan areas

Period	Metropolitan	Non-metropolitan
1947–54	147	55
1954–61	107	a
1961–6	93	178

[a] There was a net decrease of 29,892 in the metropolitan population although the WAHC completed 3,144 dwellings.
Source: Annual reports of the WAHC and censuses of population.

TABLE 56 THC completions per thousand of population increase, 1947–66, metropolitan and non-metropolitan areas

Period	Metropolitan	Non-metropolitan
1947–54	82	45
1954–61	65	164
1961–6	142	103

Source: Annual reports of the THC and 1966 censuses of population.

non-metropolitan areas in 1969 probably mean that there is a higher proportion of vacated units in non-metropolitan areas than in the metropolitan area. In 1968–9, 5 per cent of metropolitan THC completions and about 9 per cent of non-metropolitan units were vacated and therefore available for re-allocation.

The effects of area development schemes on the supply of public housing to the low income group

This section discusses whether area development schemes have resulted in the housing of socio-economic groups different from those housed under the normal low income schemes, and to what extent funds for housing which is built to promote area development compete with, or are additional to, funds provided for other public housing schemes. In short, does spending funds on area development schemes mean that there are less funds available for those on low incomes?

How various groups connected with area development in its different forms have gained priority access to public housing has been described above. The section on the SAHT in chapter 3 showed that those in public housing in South Australia (Adelaide) were of a higher average socio-economic level than those in other states. But a large proportion of those housed in pursuit of area development objectives are eligible for public housing under low income schemes. In these cases area development and social welfare objectives would result in housing similar groups, even though the objectives may be different. Much depends on whether area development schemes merely result in relocating labour within a state or provide housing for migrants from outside the state. In the latter case, area development schemes could divert the supply of public housing to those migrant groups employed by the new industries. In states where there are no significant area development schemes, the expansion of industry in an area would lead to an increase in the number of applications for public housing which would lead to an increase in the rate of public housing construction in the area, but no preference would be given to them over other applicants.

There are difficulties in measuring the comparative socio-economic status of metropolitan, non-metropolitan urban, and rural areas. Since the Commissions generally do not construct large, complete public housing areas outside the metropolitan districts, no use can be made of CD data. There is, however, extensive information available for household heads renting public housing units in all areas of the states. This is presented in Tables 57 to 61.

Table 57 presents the occupations of the household heads of rental Commission houses and flats in metropolitan, other urban, and rural areas. In all states a much higher proportion of householders in the rural areas are in the first two occupational classifications (professional and managerial and self-employed) than in either the metropolitan or other urban areas. In all states except South Australia and Tasmania the 'other urban' areas have a higher proportion of their total household heads (in the workforce) in the first two occupational classifications, than does the metropolitan area, although the differences are not nearly as great as between the metropolitan and rural areas. The rural areas, on the other hand, have a much smaller proportion of their household heads in the occupational classifications three to five (clerical workers, members of the armed forces and craftsmen and foremen) than for either the metropolitan or other urban areas. The rural areas have a higher proportion of their household heads in the lowest group: personal, domestic and other service workers and labourers. The educational data generally follow the pattern of the occupational information and show that a

TABLE 57 *Occupations of the household heads in the workforce in metropolitan, other urban, and rural, rented public housing dwellings, houses and flats, (per cent of total), 1966 census*

	Metro-politan	Other urban	Rural
	%	%	%
NEW SOUTH WALES			
Professional	2	4	9
Managerial, self-employed	5	5	5
Clerical workers	11	7	4
Armed forces	4	5	2
Craftsmen, foremen	20	18	16
Shop assistants, process workers	34	34	26
Personal, domestic, other service workers and labourers	23	25	36
Percentage of total household heads in the workforce	73	78	84
VICTORIA			
Professional	2	5	13
Managerial, self-employed	5	5	5
Clerical workers	11	7	5
Armed forces	6	6	—
Craftsmen, foremen	21	23	17
Shop assistants, process workers	32	34	33
Personal, domestic, other service workers and labourers	22	19	26
Percentage of total household heads in the workforce	73	81	78
SOUTH AUSTRALIA			
Professional	6	5	19
Managerial, self-employed	6	6	5
Clerical workers	11	7	7
Armed forces	3	—	—
Craftsmen, foremen	28	35	14
Shop assistants, process workers	28	30	27
Personal, domestic, other service workers and labourers	17	16	30
Percentage of total household heads in the workforce	80	90	90

TABLE 57—Continued

	Metro-politan	Other urban	Rural
	%	%	%
QUEENSLAND			
Professional	3	8	11
Managerial, self-employed	6	8	7
Clerical workers	10	11	6
Armed forces	8	5	—
Craftsmen, foremen	21	17	14
Shop assistants, process workers	30	30	27
Personal, domestic, other service workers and labourers	23	22	34
Percentage of total household heads in the workforce	78	82	89
WESTERN AUSTRALIA			
Professional	3	8	16
Managerial, self-employed	7	6	9
Clerical workers	10	9	7
Armed forces	4	—	—
Craftsmen, foremen	24	22	18
Shop assistants, process workers	30	33	27
Personal, domestic, other service workers and labourers	22	22	24
Percentage of total household heads in the workforce	71	85	92
TASMANIA			
Professional	5	4	11
Managerial, self-employed	5	4	2
Clerical workers	12	6	5
Armed forces	1	—	—
Craftsmen, foremen	19	21	14
Shop assistants, process workers	34	47	33
Personal, domestic, other service workers and labourers	25	18	34
Percentage of total household heads in the workforce	75	84	91

Source: Compiled from summary data supplied by the Commonwealth Statistician (cross-classification data for household heads only).

higher proportion of household heads in rural areas have university or other tertiary qualifications than in either the metropolitan or other urban areas.

The data in Table 57 do not necessarily mean that those allocated public housing in rural areas have a higher socio-economic status than those in other areas. The cross-classification data used in this table are only for rental households and a much higher proportion of public households in metropolitan areas purchase their dwellings than in either other urban or rural areas. For example, in 1968–9, 69.2 per cent of the households allocated NSWHC dwellings in the Sydney metropolitan area were purchasers compared with Newcastle (in the other urban category) 61.2 per cent and rural areas (apart from Newcastle and Wollongong) only 30.2 per cent. Since those on higher socio-economic status purchase dwellings, Table 57 understates the status of those allocated public housing in metropolitan and other urban areas.

It is very difficult to determine whether or not funds provided for area development schemes are competitive with or additional to funds provided for other types of housing. Since the amount that a State Housing Commission applies to its programme is a state decision, this decision must be analysed but there has been little research into state budgetary decision-making. The NSWHC separates funds for area development housing from

TABLE 58 Education of the household heads in metropolitan, other urban, and rural, rented public housing dwellings, houses and flats (per cent of total), 1966 census

	Metro-politan	Other urban	Rural
	%	%	%
NEW SOUTH WALES			
University qualifications	—	1	1
Other tertiary qualifications	1	1	3
Matriculation passed	4	4	6
Intermediate passed	21	21	19
Attended high school	39	41	42
Attended primary school	31	29	25
No education	1	1	1
Not stated	3	2	3
VICTORIA			
University qualifications	—	—	1
Other tertiary qualifications	1	2	3
Matriculation passed	6	7	6
Intermediate passed	13	16	13
Attended high school	29	34	33
Attended primary school	47	38	40
No education	1	—	—
Not stated	3	3	3
SOUTH AUSTRALIA			
University qualifications	1	1	3
Other tertiary qualifications	2	2	10
Matriculation passed	6	7	5
Intermediate passed	16	18	14
Attended high school	30	35	22
Attended primary school	44	36	41
No education	—	—	2
Not stated	3	3	3
QUEENSLAND			
University qualifications	—	1	1
Other tertiary qualifications	1	4	4
Matriculation passed	5	4	4
Intermediate passed	17	17	16
Attended high school	22	22	22
Attended primary school	52	50	52
No education	1	—	—
Not stated	3	3	3

TABLE 58—Continued

	Metro-politan	Other urban	Rural
	%	%	%
WESTERN AUSTRALIA			
University qualifications	—	2	2
Other tertiary qualifications	1	3	7
Matriculation passed	6	7	7
Intermediate passed	18	19	18
Attended high school	53	49	47
Attended primary school	20	17	16
No education	—	1	1
Not stated	3	3	3
TASMANIA			
University qualifications	1	1	2
Other tertiary qualifications	1	1	1
Matriculation passed	6	7	9
Intermediate passed	19	21	19
Attended high school	31	32	28
Attended primary school	38	36	36
No education	1	1	1
Not stated	3	3	3

Source: Compiled from summary data supplied by the Commonwealth Statistician (cross-classification for household heads only).

TABLE 59 *Age structure of household heads in other urban and rural rented public housing dwellings, houses and flats (per cent of total), 1966 census*

	N.S.W.	Vic.	S.A.	Qld	W.A.	Tas.
	%	%	%	%	%	%
OTHER URBAN						
Up to 19	—	—	—	—	—	—
20–29	16	17	25	20	22	21
30–39	30	28	32	30	30	29
40–49	24	25	23	24	24	24
50–59	16	17	12	16	14	15
60 +	14	12	7	10	10	10
RURAL						
Up to 19	—	—	—	—	—	—
20–29	12	23	29	32	29	27
30–39	24	32	28	29	34	26
40–49	26	22	20	18	19	17
50–59	19	12	18	14	12	18
60 +	18	10	7	6	6	11

Source: Compiled from summary data supplied by the Commonwealth Statistician (cross-classification data for household heads only).

funds used for normal low income housing schemes. Each year the state Treasury grants the NSWHC an amount under the CSHA which is spent only on low income housing, allocated to those in 'need' as described in chapter 3. While the Commission has many pressures from various sources such as other government departments like education, decentralization and the police force for the allocation of preferential housing, the Commission has 'religiously refrained from using CSHA funds' for these purposes. By 1968 a total of $16 million or 2,000 homes had been provided under these schemes.

TABLE 60 *Birthplace of household heads in other urban and rural rented public housing dwellings, houses and flats (per cent of total), 1966 census*

	N.S.W.	Vic.	S.A.	Qld	W.A.	Tas.
	%	%	%	%	%	%
OTHER URBAN						
Australia	84	74	61	86	64	82
New Zealand, England, Wales, Ireland, Scotland	11	15	25	10	23	12
Austria, Czechoslovakia, Germany, Hungary, Yugoslavia	1	3	5	1	2	2
Greece, Italy, Malta	—	2	2	1	2	1
Other	4	6	7	2	9	3
RURAL						
Australia	88	82	80	89	72	87
New Zealand, England, Wales, Ireland, Scotland	8	8	7	7	17	6
Austria, Czechoslovakia, Germany, Hungary, Yugoslavia	1	3	4	1	5	1
Greece, Italy, Malta	2	1	1	2	3	—
Other	1	6	8	1	3	6

Source: Compiled from summary data supplied by the Commonwealth Statistician (cross-classification data for household heads only).

TABLE 61 *Marital status of the household heads in other urban and rural rented public housing dwellings, houses and flats (per cent of total), 1966 census*

	N.S.W.	Vic.	S.A.	Qld	W.A.	Tas.
	%	%	%	%	%	%
OTHER URBAN						
Never married	2	1	1	4	3	1
Married	80	82	90	83	87	85
Married, but permanently separated	4	5	3	4	4	5
Divorced	2	2	1	1	1	2
Widowed	11	10	5	8	5	7
RURAL						
Never married	2	3	3	6	3	2
Married	75	82	89	87	91	94
Married, but permanently separated	6	6	2	2	3	1
Divorced	3	1	—	1	1	—
Widowed	14	8	6	4	3	3

Source: Compiled from summary data supplied by the Commonwealth Statistician (cross-classification for household heads only).

The general favouring of the country programme in the NSWHC, as in all Commissions favouring country areas, does come from general CSHA funds.

The VHC does not allocate any special funds for area development schemes, the funds coming from the general CSHA allocation. Those connected with the allocation of funds in the VHC claim that the state Treasury does not increase the initial allocation to support area development schemes. The normal loading of the building programme in country areas also comes from general CSHA funds.

The SAHT provided more finance per capita for public housing than any other state. This may mean that the Trust provides such a large volume of housing that it is able to supply units to the middle income groups—the main beneficiaries of the sale programme (area development)—without interfering with a comparatively large supply to the low income group. Since the main motive for establishing the SAHT in the first place was the expansion of industry, it could be argued that without this objective the South Australian government would not allocate such a large proportion of its total expenditure to the SAHT. This question is further discussed in chapter 7, especially Table 74 which shows that, apart from the middle income scheme (house sales), the SAHT has supplied low income public housing at a rate comparable with other Australian states.

The WAHC's policy is identical to the NSWHC's. Except for some minor schemes before 1956, the WAHC uses special state funds for the provision of housing for area development schemes. In 1967 the Minister for Housing, Mr O'Neil, said that the use of CSHA funds for area development housing was against the purpose for which these funds were intended—the housing of the low income groups—and referred to his desire to continue the spirit of the 1945 CSHA, which emphasized the use of public housing for those at the lower end of the economic spectrum. It was shown above that the WAHC has provided the largest amount of low income public housing per capita of all public housing authorities in Australia. This tends to verify the claim that the provision of separate funds for area development schemes has not curtailed funds for low income schemes.

The QHC and the THC use general CSHA finance for area development schemes, and both say that no additional amounts are advanced because of these schemes.

Conclusion

From the viewpoint of this book, the most important effect of area development policies is their influence on the distribution of the public housing subsidy. In the states where area development schemes are financed from CSHA sources (Victoria, Tasmania, Queensland and, to some extent, South Australia) is is likely that their implementation means that less housing is available for the low income group not connected with area development schemes. From the Census data presented above it is clear that area development schemes, particularly in the SAHT, result in the housing of higher socio-economic groups than is the case in the low income schemes described in chapter 4. But in the case of the SAHT it can be argued that because of the large volume of funds allocated to public housing in South Australia and the Trust's efficiency (illustrated by its double-unit programme), there is little conflict between the Trust's low income schemes and its middle income sales schemes. Certainly, any conflict is on nothing like the scale of that between the VHC's objectives of urban renewal and low income housing.

On initial analysis, the middle income occupants of the Trust's housing schemes are the main beneficiaries of the subsidized public housing supplied. But if the Trust's arguments are correct, the lower housing costs may be reflected in lower wages and the owners of the enterprises employing workers living in Trust houses may benefit the most. In weighing the gains and costs of the Trust's industrial development policies, account must be taken of the claim by the general manager, Mr Ramsay, that the cost of the SAHT subsidy to companies and middle income households is offset by the savings from the decentralization of industrial growth away from industrial areas where the external diseconomies of growth, such as pollution and traffic congestion, involve hidden costs that do not occur in the Trust's developments.

From the policy statements given above, it may appear that housing those on low incomes is not the main aim of the SAHT, and therefore the Trust cannot be evaluated on its performance in this direction. But the Housing Improvement Act in 1940, still incorporated in the Trust's charter, suggests that the Trust does have a formally stated social welfare objective similar to all other Australian Housing Commissions. Where the 1936 Act had depended on donations from concerned citizens to provide housing for those unable to afford SAHT rents (up to 1940 there had been no donations), the 1940 Act provided for widespread government assistance for those on low incomes. These two Acts—the 1936 and 1940 Housing Improvement Acts—have co-existed in SAHT policy from 1945 to the present.

The amount of subsidy in the SAHT middle income house sales scheme is less than in the Trust's CSHA programmes but is substantial. The Trust sometimes claims that since its interest rates are roughly the same as bank housing loans this means that there is no subsidy. SAHT loans are normally for a higher proportion of the dwelling cost than bank loans and are for longer repayment periods. Moreover, most of the bank finance that flows into housing loans in Australia is subsidized: the banks could get a far higher return for the funds elsewhere and their generosity is simply the result of informal Federal government direction. True, the banks do use housing loans to attract depositors but this is just making the best of an unprofitable situation. The Trust's claim that it is not really subsidizing middle income earners because its sale houses are at a relatively high interest rate is open to another objection: more than one third of Trust houses are the double units built for rental from CSHA funds and tables 22, 23, 57 and 58 show that many occupants of these houses are of comparatively high socio-economic status.

This chapter has argued that, generally speaking, the Housing Commissions load their non-metropolitan building programmes so that it is easier to obtain public housing in these areas than in the capital cities. Without a co-ordinated plan for decentralization it is unlikely that the public housing programme alone can do much to assist significant decentralization, particularly when even the public housing is typically dispersed over a large number of towns rather than concentrated in a few towns with some possibility of significant growth. In 1971 the Commonwealth and state governments agreed on a plan for rural reconstruction. Underlying this plan was a realization that the current crisis in the rural sector was not a temporary phase. Rather, it is the long-term result of a vast multitude of government schemes to avoid the consequences of the poor economic foundation of so much rural production. A basic element in the reconstruction plan is the relocation of sizeable numbers of country people to areas of significant employment growth—mainly the metropolitan areas. In view of this, the plentiful supply of public housing in country areas seems a most ineffective way to help country people. It would be better to give country people preferential access to metropolitan public housing, co-ordinated with retraining schemes and other forms of relocation assistance. This could also be in the Housing Commissions' narrow self-interest: if they keep building so many houses outside the metropolitan areas they could soon be burdened with large numbers of empty houses in declining country areas. With low cost housing it is rarely economic to remove them from their original location.

7 HOME OWNERSHIP

This chapter and the following one on rent policy evaluate the two forms of tenure available to those housed by the Housing Commissions. Two groups of criteria for appraisal of policy are listed. The first concerns allocation of available public housing in the way most efficient in assisting those on low incomes. These include capacity to pay; the principle of equity in public finance (equal treatment of those in equal circumstances); the degree of progression involved (that is, the poorer the household the smaller the proportion of income it can afford to spend on housing); and the comparison of opportunities within public housing and opportunities outside public housing, important in Australia where there is considerable government assistance to home owners outside public housing.

The second group is less important than the first, so it is given less attention here. The most important of the criteria of this group is the effect of different tenure systems on the social composition of neighbourhoods where public housing is concentrated and the policies followed to avoid what is considered an undesirable concentration of people on low incomes. Other relevant aspects include 'stigma', which is discussed at length in chapter 9 and may be important; important, too, is the possible invasion of privacy involved in collecting detailed information on the tenant's socio-economic status necessary for some rental systems; effects of various tenure systems on work incentives and on the mobility of labour are glanced at; and the effects of tenure systems on the cost of living and on general price stability may be considered since minimizing the cost of living is a major objective of any government.

The most notable feature about Australian housing policy is the emphasis and encouragement given to home ownership. A wide variety of formal and informal controls direct relatively cheap funds into home ownership finance, and the Commonwealth government administers the Home Savings Grant scheme and the Housing Loans Insurance Corporation, two recently introduced programmes to assist those wishing to own their homes. The former scheme provides grants of up to $500 towards the purchase of a home to be made at the rate of $1 for each $3 saved over a three-year period. The latter scheme insures home mortgages, thus encouraging the private market to invest in housing. In addition, the local government rates on owner-occupied dwellings are tax deductible and there is no taxation of the imputed rental income always associated with home ownership. The result of these policies and continuing inflation is that at a given time many Australians have no direct housing cost (rent or repayments on mortgages). This was shown very clearly in the Australian National University Urban Research Unit's survey in Sydney in 1969 and in Henderson's 1966 Melbourne study. In the Sydney survey, about 33 per cent of the cross-section of families interviewed had no direct housing costs.

Much of this chapter and the next on rent policy deals with the effects of inflation. In Australia, prices have nearly trebled in the 1945 to 1970 period. Obviously, home owners obtain the benefits from inflation in low housing costs. The earlier the household purchased the dwelling the lower the proportion of its income that has been spent on mortgage repayments during that period, assuming that income increased at least as fast as the price level. Moreover, the market value of the dwelling has also increased at least as fast as the rise in prices, producing a capital gain for the occupant.

State home ownership schemes before 1945

This section details the nature and extent of the home ownership schemes in the states until 1945, with special emphasis on the socio-economic status of those who obtained the subsidized housing supplied.

The Housing Board established in New South Wales in 1912 accepted the principle of home ownership and by 1943 had built 376 cottages for sale in New South Wales. In addition, the Homes for Unemployed Trust established in 1934 built 833 homes for sale from 1934 to 1944. The first functioning public housing scheme in Victoria began with the establishment of the VHC in 1938 following the recommendations of the 1937 Report of the Housing Investigation and Slum Abolition Board. This report, and the VHC until 1943, were overwhelmingly concerned with the plight of the poorest group in society—the slum dwellers. The 1937 Report said that, 'having regard to the fact that the lower-paid worker cannot pay an economic rent it is futile to suggest that any system of home purchase (which involves repayment of capital, interest charges, rates, and maintenance) will meet the housing needs of the lower-paid worker. He is not under present economic conditions a potential home owner'. It was not until 1943 that the home ownership objective was formally incorporated into Victorian housing legislation, by the amendment of the Housing Act to provide for advances for those wishing to purchase a dwelling.

The government of South Australia introduced a home ownership scheme in 1910, and by 1930 about 20,000 dwellings had been supplied under the scheme. This represented about 15 per cent of the total stock of private houses and flats in South Australia at the 1933 Census. Applicants under the scheme had either to own their own block of land or to pay a deposit of one-fifth of the value of the house and land. The loans were advanced at an interest rate of 4½ per cent per annum over a period of 36½ years. These conditions meant that the scheme did not help those on lower incomes and was generally much less favourable than the home ownership terms offered to public housing tenants after 1956. The scheme did continue until 1945 but the austerity of the depression, the disruption of World War II, and the establishment of the SAHT in 1936 meant that the 1910 Act virtually ceased granting new loans in 1930.

The first public housing scheme introduced into Western Australia in 1911 enabled workers to purchase their own homes, on low deposits and using low interest finance. From 1911 to 1939, a total of 3,017 homes were provided under the scheme, representing about 3 per cent of the total stock of housing in Western Australia in 1939. The legislation catered only for those able to afford the instalments. A spokesman for the government said in 1937 that the '. . . people who take Workers' Homes belong to a good type. They have been selected by experts of the Housing Board who seldom make a mistake . . . This is not a charity scheme'.

From 1909 to 30 June 1939 the State Housing Corporation of Queensland built 20,828 dwellings, about 8 per cent of the total Queensland housing stock in 1939. Out of the total of 20,828 dwellings, 18,536 dwellings were built under the Workers' Dwelling scheme, the remainder under the Workers' Home scheme. When discussing the legislation for the scheme in 1909 the Premier, William Kidston, insisted that it would be administered in a businesslike manner and those defaulting in their payments would have their properties resumed. There is some evidence that the houses built under the Workers' Dwelling scheme did not go to the poorest sections of society. To be eligible for a loan under this scheme an applicant had to own his own block of land and then no more than 75 per cent of the value of the dwelling was advanced. A survey of applicants who lodged applications from 1925 to 1930 showed that they had an average annual income of $564 while the average annual wage at that time was $516, and the average basic wage was $430. The Workers' Homes scheme introduced in 1919 attempted to reach a lower income group than did the Workers' Dwelling scheme. The worker had to have a deposit of only 5 per cent of the capital value of the house and land, and the capital was repayable over a longer period than was the case for workers' dwellings. But, as shown above, only 2,292 dwellings were built under the scheme between 1919 and 1939.

The first public housing scheme in Tasmania in 1919 provided for the sale of dwellings. Advances were made up to nine-tenths of the value of a dwelling and land. By 1935 it was realized that this scheme did not give many low income families an opportunity to purchase their own homes, so the government introduced a scheme enabling applicants to rent dwellings and if they proved to be satisfactory tenants for six months they would be given the opportunity of purchasing the dwelling on a no-deposit basis. By 1943 a total of 1,135 dwellings had been provided under these two schemes, most of them under the first.

As was argued in chapter 1, the home ownership schemes in the states up to 1945 were very limited in their capacity to assist those on the lowest incomes. There was still the underlying attitude that although the government should subsidize housing for the workers in the form of low-interest loans repayable over long periods of time, they were unwilling to embark on schemes that would involve further subsidy. Moreover, it was not accidental that most of the schemes referred to housing the 'workers'. Unlike the strong social welfare movement that developed in the 1930s, these home ownership schemes were not concerned with housing the poorest groups in society, those households with a very low capacity to pay.

However limited the pre-1945 home ownership schemes were, they still provided valuable assistance for some families on lower incomes able to afford the substantial deposit and repayments. The general housing problem was worsened when most of these schemes were either abolished or seriously limited with the onset of the depression in 1930. The details of the various states below will show, however, that in most states, particularly Queensland, these pre-war schemes were to continue after World War II to the present time, often with liberalized conditions.

Commonwealth and state attitudes

It has already been shown that the first CSHA in 1945 was the basis for the extensive provision of housing in the post-war period. It provided that any houses built under the agreement could be sold, but the price could not be less than the capital cost and the state would have to pay the full purchase price of the dwelling to the Commonwealth immediately. Hence a tenant of a Housing Commission house would have to find the cash price of the dwelling or else find some alternative source of finance. No doubt part of the reason why home ownership was not made more attractive in the agreement was that the Labor government which introduced the bill did not believe that selling government-built housing was a desirable policy. Mr Dedman, the Minister for Post-war Reconstruction, who introduced the bill, said, 'The Commonwealth Government is concerned to provide adequate and good housing for the workers; it is not concerned with making the workers into little capitalists'. He said, however, that the government realized the need for home ownership and pointed to the extensive home ownership schemes in the states and the Commonwealth War Service Homes scheme. But he argued that 'the principal deficiency in Australian housing policy to date has been in respect of good standard houses to be let at rents within the capacity to pay to families who cannot afford, or who are not ready, or on account of their occupations do not desire to purchase homes'.

The states wanted to sell CSHA dwellings on easy terms. After discussing schemes to facilitate the sale of houses under the first CSHA with the state Premiers in 1953, the Prime Minister, Mr Menzies, said, 'I do not want to see a state of affairs in Australia—and I am glad to gather that the Premiers do not—in which governments are the universal landlords. I think that this is a shocking position for governments to get into'. A number of factors had produced this opposition to state landlordism. The first and possibly the most important was the fact that housing had become an important state political issue and there was strong pressure from the electorate to make CSHA dwellings available for sale on more favourable terms.

A further reason was that the states were losing on their rental operations. Although the CSHA in 1945 provided for the sharing of losses sustained through rental operations (presumed to be caused by the need to provide housing at subeconomic rentals to certain groups) by the Commonwealth and the states, this operated only if the states regularly adjusted their rents to take account of increases in price levels. The states refused to adjust rents regularly, mainly because the raising of public housing rentals was an important state political issue. These facts are discussed at length in the next chapter. The results of this were summarized by Mr Cain, the Premier of Victoria, at the Premiers' Conference in 1954:

> I believe that the Commonwealth in conjunction with the States is destined to lose large sums of money unless the houses are sold, or alternatively the rents are increased substantially. We do not believe that the latter course can be adopted while rent pegging is being held as it is in most States. Therefore the only sensible thing to do is to sell the houses.

Mr Cahill, the Premier of New South Wales, expressed identical views on the matter. The decision by the New South Wales government in 1956 to sell at least 80 per cent of dwellings was made mainly because of the fear of losses sustained through rental operations. The Director of Housing in Tasmania said in 1958: 'Tasmania is trying to meet losses sustained through low rentals by selling as many houses as possible'. Closely connected with the fear of losses was the belief that tenants of rental housing took little care of the premises and hence caused large expenditures on maintenance compared with householders in dwellings that had been sold, where more care was taken and the occupant was responsible.

In addition to the above arguments for home ownership, there was a long-held belief in Australia that home ownership produced a number of favourable effects. It was these beliefs that had been the basis for the extensive state home ownership schemes operated before 1945. The philosophy of the largest of these, the Queensland Workers' Dwelling and Workers' Home schemes, was summed up in 1937 in a report of the State Advances Corporation which administered the plan. It said:

> Home ownership, whether assisted by the State or private enterprise, is undoubtedly one of the soundest bulwarks of a well organized and orderly society, and probably the best safeguard against irresponsibility and unrest; accordingly, encouragement of this sound and reproductive social work is one of the best possible acts of the body politic.

In 1948 the Annual Report of the QHC claimed: 'Unless we can restore the institution of private property we cannot escape the institution of slavery', and that home ownership was the best way to ensure a wide distribution of private property. Mr Duggan, the Deputy Premier of Queensland, said in 1953 that the Commonwealth should make it easier to purchase homes under the CSHA because a home ownership scheme '. . . would not only make a better citizenry generally but also would promote greater industrial harmony. I feel that if a workman owned his house and therefore had a great interest in it, he would be disinclined to be influenced by extraneous matters raised by a few demagogues'. Mr Gair, the Premier of Queensland, also claimed in 1954 that 'Home ownership encourages a sense of responsibility in the individual and is an antidote to any of the "isms" that may exist here. If a man is given a stake in the country his sense of responsibility and citizenship is increased'. The Premier of Victoria, Mr A. A. Dunstan, said, when introducing the 1943 home ownership bill in Victoria, that the person who could afford the deposit necessary for home purchase was '. . . invariably an exemplary citizen, a symbol of achievement, purpose, industry and thrift'. When Mr Landa, the Minister for Housing in New South Wales, wanted to boost the rate of sales in the NSWHC in 1957 he sent a circular to all those eligible saying, 'You have pride in the ownership of your refrigerator or radio—even perhaps a car. You can, and will, have even greater pride in the ownership of your home'.

The federal Labor government was removed from office at the 1949 election and replaced by the Liberal-Country Party government which had quite a different approach to the importance of home ownership. Senator Spooner, the Minister for National Development in charge of the administration of the CSHA, had a number of criticisms of the State Housing Commissions. He, and the government in general, objected to the large blocks of flats that the VHC and the NSWHC were constructing in inner areas as part of their slum clearance programmes. These objections were raised because '. . . the aim of Government housing should be to provide houses for families and we do not feel that large blocks of flats are the best places for families with young children to live'. In addition, these large blocks of flats were more expensive than houses or small blocks of flats and if they were built fewer units could be provided with the same amount of money. Spooner also claimed that the Housing Commissions were catering for many who were not really on low incomes. In 1956 he said:

> The records of tenants of Housing Commission homes show that a very substantial proportion of them are in receipt of good incomes. For instance, the large block of flats in North Sydney is something more in the nature of housing accommodation for professional people.

He saw the period from 1945 to 1955 as a time of readjustment in the housing market. It was, in his view, the period in which large-scale government assistance was necessary to overcome the housing shortage produced by the depression of the 1930s and World War II, and the period from about 1955 onwards saw an easing in the housing shortage and a lessened need for public housing. Spooner also demanded:

> When we are expending government moneys, is it not at least desirable and equitable that an appreciable proportion of those moneys be earmarked for the benefit of those who have had the courage, determination and good sense, despite very difficult circumstances, to save enough for a deposit on a home?

While the 1945 CSHA attempted to provide public housing for the lowest income group, the new agreement tried to

> . . . ensure that the financial aid that the community gives to housing will not be confined to one section only but will spread its benefits as widely as possible . . . The Commonwealth believes it is unfair and inequitable to ask the general taxpayer to subsidize to this extent [the 1945 CSHA level] rents of people living in Housing Commission dwellings.

In addition, Spooner said that since many people in public housing were not on low incomes the general taxpayer outside public housing was forced to subsidize people whose financial position was as good as or better than his own.

Spooner argued that because of the cheap finance supplied to the Housing Commissions and the restrictive effects of state rent-control legislation, little housing had been built by private enterprise in Australia since 1945. He also claimed that the sale of Housing Commission dwellings on favourable terms was undermining the sale of homes by private builders and was thus harming the building industry. Spooner saw the operations of the Housing Commissions as being in competition with the private market in housing, that is, many of those obtaining assistance from the Housing Commissions would be able to afford housing without such assistance. In 1956 Spooner approvingly quoted a report in the *Sydney Morning Herald* that claimed that the thousands of dwellings built by the NSWHC were built of poor-quality materials and would be substandard in 20 years. One of the advantages of the diversion of funds to co-operative societies was that (in Spooner's view), the dwellings would not be grouped together in public housing estates but would rather be '. . . infinitely better houses. In addition the people concerned will be able to have houses erected in localities where they desire to have them'.

Since all state governments were pressing for home ownership provisions in the standing 1945 CSHA the Commonwealth was eager to revise the 1945 Agreement and facilitate the sale of dwellings provided by the State Housing Commissions. But there were considerable differences between the states as to the terms on which the houses should be sold. By 1955 these differences were reconciled and the 1945 CSHA was amended. Dwellings could be sold to tenants on a minimum deposit of 5 per cent of the first $4,000 of the sale price and 10 per cent of the balance. The principal repayments included in the rent previously paid by the tenant could be credited to him and form part of the deposit, provided that not less than 5 per cent of the sale price was paid as a cash deposit. A maximum advance of $5,500 would be made, the maximum period of repayment was 45 years, and the rate of interest was 4½ per cent per annum. The purchase price of the dwellings could be fixed by the states and any profit or loss was a matter for the state concerned.

Complementary legislation was passed in all states except Tasmania which was not a partner to the agreement at that time. The CSHA of 1956 allowed the states to dispose of the dwellings as they liked, the only requirement being that the funds should go to the 'low and moderate income group' and the funds, carrying an interest rate of 1 per cent below the longer term bond rate, had to be paid back to the Commonwealth in 52 years. This general policy of allowing the states to determine the terms of sale of their dwellings was repeated in the renewals of the CSHA in 1961 and 1966. The 1956 CSHA also discontinued the loss-sharing arrangement that had operated under the 1945 CSHA. Further, it directed 30 per cent of all CSHA funds to the co-operative societies. Neither of the latter two policies was generally welcomed by the states.

Advantages of home ownership from the client's viewpoint

Reasons for client preference for ownership over renting may be divided into two categories—economic and social. The literature on whether or not it is cheaper to rent or buy a dwelling has reached few definite conclusions. Studies have found that the decision to rent or to buy, as far as there is an economic component in this decision, is primarily concerned with the comparison of the current direct costs (rent or mortgage repayments) of renting or owning. However, purchasers may view their dwellings as a capital investment. Some limited observations will be made on the comparative costs of owning or renting public housing dwellings in Australia. As stated earlier, in a situation of continual if gradual inflation, the home purchaser is faced with repayments that account for a progressively smaller proportion of his income, assuming that it increases at least as fast as the increase in the price level. In addition, the weekly direct costs of home ownership from a public housing authority in Australia are generally the same as rental for the same new dwelling. This is because the amortization periods for rental and purchase are usually similar if not identical, as are interest rates, although the amortization rate is generally longer for rental dwellings (53 years) than for purchase units (around 45 years). The rental includes a figure for administration, and provision for vacancy and default which are not part of the normal weekly, direct costs of home ownership. The weekly rent also includes an allowance for the cost of insurance, rates and maintenance.

It is shown, however, in the following chapter on rent policy, that, except in the VHC, QHC and WAHC, rents on older dwellings are generally not regularly adjusted to account for the increase in the value of the dwelling due to inflation or for increases in the cost of maintenance of the dwelling. On the other hand, if the occupant decides to purchase the dwelling, he will get some credit for the amount he has paid in amortization in the rental but generally he will have to pay a price for the dwelling above the 'historic' cost, and close to the current market value. Another possible incentive to rent rather than purchase a dwelling from one of the Housing Commissions is the rental rebate scheme that applies to rented dwellings in most states. This allows housing costs (i.e. the rent paid) to be adjusted to changes in the family income, particularly if the household suffers from sudden decline in income for such reasons as unemployment or the death of the breadwinner. There is no similar scheme for public housing units purchased, although a family suffering a chronic, long-term loss of income, as a result, say, of the death or desertion of the breadwinner or similar reasons, can be transferred back to a tenancy in the same or some other dwelling. Another possible reason for choosing renting over purchase is that renters may be more mobile than purchasers, and that home ownership is a barrier to the mobility of labour. The main argument is that home owners are tied to such long-term contracts that it will be difficult for them to move. However, in a period of rising property values a purchaser from a housing authority would probably be able to sell his dwelling at a price that would cover his indebtedness on the dwelling and might even produce some overall capital gain. One barrier to mobility if a house is being purchased and the occupant wants to move to another dwelling is the transfer costs involved, especially the legal fees, title search fees and government stamp duty, none of which usually accompanies a change in rental accommodation.

In 'Home Ownership Motives', *American Sociological Review*, 1948, Rosow found that financial considerations were not very important in explaining the popularity of home ownership in the United States. The major reasons for home ownership were those connected with status and prestige and emotional goals. Some of the things Rosow found to be important were the assertion of achieved status and social aspiration; assertion of individualism and independence; and emotional goals of romantic nostalgia, ego aggrandizement, pride, creativity and self-expression.

The socio-economic status of renters and purchasers

The NSWHC carried out a survey of households renting and buying cottages in a new NSWHC development at Mt Druitt, about 32 miles from Sydney. The survey covered 367 families who took up residence between June and December 1969. It showed the substantial differences in family income between purchasers and renters, supporting the hypothesis that the higher the income the higher is the propensity to purchase rather than rent. This hypothesis is also supported by the fact that 44.2 per cent of the renters owned a car while the figure for purchasers was 72 per cent.

There were also substantial differences in the number of children in households that rented and those who purchased. In the rental group 61.2 per cent of the children were under seven years of age and 20.6 per cent were between seven and 11 years of age. These families had an average of 2.8 children (under 16 years of age) per household. Of purchasers' children, 85.5 per cent were under seven years of age and 9.2 per cent were between seven and 11 years. The average number of children per household was only 1.7. There are also interesting differences between the ages of renters and purchasers (household heads). Purchasers tend to be substantially younger than renters.

Tables 62 to 67 show the characteristics of public housing home ownership areas, based on CD data. The occupational data show that the home ownership areas are only of slightly higher occupational status than the totals for the metropolitan areas given in Table 5 in chapter 3. Taking the first two occupational classifications (professional and managerial and self-employed), the home ownership areas in Table 62 are only from 1 per cent (NSWHC) to 5 per cent (SAHT) higher than for the public housing metropolitan totals. Educational and motor vehicle ownership is also only slightly higher for the home ownership areas than the metropolitan averages, and there is very little difference in marital status, age, or birthplace (for marital

TABLE 62 Occupations of the workforce in metropolitan public housing home ownership CD areas (per cent of total), 1966 census

	NSWHC	VHC	SAHT	QHC	THC
	%	%	%	%	%
Professional	4	5	11	5	5
Managerial, self-employed	9	10	13	10	11
Clerical workers	19	22	21	23	18
Armed forces	1	1	1	1	—
Craftsmen, foremen	20	20	23	19	17
Shop assistants, process workers	31	27	17	25	28
Personal, domestic, other service workers and labourers	14	14	11	17	18

Source: Compiled from summary data supplied by the Commonwealth Statistician (Collectors' District data for the total population).

TABLE 63 Education of the population (excluding children not at school and full-time students), in metropolitan public housing home ownership CD areas (per cent of total), 1966 census

	NSWHC	VHC	SAHT	QHC	THC
	%	%	%	%	%
University qualifications	—	1	1	—	—
Other tertiary qualifications	1	1	3	2	1
Matriculation passed	5	9	12	5	10
Intermediate passed	32	19	24	29	22
Attended high school	42	32	29	19	32
Attended primary school	16	35	30	42	33
No education	3	1	1	2	—
Not stated	2	2	2	2	2

Source: Compiled from summary data supplied by the Commonwealth Statistician (Collectors' District data for the total population).

TABLE 64 Motor vehicle ownership in metropolitan public housing home ownership CD areas, number of vehicles per occupied private dwelling (per cent of total), 1966 census

No. of vehicles per dwelling	Sydney	Melbourne	Adelaide	Brisbane	Hobart
	%	%	%	%	%
HOUSES					
None	28	21	12	20	22
One	60	54	64	61	59
Two	9	19	20	14	14
Three +	1	4	3	2	3
Not stated	2	1	1	3	1
FLATS					
None	a	49	a	a	a
One		29			
Two		2			
Three +		15			
Not stated		5			

a = too few flats for reliable figures.
Source: Compiled from summary data supplied by the Commonwealth Statistician (Collectors' District data for the total population).

TABLE 65 Age structure in metropolitan public housing home ownership CD areas (per cent of total), 1966 census

Age group	NSWHC	VHC	SAHT	QHC	THC
	%	%	%	%	%
0–4	13	10	11	13	17
5–9	18	13	15	13	13
10–14	17	13	13	11	12
15–19	8	12	9	11	10
20–29	10	12	9	15	16
30–39	19	13	17	13	12
40–49	10	14	14	13	11
50–59	4	8	7	7	6
60 +	2	5	5	5	4

Source: Compiled from summary data supplied by the Commonwealth Statistician (Collectors' District data for the total population).

TABLE 66 Birthplace of the population in metropolitan public housing home ownership CD areas (per cent of total), 1966 census

Birthplace	NSWHC	VHC	SAHT	QHC	THC
	%	%	%	%	%
Australia	88	80	61	75	92
New Zealand, England, Wales, Ireland, Scotland	8	11	30	20	5
Austria, Czechoslovakia, Germany, Hungary, Yugoslavia	1	2	2	1	1
Greece, Italy, Malta	1	4	1	1	—
Other	2	4	6	3	1

Source: Compiled from summary data supplied by the Commonwealth Statistician (Collectors' District data for the total population).

TABLE 67 Marital status of the population (excluding the never married) in metropolitan public housing home ownership CD areas (per cent of total), 1966 census

Marital status	NSWHC	VHC	SAHT	QHC	THC
	%	%	%	%	%
Married	92	90	93	93	92
Married, but permanently separated	3	2	1	2	2
Divorced	1	—	1	1	2
Widowed	4	7	5	6	4

Source: Compiled from summary data supplied by the Commonwealth Statistician (Collectors' District data for the total population).

status see Table 13, chapter 4; age, Table 15, chapter 4; and birthplace, Table 35, chapter 4). This does not contradict the findings in the NSWHC survey above: that few of the aged, divorced, or permanently separated purchase dwellings. The public housing areas analysed in Tables 62 to 67 contain many dwellings built up to 25 years ago. Many households could have become aged, widowed, divorced or permanently separated.

Apart from the VHC there were too few flats to produce accurate figures for vehicle ownership. Home ownership areas in the NSWHC contained 2,496 dwellings and 11,844 people; 98 per cent of the dwellings were cottages and 2 per cent flats. Of the cottages, 73 per cent were sold. Home ownership areas in the VHC contained 4,150 dwellings and 23,177 people; 93 per cent of the dwellings were cottages and 7 per cent flats. Of the cottages, 69 per cent were sold. Home ownership areas in the SAHT contained 3,374 dwellings and 13,843 people; 97 per cent of the dwellings were cottages and 2 per cent flats. Of the cottages, 77 per cent were sold. Home ownership areas in the QHC contained 756 dwellings and 3,146 people. All dwellings were cottages of which 70 per cent were sold. Home ownership areas in the THC contained 1,441 dwellings and 6,456 people; 99 per cent of the dwellings were cottages and 1 per cent flats. Of the cottages, 64 per cent were sold.

Home ownership terms and conditions, 1945 onwards

The Commissions attach varying conditions to the dwellings they have offered for sale since 1945. The level of deposits, the rate of interest, the period of repayment and the fixing of the sale price are all important determinants of which socio-economic groups will be able to purchase dwellings. Table 68 shows the number of houses sold in New South Wales and the relationship between this and completions. Yearly vacated units added to new constructions would have produced a better indicator but this information was not available.

From Table 68 it can be seen that very few houses were sold by the NSWHC before 1955. This was because, as was explained above, the Commonwealth required that if a dwelling supplied under the agreement was sold, the full purchase price had to be paid to the Commonwealth immediately. With the general shortage of low-interest, low-deposit finance available outside the CSHA, few NSWHC occupants could take advantage of the home ownership provision of the agreement. The dwellings at this time were offered for sale at cost or market value, whichever was the higher. Market value was defined as '. . . a fair figure at which the State might be prepared to sell and the tenant or other purchaser be prepared to buy, on the basis of a seller who is willing but not anxious and a buyer who is willing but not anxious'. There was a condition that the purchaser could not resell in less than seven years without the consent of the Commission but this proved ineffective because there was no penalty. The CSHA in 1955 liberalized the provisions for sale, and these terms have been presented above. The NSWHC also reduced the pre-emption period to five years. If the purchaser wanted to sell, the Commission could, if it wanted to, repurchase the dwelling during this five-year period at a price equal to the original sale price plus the value of the improvements.

The New South Wales government was most anxious to sell as many houses as possible and the Commission was required to introduce an active

TABLE 68 House sales in the NSWHC 1945–69

Year	Houses sold	Total completions	Sales as a percentage of completions
1945–6	—	1,348	—
1946–7	—	2,180	—
1947–8	—	2,716	—
1948–9	15	3,587	—
1949–50	98	3,403	3
1950–1	122	3,520	3
1951–2	338	3,842	9
1952–3	528	4,441	12
1953–4	403	5,177	8
1954–5	165	5,254	3
1955–6	733	3,655	20
1956–7	3,197	3,030	106
1957–8	3,679	3,695	100
1958–9	2,507	3,177	79
1959–60	2,701	3,502	77
1960–1	2,004	3,153	64
1961–2	2,303	4,722	49
1962–3	2,598	4,342	66
1963–4	1,521	4,364	35
1964–5	2,361	5,482	43
1965–6	1,919	5,390	36
1966–7	1,502	4,337	35
1967–8	1,872	5,223	36
1968–9	1,627	4,277	38
	32,193	93,817	34

Source: Commonwealth year books and the annual reports of the NSWHC.

sales campaign to encourage and stimulate sales. As a result of the new CSHA in 1956, the NSWHC introduced a policy whereby 80 per cent of the homes erected under the agreement were to be sold. The reduction in the proportion of completions sold after 1963 was due largely to the cessation of the 80 per cent sale rule in that year. The houses were provided on a minimum deposit of $100 with a maximum period of repayment of 45 years at 4¾ per cent interest. Dwellings were sold at the estimated cost or Rural Bank valuation, whichever was the higher. During the 1956–69 period average deposits amounted to $136. At October 1970, the interest rate on new NSWHC dwellings was 5¾ per cent per annum over 45 years, with a deposit of $100. These are very favourable conditions indeed, compared with some of the other Housing Commissions and especially with free market loan rates where the best available require about $3,000 deposit over 25 years at around 7 per cent per annum. The applicant must, of course, qualify under the normal NSWHC means test described in chapter 3. When account is taken of the very favourable conditions given to NSWHC tenants who wish to purchase their dwellings as described below, and the fact that the NSWHC concentrates on the production of saleable cottages, it must be concluded that the NSWHC does a great deal to promote home ownership.

The NSWHC also has a small scheme that allows applicants who are otherwise eligible for Commission accommodation but who own land or have a substantial interest in a block and who are unable to proceed with the construction of a dwelling to have the Commission build a standard NSWHC dwelling on the site. The other details of the scheme are identical to those outlined above for current NSWHC purchasers, and the average deposit from the introduction of the scheme in 1960 to 1969 was $104, in addition to the value of the applicant's land. A total of 535 dwellings were provided under the scheme from 1960 to 1969.

Another NSWHC scheme directed towards the promotion of home ownership, the Homes Sites Development scheme, was begun in 1961 to '. . . acquire reasonably priced land for subdivision and development and to make it available at cost to genuine home builders'. Sites could be purchased for cash or a minimum deposit of 25 per cent with the balance payable over a maximum of three years with interest of 4 per cent per annum on the outstanding balance. Applicants are considered eligible for a ballot for the land if they are married, are not less than 21 years of age, have a yearly income not exceeding $4,000, need land for the erection of a dwelling for their own residential purposes and demonstrate the ability to purchase the land in cash or terms and to erect a dwelling within two years of the transfer of the title for the land. Up to 1969, 358 sites had been provided under this scheme, which the Commission claims is only in 'rather limited demand', a statement based on the difficulty in disposing of some sites.

Table 69 shows the number of dwellings sold in Victoria compared with the total number of completions. The patterns evident from this table are similar in some ways to those for the NSWHC. There was very little selling before 1956, for the same reasons as described for the NSWHC—the unfavourable terms offered under the 1945 CSHA. From 1956 to 1961 dwellings were sold at a deposit of 5 per cent of the first $4,000 of the sale price and 10 per cent of the remainder. In 1961 the VHC introduced a scheme enabling all dwellings to be sold on an even lower minimum deposit of $200. A restricted no-deposit scheme was introduced in 1964. In 1968 all applicants, including current tenants, who wished to purchase a VHC home had to fulfil the following conditions: they had to be in need of VHC assistance, that is, not own another suitable home or have extensive assets; they must have an unmarried child under 21 years of age residing with them; in the case of current tenants, no maximum income limit applies but in the case of other applicants the breadwinner's income must not exceed $70 per week, or, where the family comprises three or more children, $80 per week. A minimum income level is set by refusing an application to purchase if the repayments exceed 25 per cent of the applicant's income. The homes are sold on a minimum deposit of $200. The period of repayment varies with the age of the applicant. The maximum term is 45 years but this may be reduced to 30 years or less. The period is determined so that half the repay-

TABLE 69 House sales in the VHC 1945–69

Year	Houses sold	Total completions	Sales as a percentage of completions
1945–6	—	1.093	—
1946–7	—	1,491	—
1947–8	—	2,179	—
1948–9	—	2,357	—
1949–50	6	2,454	—
1950–1	39	2,699	1
1951–2	26	2,970	1
1952–3	13	3,238	—
1953–4	6	3,590	—
1954–5	—	3,960	—
1955–6	1,289	4,152	31
1956–7	1,732	2,580	67
1957–8	1,336	2,414	55
1958–9	2,506	2,560	98
1959–60	2,672	2,594	103
1960–1	2,704	2,217	122
1961–2	2,125	2,400	89
1962–3	1,791	2,022	89
1963–4	1,799	2,324	77
1964–5	2,028	2,688	75
1965–6	2,219	2,686	83
1966–7	1,859	3,116	60
1967–8	1,794	2,214	81
1968–9	1,404	2,131	66
	27,348	62,129	44

Source: Commonwealth year books and the annual reports of the VHC.

ment term must be completed before the purchaser's sixty-fifth birthday. The sale prices of houses are determined by the mean of the construction cost and the estimated current replacement cost, with a maximum selling price that is varied over time. For older dwellings, therefore, the sale price will generally be lower than current market values because of the general inflation in property values. Like the NSWHC, in 1970 the VHC sold its dwellings—the few it had for sale in the metropolitan area—on very favourable conditions; deposits were $200 on an interest rate of 6½ per cent over 45 years.

In 1965 the Minister for Housing, Mr Lindsay Thompson, introduced a scheme whereby the VHC sold some of its subdivided land to prospective home builders. Up to 1969 the VHC had made a profit of $84,637 on these sales. The VHC objective is to develop its estates with a mixture of private and Commission development and make land available to genuine home builders and private developers. Sales must be made by auction or tender initially but the Commission is then free to negotiate with any interested purchaser for sites not sold as a result of these auctions. In summary, then, the VHC offers attractive conditions to home ownership applicants, providing low-interest funds repayable over long periods of time and on a low deposit.

The SAHT has three schemes for home ownership. The first scheme, introduced in 1946, provides for the sale of homes to those able to afford a deposit of about 10 per cent of the cost of house and land. This is referred to as the middle income scheme. The second scheme is the sale of imported dwellings from 1951 onwards, and the third is the programme for low-deposit ownership introduced in 1963. The last two schemes are referred to as low income schemes. Table 70 shows the sales under these various programmes.

A number of trends can be seen from this table. Although the middle income scheme led to a considerable number of sales from 1945 to 1956, the Trust built predominantly for rental. This rental housing was primarily the 'double-unit' type, consisting of two semi-detached dwellings not available for sale. The only other form of low income housing provided (except a small number of flats and temporary dwellings) was imported single units. A total of 3,606 of these dwellings were imported from 1950 to 1955, and it is the sales of some of these that appear in the table from 1953 to 1963, under the low income column. These dwellings were sold on terms with deposits and repayment conditions similar to the provisions of the 1955 CSHA on house sales. This meant that they were lower than the SAHT middle income sales scheme but higher than the 1963 low income scheme. The SAHT did not draw on CSHA funds until 1953, although it had signed the original agreement in 1945. From 1953 onwards the Trust used CSHA funds to finance its rental programme and its low income home ownership scheme. The finance for the middle income house sales scheme came from other lending authorities. The applicant purchasing a dwelling under this scheme is required to pay the Trust the full sale price of the house, by either providing money from his own resources or, in most cases, by paying a deposit and arranging the balance by giving a mortgage to any recognized lending authority. The Trust used its fund of deposits to provide a second mortgage to assist the purchaser to cover the amount between the deposit he could afford (usually a minimum of 10 per cent of house and land) and the minimum deposit required by lending authorities.

From 1963 a scheme for low income home ownership was introduced in the SAHT, enabling applicants to purchase a dwelling with a minimum deposit of $100, with repayments spread over 40 years at 6¼ per cent (1971). Of the 21,358 SAHT tenants in the metropolitan area in 1969, 15,271 were housed in the double-unit type of accommodation which could not be purchased. For both the low and middle income sales schemes there are no official 'means' tests to determine eligibility although an applicant will be advised to purchase a 'middle income' dwelling if he can afford it. There is the normal requirement that an applicant's income must be at least four times repayments for him to be allowed to purchase. All dwellings are sold at the capital cost or, in the case of the relatively small number of older dwellings, at the market value.

TABLE 70 House sales in the SAHT 1945–69

Year	Middle income scheme	Percentage of total completions	Low income scheme	Percentage of total completions	Total completions	Total sales as percentage of total completions
1945–6	12	4	—	—	308	4
1946–7	151	33	—	—	453	33
1947–8	352	41	—	—	866	41
1948–9	527	45	—	—	1,164	45
1949–50	593	39	—	—	1,537	39
1950–1	651	36	—	—	1,825	36
1951–2	770	34	—	—	2,251	34
1952–3	1,102	30	—	—	3,635	30
1953–4	993	29	1	—	3,404	29
1954–5	1,034	32	7	—	3,184	32
1955–6	1,545	50	275	9	3,115	59
1956–7	1,681	55	231	8	3,065	63
1957–8	1,726	58	259	9	2,971	67
1958–9	1,623	52	252	8	3,106	60
1959–60	1,719	55	140	4	3,137	59
1960–1	1,418	43	88	3	3,301	46
1961–2	1,431	44	33	1	3,243	45
1962–3	1,289	45	96	3	2,878	48
1963–4	1,259	44	457	16	2,857	60
1964–5	1,654	50	812	24	3,317	74
1965–6	1,727	53	886	27	3,250	80
1966–7	1,189	37	1,002	31	3,228	68
1967–8	663	28	813	34	2,400	62
1968–9	954	50	640	34	1,898	84
	26,063	41	5,992	10	60,393	51

Source: Commonwealth year books and the annual reports of the SAHT.

Home ownership policies in Queensland have been a continuation of pre-1945 policies with some extensions of home ownership to lower income groups. Table 71 gives the number of houses sold under the Workers' Dwelling scheme and under low income schemes. It shows that home sales have accounted for a high proportion of QHC completions although the figure has fluctuated greatly over time. Workers' Dwelling homes have continued to account for many QHC allocations. Under this scheme the QHC builds homes on an applicant's land, the land being mortgaged to the Commission as security for the loan to construct the house. The applicant is allowed a wide choice of designs: he may either select a standard QHC design, request the Commission to draw up a design to meet his own requirements or have the plans prepared privately. The dwellings are built by builders successful in public tenders called for their construction. Funds for the Workers' Dwelling scheme come from the Queensland state Treasury—not from the CSHA. Workers' Dwelling homes are scattered throughout the metropolitan area since they are built on applicants' land, so it is not possible to obtain CD data on the occupants.

The QHC also operates a scheme using CSHA funds for home ownership by a lower income group than the Workers' Dwelling scheme. An applicant

TABLE 71 House sales in the QHC 1945–69

Year	Workers' dwellings	Percentage of total completions	Other sales	Percentage of total completions	Total completions	Total sales as percentage of total completions
1945–6	260	62	—	—	417	62
1946–7	279	37	—	—	751	37
1947–8	282	34	391	47	840	81
1948–9	467	45	530	51	1,047	96
1949–50	360	36	372	37	1,013	73
1950–1	632	51	726	59	1,230	110
1951–2	470	23	569	27	2,076	50
1952–3	487	21	159	7	2,314	28
1953–4	407	19	77	4	2,105	23
1954–5	543	27	170	8	2,047	35
1955–6	634	36	404	23	1,754	59
1956–7	752	39	466	24	1,912	63
1957–8	694	46	674	45	1,504	91
1958–9	558	31	837	47	1,781	78
1959–60	531	37	760	52	1,452	89
1960–1	650	37	699	40	1,746	77
1961–2	673	34	567	28	2,006	62
1962–3	618	34	310	17	1,798	51
1963–4	373	20	442	24	1,876	44
1964–5	465	27	287	16	1,744	43
1965–6	317	19	536	31	1,702	50
1966–7	290	18	742	45	1,643	63
1967–8	314	18	667	39	1,716	57
1968–9	249	15	515	31	1,678	46
	13,305	35	10,900	29	38,152	54

Source: Commonwealth year books and the annual reports of the QHC.

may preselect a Commission site and arrange to have a dwelling erected according to his design or select a Commission house already constructed in the QHC subdivision. The Commissioner said in 1969 that the average deposits under this scheme were close to $1,000. There was no upper income means test on the applicants under any QHC home ownership scheme, in contrast to the effective means test applied to rental applicants described in chapter 3. In 1971 the interest rate on all QHC loans was 7⅛ per cent over 45 years.

The WAHC has pursued four house sales schemes, the main two being financed from state and CSHA funds, respectively. Table 72 gives details of these schemes. From the table it can be seen that the WAHC was selling a sizeable proportion of its dwellings, both under the state scheme and under the CSHA scheme, as early as 1951. This was because the Commission introduced a scheme in 1951 that used state funds and Commonwealth Bank funds to finance the sale of CSHA dwellings. The first two schemes to be considered are so similar that they will be treated together. They are the schemes enabling applicants eligible for, but not currently tenants of, public housing to purchase either state Housing Act or CSHA dwellings constructed by the WAHC. If the repayments would account for more than one-quarter

TABLE 72 House sales in the WAHC 1945–69

Year	State Housing Act houses sold	Percentage of completions	CSHA funds sales	Percentage of completions	Total completions	Total sales as percentage of total completions
1945–6	1	—	—	—	240	—
1946–7	9	2	—	—	535	2
1947–8	15	2	—	—	868	2
1948–9	20	2	—	—	1,036	2
1949–50	40	4	115	12	992	16
1950–1	11	1	508	39	1,288	40
1951–2	151	13	480	41	1,173	54
1952–3	455	29	309	19	1,595	48
1953–4	266	12	94	4	2,278	16
1954–5	785	27	96	3	2,955	30
1955–6	874	35	177	7	2,478	42
1956–7	353	30	294	25	1,191	55
1957–8	262	18	737	52	1,419	70
1958–9	321	26	222	18	1,218	44
1959–60	362	33	324	30	1,084	63
1960–1	519	38	572	42	1,374	80
1961–2	396	28	555	39	1,438	67
1962–3	610	33	590	32	1,845	65
1963–4	630	33	210	11	1,929	44
1964–5	887	51	180	10	1,754	61
1965–6	957	46	203	10	2,098	56
1966–7	560	37	567	38	1,500	75
1967–8	390	29	481	37	1,329	66
1968–9	539	33	373	23	1,657	56
	9,413	27	7,087	20	35,274	47

Source: Commonwealth year books and the annual reports of the WAHC.

of the applicant's income, he is not allowed to purchase. The minimum deposit has varied over time. A system of second mortgages was introduced in 1955 to lower deposits required on dwellings built under the state Housing Act to bring them to the same low level as CSHA deposits. In 1958, about 75 per cent of purchasers under the state Housing Acts paid deposits of under $200, and 40 per cent of those purchasing under CSHA at the same time paid less than $200. In 1969 the minimum deposit for both schemes was $200 and the average deposit paid was not much above this. Dwellings are sold at market value, and in 1971 the interest rate was 5⅜ per cent over 45 years for all schemes. The normal means test described in chapter 3 applies to all applicants to the WAHC, including home ownership clients. Because of this latter policy and the low deposits and favourable terms it can be assumed that the houses sold by the WAHC benefit those on low incomes although the lack of CD data on these areas prevents definite confirmation of this.

Tasmania signed the CSHA in 1945 but withdrew from the agreement in 1950 because 'We desire to build homes for purchase by tenants rather than for letting. For a number of years we have been selling houses for no deposit and we have shown no loss under that scheme. . . .CSHA has not come up to expectations in Tasmania'. From 1945 on, occupants of all dwellings, except for those on very low incomes such as the unemployed and deserted wives, were allowed and encouraged to purchase THC dwellings with no deposits and the repayments spread over 53 years. Applicants for home purchase have to prove a housing need like that applied to rental housing and described in chapter 3. Moreover, the houses were sold to

TABLE 73 House sales in the THC 1956–69

Year	Houses sold	Percentage	Total completions
1956–7	207	38	541
1957–8	398	87	458
1958–9	247	60	410
1959–60	311	72	430
1960–1	329	70	469
1961–2	354	72	492
1962–3	311	59	531
1963–4	431	78	555
1964–5	532	91	586
1965–6	464	85	544
1966–7	460	77	595
1967–8	595	90	665
1968–9	601	100	604
	5,240	76	6,880

Note: Tasmania was not operating under the CSHA from 1950 to 1956.

Source: Commonwealth year books and the annual reports of the THC.

applicants at the capital cost of the dwelling, which meant that the dwelling was usually sold at less than the current market value. Vacated units reoccupied are sold at the current market price less 1 per cent per year depreciation until the price equals the cost. The repayments on a dwelling include an amount for insurance and rates and taxes. These conditions for sale, possibly the easiest terms of all State Housing Commissions, help to account for the large percentage of sales evident in Table 73.

Another scheme introduced in 1965 enables applicants to purchase dwellings with more amenities such as garages attached and hence generally costing more than the normal THC dwellings. Up to 9 April 1969 the average deposit for these dwellings was $300. In 1967–8 these dwellings accounted for about 4 per cent of the total completions of the Commission.

Sales to existing tenants

While the above analysis has been concerned with the conditions attached to the sale of dwellings to someone outside public housing, this section looks at the policies towards tenants currently in public housing who wish to purchase the dwelling they are renting. Only houses are for sale—not flats. Because of the limits on data available attention is restricted to the sale of dwellings completed under the 1945–56 CSHA. Since the THC was not in the CSHA for most of its duration no figures are available. Generally, all states provide attractive conditions to induce current tenants to purchase the dwellings.

Up to 1969 most states had sold a large proportion of their dwellings built under the CSHA 1945–56. The NSWHC had sold 10,047 out of 33,950 saleable units (excluding flats); the VHC, 11,875 out of 28,076; the WAHC 3,105 out of 11,773; the QHC 1,964 out of 9,456; and the SAHT 529 out of 15,548. The reasons for the small proportions in the QHC and the SAHT are discussed below.

In the NSWHC the restrictive conditions of the first CSHA made it difficult for the sitting tenant to purchase his dwelling. From 1955, however, he was able to purchase the dwelling on the same terms as those outside public housing, although the terms for dwellings built under the 1945 Agreement were not as attractive as for those built under the 1956 Agreement. (They were the same as in the 1955 Agreement described above.) However, in 1961 the government decided to permit the sale of all 1945 Agreement dwellings, that is, dwellings built between 1945 and 1955, on the following terms: $100 deposit, no limit on the amount of outstanding indebtedness, 4¾ per cent interest rate, a maximum repayment period of 45 years, and a sale price deposit for both schemes of $200—and the average deposit paid was not much above this. Dwellings were sold at the higher of the cost or the market valuation at the date of taking up tenancy. In 1965 this system was altered so that tenants of 1945 Agreement dwellings could no longer purchase them at the valuation at the time of initial tenancy. Instead they had to pay the higher of the cost or the Rural Bank's current valuation (usually a little below current market value) at the date of application to purchase. Furthermore the Commission did not actively seek their sale as was the case before 1965. They sold only when the tenants approached the Commission. The terms of sale of these 1945 Agreement dwellings since 1965 have been similar to the terms for all other dwellings. The average deposit on 1945 CSHA units during 1968–9 was $143 while the average deposit from the inception of the scheme in 1956 to 1969 was $136. There is no pre-emption period on dwellings currently sold by the Commission. From 1956 to 1961, tenants of 1956 Agreement houses could buy their dwellings at the same rate as the applicants outside, described above.

From 1955 onwards all tenants who subsequently purchased their dwellings were able to gain credit for the amortization of the capital component of the rent paid (less any rebates of rentals granted), this sum being usable as a deposit on the dwelling. All the NSWHC sales of 1945 CSHA dwellings are to existing tenants and this also applies generally to most other states.

Like all the other Commissions the NSWHC applies no upper means test on house tenants wishing to purchase. A lower income limit applies since tenants must be able to afford the deposit, if any, and the weekly repayments should not account for more than 25 per cent of income. The VHC also allows the existing tenants to purchase their houses. Like the NSWHC, the VHC allows these tenants an amortization proportion of the rental they have paid. The sale price, deposit and so on are the same as for applicants who are not tenants, and are described above. The SAHT allows existing tenants to purchase their dwellings but since this applies only to the comparatively small number of rental cottages and double units are not for sale, this policy is not nearly as important in South Australia as in other states.

The QHC allows existing tenants to purchase their houses on similar terms to the above schemes, except that the applicant can provide a minimum down-payment of $50 and at least $2 a week extra rental until the required deposit (as 'low as possible' and usually about $500) is accumulated. Tenants can purchase their houses at current replacement cost less the amount of capital amortization that they have paid in rent while a tenant. The Commissioner pointed out in 1969 that since the normal allocation system ensured that only very low income applicants were admitted to rental homes, the number able to afford to purchase their dwellings could be reduced. By 1969 only 1,964 out of 9,456 saleable dwellings built under the 1945–56 CSHA had been sold.

The WAHC enables those occupying Commission dwellings to purchase them if they so wish. If the tenant decides to purchase within the first twelve months of the life of the dwelling the selling price is the cost of the dwelling plus the current value of the land. Tenants who do not decide to purchase the dwelling during this twelve-month period and tenants of dwellings older than one year may also apply to buy, but the purchase price is based on the cost or current valuation of the dwelling, whichever is the higher. In this latter case the tenant is allowed a credit equal to the principal repayment element contained in the rent which he has paid while in occupation, and this may form the whole or part of the required deposit. Usually a tenant who has been in a dwelling for six or seven years has accumulated the required deposit in this manner. The THC allows tenants to purchase on no deposit as with normal applicants but does not allow any specific amortization allowance for rental paid. The sale price, however, takes account of the time spent in the dwelling since it is set at the current replacement cost less accrued depreciation.

Home ownership and those on the lowest incomes

One effect of home ownership policies is that the Commissions sell many of their older dwellings, built at much lower than current costs. They thus gradually lose their stock of low rental dwellings (if rents are related to costs) or lessen the gains from averaging rents over their older and more recent housing in order to lower rents on newer housing and, in an effort to spread the benefits of inflation and increasing land values, over a wide group. But the following chapter on rent policy shows that averaging is fairly rare in any case and the benefits of inflation largely accrue to the comparatively small minority who occupy older dwellings.

Another effect of home ownership policies is that the sale of dwellings usually produces a profit, mainly because dwellings are generally sold at current market value, often substantially above cost due to inflation and increasing land values. Deposits and setting interest rates above CSHA rates, and the terms of lending below the CSHA term of 53 years, are also sources of income. These profits have been most marked in the NSWHC, the VHC and the WAHC. They have generally been invested in the construction of additional public housing units, especially units for the aged. It could also be argued that since there is no means test on rental dwellings once the applicant has been admitted to the unit, the sale of dwellings does at least produce some profits from relatively high income tenants which may be used for other purposes, compared with the frequent losses on rental operations. In other words any 'rich' tenants—tenants who substantially increase their incomes after admission to public housing—are likely to obtain a bigger subsidy under a rental system as practised in Australia than under the system of home ownership. On the other hand, without the possibility of buying, these rich tenants would be more likely to vacate the public housing and thereby release it for families who need it.

One possible effect of home ownership policies is that the applicants who purchase the public housing dwellings may sell the dwellings to outside groups. No Commission has a pre-emption period of more than five years after the initial sale. Information on this matter is very difficult to obtain. The NSWHC has some isolated data on reselling in some of its older estates but it is not known how common this practice is. The Commission found that 64 dwellings under the 1945 CSHA had been purchased from the Commission for an average selling price of $4,520, while the average sale price (around 1964) was $9,562, an average gross profit of $5,042 per dwelling.

Another important question is whether or not the Commissions have given priority to certain groups as a result of home ownership schemes. From 1945 to 1956 the NSWHC sold comparatively small numbers of houses, and the general emphasis was on rental accommodation. In 1956, however, as already stated, a decision was made by the state government to sell at least 80 per cent of the dwellings completed by the Commission in the future. This meant that those able to afford to purchase gained admittance to public housing after less waiting time than those unable to afford ownership. By 1963, when the decision was changed, the average person allocated a dwelling in Sydney for sale had been on the waiting list for an average of four years, while the average person able to afford only an economic rent had waited an average of six years and the person unable to afford even an economic rent (i.e. eligible for a rental rebate) had waited an average of eight years. From 1963 to the present, an eligible applicant is admitted to a common list. When he reaches the point of allocation he chooses whether to rent or purchase. The building programme was designed so that as far as possible a balance was struck between inner area flats, middle area flats, and cottages for sale or rent in outer areas. This was discussed in chapter 4.

From 1945 to 1956 the VHC, like the NSWHC, sold few of its dwellings mainly because of the restrictions of the CSHA. The emphasis in this period was on the provision of rental dwellings. Applicants wishing to purchase did not obtain access to public housing any sooner than rental applicants. Home ownership is a stated objective of the VHC, but there appears to be some conflict for priority between this and the Commission's slum clearance objective. In 1965 the Minister for Housing, Mr Lindsay Thompson, said that home ownership was an important objective of the VHC. The slum clearance activities of the VHC have increasingly meant that flats—more recently high-rise flats—have become the major form of public housing available in the metropolitan area. Flats cannot be purchased. While the waiting times for flats were from six to eighteen months, the waiting time for cottages was more than five years. This analysis applies only to the metropolitan areas of Melbourne. Waiting times in country areas are similar for rental or purchase applicants but a political directive that the VHC must sell at least 50 per cent of the annual completions means that purchasers sometimes have a shorter waiting time than tenancy applicants.

From 1945 to the present there has been virtually no waiting time under the two home ownership schemes in Queensland that concern applicants outside public housing. This is because the QHC places considerable importance on home ownership—the Commissioner said in 1969, 'We build to sell and what we don't sell we rent'. Chapter 3 showed that the allocation system for rental housing operated by the QHC resulted in short waiting times for the lowest income group but long, virtually endless waiting times for those who did not want to buy, and therefore wanted to be admitted to rental houses, but were not in great and immediate need. The QHC has always concentrated on the construction of cottages, suitable for purchase.

Since 1946, the applicants under the SAHT's middle income home scheme have been able to obtain access to public housing much sooner than rental applicants. But it is doubtful whether this middle income scheme is directly comparable with the rental schemes. As pointed out above, this scheme is not financed from CSHA sources, and, perhaps more important, the SAHT provides as many houses per capita increase in population under its low income schemes as do most other states. However, valid comparisons can be made between the low income rental schemes in other states and the rental schemes operated by the Trust. Applicants for homes under low income home ownership scheme introduced in 1963 have had to wait approximately the same time as rental applicants. In many areas the waiting time for rental applicants is actually shorter. In 1967 the Trust stated that although it agreed that society should have a wide distribution of property and hence home ownership, this did not mean that everyone had to own his own home. 'The fact is', said the Trust, 'in a migrant receiving industrial expanding community there must be a new flow of rental houses always available'. Table 74 shows that apart from the middle income schemes referred to above the SAHT has supplied a considerable amount of housing under its low income schemes. Excluding the middle income sales scheme, the SAHT has provided 17 per cent of total completions since 1945, compared with an average for all the Commissions of 14 per cent. On the other hand, Queensland has built only 11 per cent of the total (excluding units supplied under the Workers' Dwelling scheme). The figures for the NSWHC, VHC, WAHC and the THC in Table 74 are the same as those in Table 2, that is, they refer to the Commissions' low income schemes.

From 1945 to 1969 the WAHC has maintained approximately equal waiting times between its rental applicants and those desiring to purchase. Like the NSWHC since 1963, the WAHC maintains a common waiting list, except for those in great need who are granted rental accommodation almost immediately. When the applicant's turn is reached he can choose whether to rent or purchase a dwelling. The only exception to this is a small scheme in which the Commission grants an applicant finance to buy a privately built home. There is virtually no waiting time for this scheme. In 1968, the WAHC decided to concentrate on building large amounts of high-rise and semi-detached dwellings in the metropolitan area. This will probably make waiting times for those wishing to purchase longer than for those wishing to rent. The rationale for this change in policy away from cottages with the option of purchase to flats and semi-detached—non-saleable—dwellings was discussed in chapter 4.

With the exception of the small, relatively high deposit scheme discussed above, the THC has always given rental and home ownership applicants

TABLE 74 Housing Commission completions, low income schemes, as a percentage of total completions of houses and flats, 1945–70

Year	N.S.W.	Vic.	S.A.	W.A.	Qld	Tas.	Total
	%	%	%	%	%	%	%
1945–6	24	30	22	28	5	30	21
1946–7	18	20	14	30	6	7	15
1947–8	18	18	17	31	5	14	16
1948–9	19	16	16	32	6	9	16
1949–50	17	16	19	27	7	11	15
1950–1	17	13	17	24	5	16	14
1951–2	16	12	19	17	14	19	15
1952–3	17	15	28	20	17	17	18
1953–4	19	16	32	35	19	18	20
1954–5	18	16	29	32	18	19	20
1955–6	13	17	20	30	15	21	17
1956–7	13	12	19	22	16	19	15
1957–8	14	11	16	22	11	18	14
1958–9	11	10	17	20	14	15	12
1959–60	10	10	15	17	9	16	11
1960–1	9	8	18	21	10	18	11
1961–2	15	10	19	23	13	19	15
1962–3	14	8	15	26	12	20	13
1963–4	13	9	14	23	14	21	13
1964–5	14	9	13	19	9	21	12
1965–6	13	9	12	24	10	22	12
1966–7	12	10	19	15	8	20	12
1967–8	13	6	17	11	9	18	11
1968–9	9	6	10	9	8	20	11
1969–70	10	7	17	11	10	16	10
1945–70	14	11	17	21	11	18	14

Source: Annual reports of the Housing Comissions and CBCS.

equal waiting times except in cases of urgent need, in which event the applicant was given priority access to public housing. Priority access has been discontinued since 1969 and the present system is based completely on waiting times, still maintaining the same waiting times for sale or rental applicants.

Social mobility in public housing

Although social mobility within public housing is an important subject, it is very difficult to measure. In the absence of resources for large-scale sample surveys, some use was made of CD data to test the hypothesis that older public housing areas were of higher socio-economic status than more recent areas, suggesting that there had been upward social mobility amongst public housing occupants and that many of these groups had remained in their public housing unit. This involved dating public housing areas according to the time of initial construction, often a difficult process. Since specific CDs were printed out it was possible to compare the socio-economic status of all CDs, and any that were markedly different from the public housing average were analysed to see if they had been built a considerable time—generally before 1958. In addition, all the pre-1958 complete NSWHC CDs were compared with the average and totalled to form the 'pre-1958 areas' in the following tables. The same was done with the pre-1958 VHC CDs.

Generally, the evidence suggested that there was little difference in socio-economic status between older areas and more recent ones or the metropolitan public housing CD average. Tables 75 to 80 present data for the totals for selected older public housing areas in Sydney and Melbourne, and the metropolitan totals repeated from earlier tables. VHC pre-1958 areas have 18 per cent of the workforce in the first two occupational classifications (professional and managerial and self-employed) compared with 13 per cent for the VHC metropolitan total. The figure of 18 per cent in older areas is 3 per cent above the overall figure for VHC home ownership areas given above in this chapter. The pre-1958 NSWHC areas have only

TABLE 75 Occupations of the workforce in metropolitan public housing CD areas built before 1958 (per cent of total), 1966 census

Occupation	NSWHC pre-1958 areas	NSWHC metro. total	VHC pre-1958 areas	VHC metro. total
	%	%	%	%
Professional	4	4	5	4
Managerial, self-employed	9	8	13	9
Clerical workers	23	19	23	20
Armed forces	2	2	1	1
Craftsmen, foremen	17	18	17	18
Shop assistants, process workers	27	30	27	29
Personal, domestic, other service workers and labourers	18	17	16	17

Source: Compiled from summary data supplied by the Commonwealth Statistician (Collectors' District data for the total population).

TABLE 76 Education of the population (excluding children not at school and full-time students), in metropolitan public housing CD areas built before 1958 (per cent of total), 1966 census

Occupation	NSWHC pre-1958 areas	NSWHC metro. total	VHC pre-1958 areas	VHC metro. total
	%	%	%	%
University qualifications	—	—	—	—
Other tertiary qualifications	1	1	1	1
Matriculation passed	6	5	9	8
Intermediate passed	30	29	18	16
Attended high school	40	39	34	35
Attended primary school	22	23	34	37
No education	—	1	1	1
Not stated	2	2	2	2

Source: Compiled from summary data supplied by the Commonwealth Statistician (Collectors' District data for the total population).

13 per cent of the workforce in the first two occupational classifications, only 1 per cent above the metropolitan average. These older Commission areas in Sydney and Melbourne consisted of flats and rented and sold cottages.

In Tables 75 to 80 the pre-1958 areas in the NSWHC total 13,164 people and 3,492 dwellings, of which 61 per cent were cottages and 39 per cent flats. Of the cottages, 39 per cent were sold. Pre-1958 areas in the VHC contained 26,718 people and 6,565 dwellings of which 77 per cent were

TABLE 77 Motor vehicle ownership in metropolitan public housing CD areas built before 1958, number of vehicles per occupied private dwelling (per cent of total), 1966 census

No. of vehicles per dwelling	Sydney pre-1958 NSWHC	Sydney total NSWHC	Melbourne pre-1958 VHC	Melbourne total VHC
	%	%	%	%
HOUSES				
None	31	31	25	26
One	51	57	48	53
Two	14	10	20	15
Three +	2	—	5	3
Not stated	1	2	2	2
FLATS				
None	55	61	56	57
One	38	32	37	34
Two	3	3	3	3
Three +	—	—	—	—
Not stated	3	5	3	6

Source: Compiled from summary data supplied by the Commonwealth Statistician (Collectors' District data for the total population).

TABLE 78 Age structure in metropolitan public housing CD areas built before 1958 (per cent of total), 1966 census

Age group	NSWHC pre-1958 areas	NSWHC metro. total	VHC pre-1958 areas	VHC metro. total
	%	%	%	%
0–4	7	14	7	10
5–9	10	17	9	13
10–14	14	12	13	14
15–19	13	8	14	13
20–29	10	12	12	11
30–39	14	16	10	12
40–49	16	10	16	14
50–59	10	6	11	8
60 +	7	5	8	6

Source: Compiled from summary data supplied by the Commonwealth Statistician (Collectors' District data for the total population).

cottages and 23 per cent flats. Of the cottages, 56 per cent were sold.

Some explanations can be suggested for the generally negative findings on the social mobility hypotheses tested in this section. These explanations are, of course, highly speculative and extensive research involving interviewing residents in many different public housing areas would be necessary to verify them. The first possibility is that there is little intragenerational upward social mobility in Australia. In other words, few of the initial occupants of public housing units experience significant upward mobility. This is partially supported by the comparatively low educational levels of the population in public housing (since education is traditionally closely allied with upward mobility). Another possibility is that Australian public housing units are of such comparatively low standard, in the dwelling itself, the level of amenities in the surrounding area, and/or the quality of the social environment, that households who substantially improve their socio-economic status leave public housing and obtain higher-quality housing in the private market. The literature on this matter generally suggests that with changes in long-term income a household will increase the amount

TABLE 79 *Birthplace of the population in metropolitan public housing CD areas built before 1958 (per cent of total), 1966 census*

Birthplace	NSWHC pre-1958 areas	NSWHC metro. total	VHC pre-1958 areas	VHC metro. total
	%	%	%	%
Australia	90	88	89	83
New Zealand, England, Wales, Ireland, Scotland	7	8	7	9
Austria, Czechoslovakia, Germany, Hungary, Yugoslavia	1	1	1	1
Greece, Italy, Malta	1	1	2	3
Other	2	2	2	3

Source: Compiled from summary data supplied by the Commonwealth Statistician (Collectors' District data for the total population).

TABLE 80 *Marital status of the population (excluding the never married) in metropolitan public housing CD areas built before 1958 (per cent of total), 1966 census*

Marital status	NSWHC pre-1958 areas	NSWHC metro. total	VHC pre-1958 areas	VHC metro. total
	%	%	%	%
Married	83	88	88	87
Married, but permanently separated	5	4	4	4
Divorced	2	—	—	1
Widowed	10	7	8	7

Source: Compiled from summary data supplied by the Commonwealth Statistician (Collectors' District data for the total population).

that it spends on housing. One important factor in the decision to vacate public housing would be the large difference in costs between public and private housing. The public housing subsidy is generally so substantial that the household would require very substantial increases in income to be able to obtain higher-quality private housing without spending a higher proportion of its income. Some of the aspects of public housing developments that may discourage upwardly mobile households from remaining in public housing are discussed in chapter 9.

The diversion of funds to co-operative societies

In the 1956 CSHA the Commonwealth government directed that a proportion of the funds advanced under the CSHA was to be diverted to co-operative societies. This proportion was to be 20 per cent in the first year of the new agreement and 30 per cent from then on. This provision has been retained in the 1961 and 1966 CSHAs. The Commonwealth has established 30 per cent as a minimum and has attempted to persuade the states to divert more, but the states generally resist this. This section examines some of the reasons for this decision and some of the effects of the policy.

Senator Spooner claimed in 1956 that, because the funds allocated to the building societies were generally lent for periods of 30 years whereas the funds provided under the CSHA had to be repaid in 53 years, the societies would be able to form a revolving fund that would enable more dwellings to be financed than if they were used by the Housing Commissions who generally sold on terms of 45 years or, in the case of Tasmania, 53 years. Spooner also argued that the co-operatives would thus be able to build twice as many homes as the Housing Commissions. While exact data on this matter are unavailable some limited observations can be made. Firstly, as the Premier of South Australia pointed out in 1955, the SAHT (and other Commissions who operate as tract developers) was able to obtain large economies of scale both in housing costs and the cost of associated services because it built its houses generally in large groups. This is an important economy which usually does not exist when houses are purchased through co-operatives. Secondly, the Housing Commissions sometimes make substantial profits on the sale of dwellings, enabling them to reinvest these funds in the provision of additional low income housing. Thirdly, however, the funds diverted to the co-operative societies could otherwise have been used for slum clearance activities, particularly in Victoria, and this would probably have meant that substantially fewer dwellings would have been provided than when they were used by the co-operatives. This is because of the high cost of high-rise flats compared with cottages or small home units provided by the co-operative finance.

One objective of the diversion of CSHA funds to the co-operative societies was to encourage the growth of such societies. Spooner told the societies that the CSHA funds were not intended as a substitute for finance obtained from other sources and that the purpose of the CSHA funds was to spur them on to get more outside money. He warned that the amount that would be available to the societies from the CSHA funds would be very largely influenced by what they did in other directions. There is evidence that the non-CSHA sources of finance for the co-operatives have been declining since 1964. In 1964–5, the proportion of co-operative funds obtained from CSHA sources was 42 per cent. By 1968–9 it had increased to 55 per cent and there were signs in 1969 that this dependence on CSHA funds could increase rapidly.

Since 1956 the main non-CSHA sources of finance for the co-operatives have been the Commonwealth Bank and the state savings banks in some states. The decision to supply this money has been largely the result of governmental directives, since these banks are government-owned and operated. These organizations are also direct lenders for housing. Henderson claims that the type of person obtaining a loan from a co-operative society is often identical with the savings bank client and that this may be a reason for the decline in finance from the savings banks in Victoria. Lending for housing is an important source of goodwill for savings banks so that they may not be willing to lend it through co-operatives at the same or a lower rate of interest to people identical in income to their clients.

When the 1956 CSHA was introduced and the co-operatives received 30 per cent of the funds, Spooner assumed that the total amount of allocation under the CSHA would remain the same so that, in effect, the money given to the co-operatives would come from funds that would otherwise have been given to the Housing Commissions. Since there are no data on the decision-making process in the state governments which decide the overall amount under the CSHA little can be said on this matter. But the percentage of completions built by the Housing Commissions has been falling since 1957 and the diversion of funds to the co-operatives is possibly one part of the explanation. The state governments have not noticeably increased the overall proportion of their works and housing vote allocated to the CSHA after 1956.

Describing the functions of the advancement of CSHA funds to the co-operative societies, the Minister for Housing, Dame Annabelle Rankin, said in 1969:

> The moneys in the Home Builders' Account are used by the States to provide loans through building or housing societies or other institutions to those seeking to buy or build their homes. Because the Commonwealth makes these moneys available at a concessional rate of interest, it asks the States to confine the loans to home-seekers of low or moderate means. Thus, not only does the Home Builders' Account provision in the Housing Agreement encourage private home ownership by promoting the maximum development of building societies; it also relieves the State Housing Authorities of the burden of providing housing for the low to moderate income families who are assisted with the loans.

There is little information on the characteristics of borrowers from co-operative societies but some figures are presented here. Generally the interest rates, period of repayment and loan limits make them more expensive than the home ownership terms offered by the Housing Commissions, the only comparable schemes being the QHC workers' dwelling policy and the SAHT middle income scheme.

In 1969–70 a study was made of the characteristics of 1,368 New South Wales borrowers from co-operative societies which were in receipt of funds from the CSHA. While the income levels are higher than for applicants for NSWHC allocations, perhaps the most instructive figure is the low ratio of the loan to the valuation of the house and land. Since valuation usually is less than actual cost this probably underestimates the proportion of cash required for the granting of the loan. Some 70 per cent of applicants required at least 25 per cent of the total value—that is, almost $3,000 deposit since most loans are for about $9,000. This means that people on low incomes could not normally raise the deposit on, and therefore benefit from, such a loan.

In 1968 R. F. Henderson, Professor of Economics, University of Melbourne, said in the *Report of the Co-operative Housing Committee of Review* that,

> From information furnished this Committee, it is apparent that many Societies are now assisting a considerable number of people who ought to be able to obtain loans from their banks or other institutions. In other words, banks and other lenders are being asked to provide funds at a lower rate of interest, the benefit of which will be gained by many people not entitled to it. For example the Committee found that, out of 20 recent advances by one group of societies only seven had incomes below $60 per week, three cases were from $80–$90, three others $90–$100 and in one case $120.

This was at a time when the ceiling limit in income in the VHC was $70 per week for a family with more than three children and $60 for others.

Conclusion

How does Australian home ownership public housing policy rate on some of the more important criteria listed in the introduction to this chapter? In the most important area, the supply of the public housing subsidy to those on the lowest incomes, there are many schemes which do not rate highly. The THC and the WAHC are the two Commissions which supply home ownership dwellings to applicants not already Commission tenants without reducing the supply of housing to the lowest income group. This is because, in both states, home ownership applicants are subject to the same means tests as rental applicants and the deposits and repayment in both Commissions are very favourable, more so in the THC. In addition, both Commissions ensure that both renters and purchasers gain access to public housing in roughly the same period of time. The WAHC emphasis on non-saleable multi-unit accommodation since 1969 will probably mean that those wishing to rent will be given quicker access to public housing compared to those who desire to purchase. In general, the NSWHC has provided home ownership dwellings on favourable conditions to new applicants not already Commission tenants and application of the general NSWHC means test probably ensures that the housing is allocated to the low income group. On the other hand, the Commission gave great priority to home purchasers between 1956 and 1963. Although the VHC attaches favourable conditions to its public housing units, the deposits being low and the interest rate and period of repayment attractive, the emphasis on slum reclamation in the Melbourne metropolitan area means that flats not open to purchase are the main form of public housing available. The implications of this have been discussed in the chapter on slum clearance above.

The SAHT and the QHC have used home ownership policy quite differently from the other four Commissions. In the SAHT, the main form of low income housing until 1963 was the double-unit dwelling, not available for sale. Since 1963 there has been a low income home ownership plan but considerable emphasis is still placed on the middle income sale scheme introduced in 1946 and of substantial magnitude to date. The effects of the scheme in allocating subsidies to the middle income group were discussed in chapter 6. What is clear, however, is that although the SAHT does give middle income purchase applicants priority in access to public housing, it builds a large volume of low income housing, much of it for rental only (the double unit), compared with other states. The QHC has the least favourable terms for low income home ownership. Comparatively high deposits mean that probably only middle income applicants are able to purchase their homes from outside public housing, probably leaving a substantial group not so badly off as to qualify for QHC rental housing but not affluent enough to afford the deposit for a purchase dwelling. In contrast to the SAHT, the QHC does not build a very large number of rental dwellings so that the strong priority given to purchasers probably has a serious effect on the volume of funds available for low income rental housing.

The Commonwealth Home Savings Grant scheme may mitigate the comparatively high deposits required under the QHC Workers' Dwelling scheme and, to a less extent, under the SAHT middle income scheme. The home savings grant gives a tax-free grant of one dollar for every three dollars. saved towards a first home over three years, up to a maximum grant of $500. The grant is not payable on dwellings built under the CSHA and hence is limited in public housing to the QHC Workers' Dwelling scheme, the SAHT middle income programme, and the WAHC state Housing Act dwellings.

For the tenant in public housing who wishes to purchase the unit, all Commissions offer very favourable terms. Since no means test is applied when they request to purchase this may mean that households who were initially in need of housing assistance but improve their economic position after entry into public housing are not only not asked to leave or pay additional rent but are also given the opportunity to purchase. Given the fact that this dwelling is then no longer assisting the low income group it could be argued that the dwelling should not be sold on such favourable terms and the additional revenue obtained from selling it at a higher price should be used to supply more low income housing.

The diversion of funds to the co-operative societies ranks as one of the major influences on the reduction in the supply of low income public housing. Except possibly for SAHT middle income clients, the occupants of workers' dwellings in the QHC and possibly the QHC sale schemes generally (sales to existing QHC tenants excluded), and the 'rich tenants' in any Commissions (tenants who have improved their socio-economic status after entry to public housing and purchase the dwelling), public housing occupants seem to be considerably below the socio-economic status of those who obtain loans from the co-operative societies receiving CSHA funds.

Like the aged persons' home scheme relying on voluntary agencies, the co-operative societies' policy has been a failure. There are no effective methods of allocating the money to the poor through co-operative societies except, perhaps, by the WAHC which has had more courage than anyone else in trying to ensure that the CSHA funds go to those in some need. In theory, the funds that go to co-operatives could be used to provide housing for those on very low incomes; Spooner was correct in that. With continual inflation and mortgage insurance, very little unemployment and comparatively high family incomes of many of those classed as members of the low income group, lending funds to those on low incomes is a very safe proposition. The State Housing Commissions show that. Even the old rule about the repayments not exceeding one-quarter of the household's income is not valid since, with inflation, even a 10 per cent maximum may be excessive.

Why have the co-operatives not helped the poor? Firstly, their administration is very decentralized. Often they are small groups of people who wish their loans to go to people they know. There are many stories of how they are connected, unofficially of course, with certain building companies so that purchase of only a particular house carries the subsidized loans. Allocating the funds under the co-operative society loans must be one of the last remaining areas of middle class patronage, rivalled only by the activities of the private health funds. The system of rationing also prevents the loans from going to the poor. To those handing out the loans it seems eminently rational to distribute $80,000 as ten $8,000 loans rather than eight $10,000 loans. True, in this way they produce more houses, but they also force up the required deposit—though for them this probably makes administration easier since they know that anyone with enough for the deposit is a safe lending risk. But perhaps the most important reason is the ideological basis for the co-operative movement: help should be given to those who attempt to help themselves and the man with $3,000 deposit has obviously helped himself more than the man with $50. The Commonwealth would probably prefer to scrap the diversion of funds to co-operative societies but politically it is very difficult. The whole complexity of the matter prevents it from becoming an important issue. The Commonwealth could, however, exercise much more courage in forcing the co-operatives to divert their CSHA funds to the poor. It could start with a thorough survey of who benefits from the co-operatives, such as the Nimmo committee on health, instead of just writing letters to the societies.

Home ownership policies generally do not rank very highly for effectiveness in relating housing costs to capacity to pay according to accepted welfare principles, especially equity and progression, explained at the beginning of this chapter. With continual inflation the level of housing costs of home-owning families varies according to when the household purchased the dwelling—the earlier it bought, the lower the costs. Generally this means that older households have lower costs and, assuming that children appear early in the marriage cycle, high housing costs coincide with the expenses of rearing children, and by the time the household has completed rearing the children, real housing costs will be lower. Since a high proportion of private houses are owner-occupied, public housing home ownership policies score highly on the criterion of offering opportunities equal to what is available in private housing. Unlike the rent policies to be discussed below, home ownership schemes do not permit repayments to be adjusted in accordance with households' varying capacity to pay, except that if a household suffers some catastrophic loss of income—for example, the breadwinner dies or deserts—the Housing Commissions can transfer the household to a rental unit. The Commissions generally apply the 25 per cent rule in determining whether or not a household can afford house repayments. The merits of the 25 per cent rule are discussed in chapter 8. Some writers have questioned the validity of this rule since the inflationary process means that so long as incomes increase in accordance with the general increase in the price level, many households soon pay gradually less than one-quarter of their incomes on mortgage repayments. If the repayments rose in accordance with the level of income, repayments could be averaged over the period of the loan. The average weekly proportion of income spent on housing costs in the early part of the repayment period would be lower than under conventional mortgage arrangements. With rising property values and with mortgage insurance there would appear to be little rationale for requiring deposits for home ownership except that this produces additional funds which can be invested in additional dwellings. It may also encourage households to save.

Public housing home ownership policies have two generally positive effects. Firstly, they usually mean that the social composition of an area varies more widely than would be the case if the area were occupied entirely by tenants and probably also that the population is less mobile than in tenanted areas. The implications of this are discussed more fully in chapter 9. Secondly, home ownership policies have been the main source of

Housing Commission profits and, given the financial arrangements for the supply of public housing in Australia, discussed more fully in the next chapter, these profits have played a very important role in supplying public housing to those on the lowest incomes.

8 RENT POLICY

The criteria used in evaluating Housing Commission rent policies are similar to those applied to home ownership policies. The first section of this chapter outlines the development of the main objective of Australian public housing: all households should be able to obtain adequate housing at a price they can afford to pay. From this generalized statement of the objective the next section describes four rent systems: market rentals, and the historic costs, averaging, and rebate systems. The third section looks at a subject very closely connected with rent policy: who bears the responsibility for the losses involved in housing those unable to pay normal Housing Commission rents? This could be any of a number of groups: the sitting tenant in the Housing Commission benefiting from the historic cost rental system, the rich tenant, other Commission tenants, the Housing Commission home purchaser, or the taxpayer generally, through either the state or federal governments.

The capacity to pay—the development of an idea

As was outlined briefly in chapter 1, public housing policy gradually moved from an emphasis on home ownership—not for those on the bottom of the income ladder—to a complete acceptance that the government would have to provide adequate housing for many on low incomes, even though this would involve large losses. The first public housing scheme in New South Wales, Dacey Gardens, completed in 1923, did not provide housing to those on low incomes regardless of the losses involved. When introducing the legislation establishing the suburb in 1912, J. R. Dacey, the Treasurer in a Labor government, said that:

> In this free Australia there is no submerged tenth and I do not want to carry out a scheme which would enable people to put their heads in the air and say 'that is where the working class live'. No one is allowed to live there who has more than a certain income. We do very well for that sort of person . . . the houses will be let regardless of occupation . . . I want this thing to be self-supporting. I want no element of charity or condescension about it. The tenant who gets one of our houses and pays what is a fair amount on the capital expenditure is under no compliment to the State and I do not think that the State should be under any compliment to him either. It is a purely business transaction.

The last chapter showed that home ownership schemes between the wars (1919 to 1939) were not concerned with the lowest income group. In the 1930–45 period the housing reform movement accepted the losses involved in housing those on low incomes and the 1937 Report in Victoria stated that 'slum reclamation is a social service and not a cold profitable or commercial proposition. The "profit" is on the side of better citizenship and a healthier community'. When introducing the 1937 Housing Bill in New South Wales the Premier, Mr Stevens, said that, in addition to schemes for promoting home ownership,

> . . . the second section of the housing policy relates to a small but important minority of the population who live in circumstances of some distress or insecurity. Folk in these circumstances are all too frequently not in a position to help themselves, because of their misfortune or disabilities. They are generally housed in substandard habitations, often in congested areas, or in undesirable locations. On the whole, they are not in a position to pay a commercial rental, and too often they live in conditions of primitive squalor, destructive alike to their own well-being and that of their children. It is not, in general, possible to improve the housing of these indirectly by encouraging private enterprise or by providing easy means of finance. To cope with the position properly it is necessary for the Government to assume a direct responsibility, not as a business proposition, but as a social service.

The Minister for Post-war Reconstruction in 1945, J. Dedman, said when introducing the first CSHA Bill in 1945,

> In the history of Australia there have been few, if any, instances where a working man on the basic wage or less has been able to obtain a new dwelling of good standard for his family needs for a rent of one-fifth of his income.

Rental systems

The Commissions use three rental systems: historic costs; rental averaging; and rebate rentals. This section looks also at another rental system—market rents—which are not currently applied by any Commission but are useful as a comparative benchmark.

Market rentals

A market rental plan means that there is no subsidy on the rental, which is the same as the rental for private accommodation of similar standard. A market rental system could have a useful place in forming Housing Commission rent policy and is therefore discussed briefly below even though no Commission actually implements it.

Market rentals would be based on the market value of the dwelling and would represent the return the Commission could obtain if the dwelling were rented on the open market. This rent would include a competitive return on capital invested and hence there would be no subsidy on the dwelling. A market rental system could be useful in ensuring that those households who improved their economic position after entry into public housing did not continue to gain the benefit of the government subsidy, as occurs at present. There are problems involved in applying such a system. Even supposing one decided on a reasonable definition of what measures were to be taken into account in defining economic welfare (discussed above) there would still be the time-consuming and expensive task of collecting information from all the households in public housing. A fair system would require at least information on income, family size, assets and outgoings. Such widespread collection of information could be considered an invasion of privacy and, depending on the number of tenants who would be paying market or near-market rents, the cost of information collection could exceed the additional revenue. Since the conditions for the purchase of a dwelling, once a household is admitted to public housing as a tenant, are so generous it could be assumed that most of the 'wealthy' tenants in public housing would decide to purchase their dwellings, making the application of a market rental system a doubtful method of increasing revenue. This latter argument would not apply to occupants of flats which cannot be purchased.

The application of a market rental system could also act as a disincentive for a household to improve its economic position, as any such improvement would be followed by an increase in rental. It would probably also encourage the better-off tenants to leave public housing and so create low income ghettos, depending on how rents are adjusted with increases in income. All representatives at the Housing Ministers' Conference in 1968 endorsed the views of Mr Meagher (Victorian Minister for Housing) when he gave reasons for not penalizing people by either a higher rent or by eviction when they improved their economic position after entry into public housing.

> We think that it is a wholly good thing that people who start off with a low income eligibility and in a fairly poor environment should improve themselves and so have an incentive to improve the properties in which they live. It provides a better balance in the type of people living in this accommodation. We do not ask them to move; we are in favour of them improving themselves.

Much the same view was repeated in 1964 when the NSWHC stated that penalizing those who improve themselves would prejudice the '. . . social character of our estates, which have been retained at a high level [that] should not be diminished by making them increasingly and progressively poorer single class settlements'.

The advantage of a market rental system is that it promotes internal equity inside public housing by making those better off pay a higher rent than those worse off. Leaving aside the question of the capacity of a household to pay a rent, a market rental system would be an excellent way of deciding the respective rents of different dwellings since the different facilities would presumably be reflected in the market rental.

Historic costs

Of the three types of rent schemes used by the Commissions, the historic costs method is the most widespread. It is used in all Commissions except the VHC since 1963 and the WAHC since 1965. The basis of the historic cost system is the conditions under which the Commonwealth advances funds to the states under the CSHAs from 1945. Although the specific terms of these agreements differ considerably, in all agreements the Commonwealth advances loans to the states repayable at below market interest rates over 53 years. The historic cost system places a rent on a dwelling built under the CSHA sufficient to cover all outgoings by the Commission on that dwelling. Thus the rent incorporates a fixed component—the repayment of the capital cost over 53 years including the interest rate ruling under the CSHA at the time of construction—and variable components—rates, maintenance, insurance, administration and an allowance for vacancies and defaults—all of which rise with the general increase in the price level. Rents that are sufficient to cover all these components are termed 'economic rents' and, with continual inflation, frequent adjustments are necessary to raise older rents to economic levels. Some Commissions do this but many of them using historic costs do not. Some increase uneconomic rents only when an older dwelling is vacated, a practice known as 'vacancy rents'.

It has been stated above that the Commissions would have to increase rents regularly to cover the increases in variable costs, primarily because of inflation. Even if the Commissions adjust the rents on older dwellings so that they cover all outgoings on them, their rents will still be lower than current dwelling rents because of the lower capital costs of the old dwellings and the generally lower interest rate. Few states have regularly adjusted historic cost rents to take account of changes in variable costs (rates, maintenance, etc.). The reasons for the different adjustment policies between the states are discussed later in this chapter.

Because the NSWHC has not adjusted rents on older dwellings regularly the rental income from these dwellings is insufficient to cover the total outgoings, that is, the amortization of capital payment, the interest, and the variable costs (rates, etc.). The SAHT has attempted to adjust rents but has not succeeded in raising them enough for rents on earlier dwellings to cover outgoings. Some adjustments were made in 1968 and there appears to be some averaging of rents. The WAHC consistently adjusted its rentals from 1945 to 1965 so that its rentals usually reflected the full historic costs of its dwellings. Since 1965 the Commission has averaged its rentals. From 1945 to 1955 the VHC had not adjusted the rentals on any of its units except when a dwelling was vacated. The widespread inflation during this period made the initial historic costs rental on the older dwellings insufficient to meet the outgoings. The first adjustment was made in 1955. Further adjustments were made in 1957 but there were no more (on sitting tenancies) until the averaging system was introduced in 1963. The THC did not adjust rents on existing tenancies from 1945 to 1965. Some adjustments were made to raise rents on older dwellings to the level of full historic costs in 1965–8 but these adjustments ceased in 1968 and in 1970 rents on about 300 homes were still in need of extensive adjustment to cover all outgoings. In contrast to other states, the QHC has consistently adjusted rents to take account of changes in variable costs. Mr T. A. Hiley, the Minister for Housing, said in 1962: 'I am the Treasurer as well as the Minister for Housing and any element of subsidy in Housing Commission rents in this State will be over my dead body. We get the full rental'.

Even where rents are adjusted fully for changes in variable costs, there can be large variations in weekly rents between dwellings because of the large increases in building costs and interest rates from 1945 to 1968. In 1968, for example, economic rentals for similar accommodation in QHC ranged from $4.75 to $16.30 depending on when the dwelling was built.

Generally, the highest rent levels charged by the Housing Commissions are vacancy rents and the rents on dwellings recently completed. In all Commissions except the WAHC, the QHC and the VHC until 1963, rents of vacated dwellings are raised so that the incoming tenant faces a higher rent than the departing tenant. Faced with extreme difficulty in adjusting the rents of tenants in occupation, the Commissions see vacancy rents as a method to adjust rents while avoiding the opposition to general increases. The NSWHC has revised the rents on vacated dwellings since 1945. The new rent is generally above the historic cost level and it is argued that these new rentals are 'reasonable at the time having regard to the nature of the premises, rental levels generally, location, etc.'. While the rents are above the level necessary to cover all outgoings on the property, they are below the rents of comparable newly constructed Commission dwellings of similar quality. The SAHT applies a similar vacancy rent system to that of the NSWHC. The THC bases its vacancy rents on the current valuations minus 1 per cent per annum for the life of the dwelling provided that this figure is not less than the original cost.

The inequity in an historic costs system is that it concentrates the benefits of inflation among the occupants of older units, the exact amount of the benefit depending on the degree of rental adjustment and the date of initial occupancy. A vacancy rent system leads to wide differentials in rents of dwellings in the one estate and even adjacent units, causing possible ill-feeling between tenants. Historic cost systems (including vacancy rents) do not benefit households during their initial period of residence in public housing, although, as was pointed out above, this may be the time when the family resources are most strained due to the arrival of children. The lack of adjustment of rents to cover even the variable costs on a dwelling may discourage households from purchasing the unit.

Another important feature of the historic costs system is that, even if rents are fully adjusted for changes in variable costs, the total rent revenue will not cover the losses incurred on rental rebates on the housing for those in most need. With the 1945–55 CSHA the Commonwealth took responsibility for three-fifths of these losses but the 1956 and subsequent agreements made no provision for this. Since the Commonwealth's partial reimbursement of losses was conditional on the states fully adjusting rentals for movements in variable costs, these payments by the Commonwealth have been largely restricted to Western Australia and Queensland. Since a householder would lose the benefits of the low rent on his old dwelling if he moved, the historic costs system may lessen labour mobility.

The historic cost rental system, the basis of all State Housing Commission rental systems for at least some of the 1945–68 period, involves developing accurate estimates of the costs of each dwelling, or else relatively small groups of similar dwellings built at similar times. This has proved to be a somewhat difficult, expensive and indeterminate process. Considerable numbers of staff are occupied in estimating costs. The 1956 Royal Commission into housing in Victoria claimed that many estimates of capital costs of dwellings were inaccurate. Irregularities were also discovered by the Commonwealth Grants Commission in investigations into the THC in 1958.

Rental averaging

The second basic rent system used by the Commissions is the practice known as 'averaging rents'. Under this system, applied in the VHC since 1963 and in the WAHC since 1965, the rents are not directly related to when the dwelling was constructed, but a set rent is applied to dwellings of particular sizes. The revenue from an averaging system may or may not exceed the revenue from a full economic rental scheme, depending on the level of rent charged.

Averaging was possible under the original CSHA in 1945. Clause 6 of the first schedule of the agreement provided that the authority might fix as the rent of a dwelling an amount which is greater or less than the amount fixed under the historic costs formula but the total of all such rents should not be less than the total sum of all economic rents fixed in accordance with the economic rent formula. Since the 1956 and subsequent agreements do not make any provision for the setting of rentals the states are free to average rentals if they so wish. The 1956 Royal Commission into housing in Victoria recommended that the VHC average rents on all its dwellings, the basis for rental determination being the numbers of bedrooms rather than the age of the dwelling, its situation or other such factors. Rents were not averaged until 1963, when the rents on most older dwellings were raised while rents on more recent dwellings were below those which would have applied had the general CSHA historic costs principle applied. Out of 31,795 tenancies the VHC increased the rents on 1,426 dwellings by a total of $24,333 (per year) and individually by amounts up to $1.99 per week; 1,292 were decreased and 22,331 were not changed. Rents were again increased in 1966, 1968 and 1970, the objective being to make the income from rents less rebates equal to the outgoings. The increase in 1970 made the VHC rental on a one-bedroom unit $11.30, $11.80 on a two-bedroom unit and $12.30 on a three-bedroom dwelling (house or flat). From 1965 the WAHC also averaged rents in a similar way to the VHC.

Averaging rentals does result in internal equity in the sense that there is one rental for each type of dwelling (bedroom size). It results in spreading the benefits of inflation over a wider group than historic cost rents. It may also encourage the household to purchase the dwelling since by doing this it generally gains the benefits from inflation. The problems do arise of actually deciding the price to be charged for accommodation of a certain size and what allowance should be made for accommodation of different quality. This latter aspect can be of some importance since the stock of public housing is likely to consist of dwellings of considerably different quality. In the VHC, for example, it has been found that high-rise flats, with lifts, mechanized garbage disposal, central heating and laundries on each floor are much more popular amongst tenants than walk-up flats without these amenities. High-rise tenants paid about a dollar per week more than those in the walk-up flats, to cover the running costs of the central heating and hot water services. A similar problem would arise if the NSWHC decided to average rents. The older dwellings tend to be located in suburbs that are now considered highly desirable—places such as Maroubra and North Sydney. The new developments are in areas in the western suburbs, like Mt Druitt, 32 miles from Sydney. These problems could be overcome by using market value as a standard for comparison. One advantage of averaging is that it removes the necessity to keep detailed accounts for the various properties according to when they were built. The historic costs system results in the Commissions having many different accounts with many different rates of interest, maintenance factors and so on.

There is a negative side to VHC rental averaging. Despite claims to the contrary, the VHC does not have the cheapest rents of any Australian Housing Commission. Even on newly constructed dwellings the WAHC and SAHT rents are considerably cheaper. The VHC slum clearance programme is the reason for this. In the VHC the total rental revenue is designed to pay for all the outgoings on the stock of rental housing, including the very high cost of high-rise ventures such as Park Towers referred to in chapter 5. This means that the residents in the older dwellings have to subsidize the cost of high-rise flats. In comparison, the WAHC and to a lesser extent the SAHT practise forms of rental averaging which do not involve supporting high-cost dwellings and so have considerably lower rents than the VHC. The comparatively high rents on SAHT flats reflect the middle income status of the clientele. The high average of rents in the VHC is yet another means of disguising the costs of the high-rise programme.

The foregoing analysis has shown that while some states, particularly Western Australia and Queensland and more recently Victoria, have been able to adjust rents regularly, other states have rarely done so. From the available evidence it appears that the key variable is the attitude of the state politicians, both the government in power and the Opposition, towards the increases in Housing Commission rents. Some state politicians feel that they are sufficiently strong politically to be able to withstand the possible backlash from a rental increase. This has been the case in Victoria although, given the political strength of the Victorian Liberal Party since 1956, it is in some ways surprising that Housing Commission rents were not increased earlier than they were. The process can depend on what action the Opposition takes on the rent increase. If the Opposition decided to make the matter an important issue the ruling party could be reluctant to adjust rents. Generally, however, it can be said that all the administrators in the Housing Commissions are eager to raise rents at least to cover total expenditure on dwellings under the CSHA formula; and in almost all cases the politicians in charge of the Commissions and the cabinet generally are eager to raise rents to take account of inflation but are afraid of the political consequences of doing so. After all, if they do not obtain additional revenue from rents the Commissions may be forced to curtail the housing of needy groups such as the aged, or become a drain on the already strained state Treasuries. This latter expedient is all the more likely given the difficulty of recouping three-fifths of losses from the Commonwealth, discussed below. It was noted in the last chapter that the desire to sell public housing units was partially a state government measure to overcome the difficulties of rental increases.

There are no clear patterns on the differences in rental policy between Labor and non-Labor (Liberal and/or Country Party) governments. In New South Wales the Labor Party, which ruled from 1941 to 1965, was very reluctant to raise NSWHC rents but the Liberal Party, which gained power in 1965, was hardly any more flexible, which is particularly surprising given the fact that with the decline of rent control, partly through the passage of time and partly through the policies of the Liberal Party, rental increases lost some of their political importance. The Labor Party has not ruled for long in Victoria, so it is impossible to make comparisons. In South Australia both the Labor and non-Labor governments have been unwilling to raise SAHT rents in any substantial way. Nor has either party in Tasmania. Queensland has adjusted its QHC rentals regardless of the party in power, possibly reflecting the influence of the QHC bureaucracy. Similarly, the WAHC has adjusted its rents regardless of the political complexion of the party in power.

Increases in Housing Commission rents have to be seen against the general background of the fact that price stability has been a major governmental objective in Australia. Probably as a result of the importance attached to price stability, but also because of political rivalry, Housing Commission rent increases are important issues in state politics in a number of states. In Tasmania, for example, from 1948 to 1965, the rents of THC dwellings were not adjusted for existing tenancies, despite pressures and criticism from the Commonwealth Grants Commission. Finally, in 1965 the THC decided to adjust rents up to the levels of full historic cost. In 1969, however, the government was defeated. At the 1970 Housing Ministers' Conference, the Minister for Housing in the Liberal government in Tasmania (Mr Clark) said, 'I am very pleased to be able to be here today completing the team and it is, in part, because of a promise we made less than a year ago that I am here. That promise was that, in the life of the present Parliament we would not increase departmental charges for rents'.

A similar sequence of events occurred in the NSWHC. In 1963, after 18 years of state reluctance to adjust rentals on Housing Commission units, the NSWHC managed to convince the Labor cabinet not only that the Commission should be allowed to increase the rents on older dwellings, but that this process should be an annual affair, presumably removed from the political. arena. However, Housing Commission rents became an important issue in the 1965 state election and the sitting Labor government was defeated and replaced by the Liberal government which as part of its platform had said that it would not increase NSWHC rents during the life of that parliament. Probably as a result of NSWHC overtures to the Opposition, Commission rents were not an issue in the 1968 state election and this paved the way for rental increases in 1969, when the Commission was given the power to increase rents up to the 'economic [historic costs] level up to a maximum of fifty cents per dwelling per year'. It is arguable that this arrangement could be upset by a change in the political balance in the state.

Until about 1956 general rent control was in force to varying degrees in most Australian states, and the chairman of the VHC said in 1953:

> The Commission (VHC) has realised therefore that although it is empowered to adjust rents of houses constructed under the CSHA and is not restricted under the various restrictions of the Landlord and Tenant Act, it would have been embarrassing to all governments which have been in office since the Agreement was introduced to have raised rents of Commission houses while a ban existed on similar private action.

The Chairman of the VHC claimed that the minor adjustment of VHC rents in 1956 precipitated a Royal Commission and, when the rents were adjusted again in 1958, 'Protests were received from many tenants and pressure groups waited on members of Parliament. It was a hectic time for all'.

A number of reasons can be given to explain why the VHC began averaging rentals in 1963. Possibly the most important is the political strength of the Liberal Party in Victoria. Since the Labor split in Victoria in 1955 the Liberal Party has increased its power. In addition to this, the VHC's emphasis on slum clearance has meant that, if rents were not averaged, a subsidy for slum clearance above what the state government already gives for the acquisition and clearance of areas would have to be introduced, because of the capital cost of the high-rise flats. The economic rentals were around $22 for the Park Towers project described in chapter 5. Since the Commonwealth refused to supply this subsidy the state Treasury was the only alternative source. The increasing cost of rental rebates was also an important consideration, as was the desire to generate funds to modernize the stock of older dwellings. In addition, the government revised the basis for home sales by the Commission, the effect being to reduce the profits from this source. The emphasis on high-rise flats in the metropolitan programme meant that profits from the sale of dwellings would eventually fall as the stock of saleable units was depleted. The VHC produced overall losses in 1963–4 ($30,000) and in 1964–5 ($270,000) which supported the claims made by the VHC that the failure to adjust rents would lead to losses. The SAHT faces political difficulties in significant rent increases. The QHC and the WAHC, both under non-Labor governments, face criticism from the Opposition when they adjust rents but they do so none the less.

Rebated rentals

The third rent system used in the Commissions, in conjunction with both historic cost and averaging schemes, is the method of rebating rents. This is directed at those whose capacity to pay is so low as to fall short of the normal historic cost rent or the averaged rent, whichever is applicable. It sets a rent below these two rents so that, ideally, the household pays only what it can afford. The rentals calculated according to the 'historic costs' rental formula or from either form of averaging are maximum rentals. If these rentals amount to more than a certain proportion of the tenant's income, he is entitled to a rental rebate. The standard rental rebate formula included in the CSHA in 1945 and continued in most Commissions today was based on the Commonwealth basic wage and the child endowment scheme. It was assumed that the basic wage was a relatively accurate measure of the cost of maintaining a minimum standard of living, and that the child endowment scheme removed the necessity for rents to take account of the number of children in the family. The formula operated by measuring the 'family income' and then assessing capacity to pay. The family income was determined by adding together the whole of the gross weekly income of either the tenant or a related person in the dwelling (whichever was the higher), two-thirds of the gross weekly income of the next highest income earner in the dwelling, and one-third (but not more than $3 for each person) of the gross weekly income of all other persons resident in the dwelling. Maternity allowances and Commonwealth child endowment are not included in the definition of income. The weekly rent payable varies with the level of family income. When the family income is equal to the basic wage the weekly rent is one-fifth of the income. When the weekly income is above the basic wage, the weekly rental is one-fifth of the basic wage plus one-third of the difference between the basic wage and the family income. When the income is below the basic wage the weekly rental payable is one-fifth of the basic wage minus one-fourth of the difference between the family income and the basic wage. The minimum rent payable is 80 cents. The effect of this scale is that those on incomes below the basic wage pay a lower percentage of their income for rent than do those who earn more than the basic wage. This is shown in Table 81.

The Commissions apply special rentals to the aged units usually constructed from non-CSHA funds. The rentals on these units are approximately the same as would apply under the normal CSHA rental rebate system. They are set so that they account for about one-fifth of the pensioner's income.

The rental rebate scheme has been applied in the NSWHC from 1945 to 1968, but the basic wage level, of course, has changed over time. However, in the NSWHC from 1956 until 1963 the rental rebate scheme did not apply to any new dwellings built under the CSHA. This meant that only those households who could afford full economic rentals were allocated to these dwellings. Those unable to afford these rentals and requiring a rebate had to wait for vacated 1945–55 Agreement dwellings. Moreover, if the applicant required a rebate after admission to a 1956 CSHA dwelling he had to be transferred to a 1945 dwelling. The general effect of this decision not to allow rebates on new dwellings was to lengthen considerably the waiting times of those groups who could not afford the rentals, the lowest economic group on the waiting lists. The rebate system as currently applied in the NSWHC appears to benefit mainly aged pensioners, widow pensioners, deserted wives and invalid pensioners. At 30 June 1969 rental rebate cases accounted for about 13 per cent of all rental households in the NSWHC.

The VHC has applied the same rental rebate system as that used by the NSWHC from 1945 to date, with no interruption. Aged pensioners form a larger proportion of those receiving rebates in the VHC (55 per cent) than in the NSWHC. This is because the VHC constructs its aged housing from normal CSHA funds so that all occupants of these units are classed as rental rebates

TABLE 81 Rent payable on assessed family income under CSHA schemes

Assessed family income not exceeding	Maximum rent payable	Rent as percentage of income
$	$	
10.35	0.80	8
15.15	2.00	13
20.15	3.25	16
25.15	4.50	18
30.15	5.75	20
35.15	7.00	20
40.10	8.60	21
45.05	10.25	23
50.15	11.95	24
55.10	13.60	25
60.05	15.25	25
64.40	16.70	26

Source: NSWHC schedule of rent payable 25 October 1968 on basic wage of $35.85 per week.

cases. At 30 June 1969 about 19 per cent of tenants were on rebates. This is a higher percentage than in the NSWHC and could partially be due to the VHC averaging system which meant that some households who were previously on a low historic cost rent were transferred to a higher rent, thus making them eligible for rebate.

From 1956 the SAHT has operated a scheme that is similar in operation to the CSHA rebate formula although it is more flexible in its consideration of the circumstances of each case. In addition to this rebate system for tenants already in a Trust unit, there is a system that attempts to allocate the older and cheaper dwellings to those in need of rebates, although this policy is in some conflict with the general policy of raising the rents on vacated dwellings, described above. The groups on rebates in the SAHT are similar to those in other states, but the absence of any group of those employed on low incomes suggests that the rebate system does not apply to these groups. The rent structure of the SAHT is generally the lowest of all the states, so only about 7 per cent of tenants are on rebates, the lowest of all states. The rentals on the double units constructed in 1968–9 are about $8.75 for a three-bedroom, semi-detached unit. Those on a weekly family income of $40 would not be granted a rebate on this rental in the SAHT.

Like the NSWHC, the WAHC has operated the standard CSHA formula since 1945. At 30 June 1969 about 14 per cent of WAHC tenants were on rebates. The THC applied the standard CSHA rebate formula until 1961 when a modified scheme was introduced. The new scheme was designed to reduce the cost of the rebates to the state Treasury. The new scheme provided that the standard CSHA scheme would apply except that (1) the maximum rental rebate with respect to any dwelling was to be $5.60; (2) no rental rebate should be granted when the family income exceeded $37.60 per week; and (3) the minimum rental on any dwelling was to be $2 per week. (Family income was to be calculated by taking the whole of the income of the tenant and spouse, one-half of the income of any relative living in the house, but not exceeding $8 per week, and one-third of the income of any other occupant of the dwelling, but not exceeding $4 in any one case.) This probably means that those on low incomes but in employment do not receive rebates. This policy may be partially offset by granting low income applicants in need of a rebate older and cheaper dwellings, but this is in some conflict with the vacancy rent system discussed above.

At 30 June 1969 about 20 per cent of all THC tenants were on rental rebates, the highest proportion in all the states, probably reflecting the THC policy of encouraging a high proportion of applicants to purchase their dwellings, thus leaving only those on comparatively low incomes to rent. Since 1961 the THC has taken into account the tenants' hire-purchase commitments, and the value of these commitments is deducted from the amount of rebate that may otherwise have been approved. The THC claimed that

> . . . in those cases in which it is called upon to subsidize rentals because of the sub-economic incomes of the occupiers, the latter should not, because of the

subsidy, be placed in a financial position where they can enter into contractual commitments for the acquisition of luxury equipment such as television sets, radiograms and refrigerators.

The QHC has applied the standard CSHA rebate formula to dwellings constructed from 1945 to 1955 under the CSHA but not to dwellings built since then, all such dwellings bearing the full economic rental under the CSHA formula. The 1945 Agreement dwellings are allocated to those in 'need' of a rebate under the CSHA formula. When television was introduced into Queensland the QHC refused some tenants who were in arrears permission to install television sets. The Treasurer explained in parliament in 1959:

> When the advent of TV was imminent, enquiry was made into its effects on tenants in other States. We were advised that it had a very adverse effect on arrears. Rental arrears have been fairly level at approximately $160,000. Even at that level the Commission finds it necessary to eject a few tenants for unpaid rent. Should the level of arrears be allowed to rise it would have two equally unfortunate effects. There would be less money available for new homes; some existing tenants who are already struggling would have to be evicted. Accordingly, the Commission has sought in the interests of the tenants as well as the State to restrain people who cannot meet the present rental obligations . . . from burdening themselves with new obligations. We cannot afford to allow rental arrears to finance television.

In 1966 the Minister for Housing (Mr Bjelke-Petersen) said in parliament:

> As I see it, in these days there are so many things that people think they must have—for example, to own a motor-car has become almost a necessity—and it is very nice indeed to have them; but this does make it difficult for many people to pay what the Commission believes to be an economic rent.

No figures are available on the number of tenants on rebates at a point in time, but 1,658 were granted in 1968–9, some for only part of the year, this being about 11 per cent of QHC tenants.

Tying rebates to older dwellings

In the period up to 1956 the SAHT allocated cheaper pre-1945 dwellings (the Trust started building units in 1937) to low income families at the historic cost rental. In effect, these families received rebates similar to those in the states operating under the CSHA rebate scheme. This process of allocating older and cheaper dwellings to low income households continues although in some ways it has been replaced by a rebate system discussed above. As stated above, the QHC does not grant rebates on CSHA dwellings built since 1956. Hence households unable to pay the full economic rental have to accept an older dwelling and if in need of a rebate have to wait for a 1945–55 CSHA unit for which the Commonwealth contributes three-fifths of the losses. The NSWHC had a similar policy from 1956 to 1963. Households who could not afford to pay full economic rents were allocated vacant 1945 CSHA dwellings. The result of this, as mentioned above, was that in

1963 when the policy decision was changed the waiting time for home ownership applicants (80 per cent of all new dwellings had to be sold) was four years, for those able to pay 'economic rents' six years, and for those unable to pay economic rents eight years.

Tying rebates to particular dwellings may also create problems in that quite often the need for a rebate appears after the applicant has been allocated a full rental dwelling. In this situation he has to transfer to another dwelling. It may also affect the social character of an area. The poorest households will congregate in the districts that contain the older low rent housing, and, given the normal Australian public housing practice of developing large estates, this may lead to the highly 'stigmatized', generally unsatisfactory social environments discussed in chapter 9. In 1970 the NSWHC gave priority to households able to pay full rentals in the slum clearance project in Waterloo. This was partially because this would reduce the rebate level on these fairly expensive units and would also prevent the congregation of an excessive number of female-headed households (deserted wives, widows, etc.).

Rental levels at the 1966 Census

Although the following statistics are not the most desirable they are the best available and do show some of the significant differences between the states. Public housing rent levels are strongly affected by three main forces: the number of tenants on rental rebates; the level of adjustment of historic cost rents or averaging; and the level of building costs reflecting the size of the dwelling, differences in factor costs (land, labour, materials) and type of dwelling (high-rise flat or cottage, etc.). Table 82 shows that there are substantial differences in rent levels (per room) among the Commissions. The highest rent levels for houses are in the THC. This appears to contradict the above argument that a high proportion of THC tenants were on rebates and the THC did not regularly adjust rents. This comparatively high figure is possibly due to the high vacancy rate in the THC noted in chapter 2, which

TABLE 82 Rent per room in 3–6 room houses and flats, metropolitan areas, 1966 census ($ per week unfurnished)

	House		Flat		Margins between government and private	
	Tenant p.h.*	Tenant private	Tenant p.h.	Tenant private	Houses	Flats
N.S.W	1.56	2.00	2.11	3.41	0.44	1.30
Vic.	1.73	2.57	2.00	4.07	0.84	2.07
S.A.	1.34	1.88	2.41	2.84	0.54	0.43
Qld	1.66	1.98	2.73	3.08	0.32	0.35
W.A.	1.49	2.03	2.14	3.40	0.54	1.26
Tas.	1.81	1.87	2.53	2.74	0.06	0.21

* Public housing.
Source: CBCS.

may allow the THC to increase its rents on many of its dwellings. The next highest rent level for houses was the VHC although it had the lowest rent for flats. The high rent on VHC houses is possibly due to averaging while the low rent on flats may be due to the comparatively high numbers on rebates. The QHC has the next highest house rents, reflecting the policy of frequently adjusting rents on older dwellings and not giving rebates on post-1956 dwellings. The comparatively high figures for QHC flats reflects the lack of QHC aged housing and the fact that most flats have been built since 1956 and therefore do not qualify for a rebate. The NSWHC and the WAHC have similar rent levels, suggesting that the averaging scheme in the WAHC has produced an average rent similar to the average rent in the NSWHC.

Mainly because of the supply of low-interest, long-term finance, the 'economic' rents on CSHA dwellings are below those in the private market for equivalent accommodation, but precise information on this is lacking. Table 82 also shows average rent levels per room for government and private houses and flats from the 1966 Census.

The 1966 Census also showed that rent levels in public housing varied between the states. This is partially shown in Table 82 but is clearer in Table 83. The very wide dispersal of rents shown clearly in Table 83 is only partially due to the differences in building costs and accommodation types. It is the natural result of the policies pursued above in this chapter, especially the widespread failure to adjust rents to take account of inflation.

Who provides the subsidy?

The Commonwealth government has had wide powers over public housing rent levels since the first CSHA in 1945. It is the Commonwealth that sets the interest rate and repayment period on the loans that are the basis of the CSHA. Loans under the first CSHA from 1945 to 1955 carried an inter-

TABLE 83 Public housing rent levels, houses and flats, metropolitan areas, 1966 census ($ per week unfurnished), percentage distribution

	Houses						Flats					
	N.S.W.	Vic.	S.A.	Qld	W.A.	Tas.	N.S.W.	Vic.	S.A.	Qld	W.A.	Tas.
$												
0–1.99	1	1	—	2	3	2	4	7	1	3	15	4
2–3.99	3	2	3	3	6	6	24	19	23	1	21	24
4–5.99	14	3	22	5	15	8	8	7	6	6	9	10
6–7.99	31	21	60	27	41	16	16	18	8	22	25	2
8–9.99	40	57	10	43	30	25	29	16	14	13	16	18
10–11.99	8	10	3	16	2	36	13	28	28	36	2	27
12–13.99	—	1	1	1	1	1	3	1	17	15	2	14
14–15.99	—	1	—	—	—	—	—	1	2	1	2	—
16–17.99	—	1	—	—	—	—	—	1	—	—	—	—
18–19.99	—	—	—	—	—	—	—	—	—	—	—	—
20 +	—	—	—	—	—	—	—	—	—	—	—	—
Not stated	3	3	2	3	2	3	3	3	2	3	3	2
Average rent $ per week	7.78	8.84	6.68	10.65	7.01	8.66	6.95	7.33	8.25	9.73	5.78	7.80

Source: CBCS.

est rate of 3 per cent and a repayment period of 53 years. The rentals of public housing units were based on these terms, with provisions made for maintenance, administration, rates, vacancies and default. From 1956 to 1968 the CSHA interest rate was about 4 per cent per annum, but with the large general rises in interest rates in 1970 the CSHA level rose to 6 per cent.

While the various rent schemes in the Commissions have generally attempted to provide adequate housing within the household's capacity to pay they have also tried to minimize the losses involved in doing this. This section looks at the profits and losses made by the Commissions. 'Profit' here means the difference between the Commissions' income and expenditure. The main expenditures are the repayment of the capital cost and interest repayments on CSHA advances and the various expenses on rental dwellings—rates, maintenance, insurance and administration. The main income received by the Commission is repayment for houses sold and rents paid by public housing tenants. The Housing Commissions make profits from the sale of dwellings and of land for industrial, commercial or public services (such as schools), the land usually being in estates newly developed by the Commissions; and the investment of cash reserves for maintenance and other reserves for rental housing. The profits are used mainly to cover losses due to rental rebates, for the construction of housing for the aged, for public housing generally, and for meeting the contributions demanded by service authorities such as the water supply authorities which cannot be supplied from CSHA funds.

The breakdown of the 1945 formula for recoupment of losses and the absence of any recoupment formula in the 1956–66 CSHAs is an important explanation for the particular building programmes undertaken by the states. The responsibility for losses, especially in housing for the aged, the dominant type of sub-economic rental tenant, has become an important political issue between the Commonwealth and the states as has been described in chapter 4. The Housing Commissions usually make losses on rental operations, due to both the failure to adjust rentals on older dwellings to cover inflation and the cost of rebates granted. But they have generally made profits on house sales. The main exception to this generalization is the THC, which has consistently made losses overall because (a) rentals have generally not been adjusted to cover all outgoings on particular properties; (b) the rebate system is costly; and (c) even houses sold have been sold at a loss because deposits have not been required and prices have been low. Its losses have been recouped from capital reserves or from consolidated revenue. This has caused considerable embarrassment to the THC since the Commonwealth Grants Commission makes allowance for these losses in assessing the amount that Tasmania should receive in grants and consistently criticizes the THC for making losses. The emphasis on the sale of dwellings by the THC was largely from the desire to cut the losses from rental operations.

The 1945 CSHA provided that the Commonwealth and the states would share any losses under the agreement that resulted from allowing rental rebates to tenants unable to afford economic rentals. Since rentals were set equal to the economic rental, a loss would result if there were any rebates, unless the Commissions made profits somewhere else in their operations. The Commonwealth would meet three-fifths of such losses and the states two-fifths. This sharing of losses by the Commonwealth was conditional on the states adjusting rentals to take account of increases in such costs as administration, rates and taxes. If this was not done the losses would have to be borne by the states. Since the states seldom adjusted rents to take account of inflation, the Commonwealth refused to contribute to these losses. Since 1945 the Commonwealth has paid out only about one and a half million dollars to the states under the loss-sharing arrangements. The QHC has received about one and a quarter million of these Commonwealth funds, the remainder being divided between the WAHC and the THC. The QHC is the only Commission to have channelled rebate cases continually into its stock of 1945 CSHA dwellings, thus inflating the proportion of the households in these units on rebates. The WAHC has generally covered its rental losses through house sale profits.

The recoupment of losses by public authorities is an important and perennial subject in the literature on public authority economics. On the one hand there is the desire for efficiency in the authority concerned, and on the other the fear that the possibility of losses may affect the authorities' social objectives—in the case of the housing authorities, the housing of those on low incomes. This conflict between equity and efficiency has no simple solution. The original CSHA formula for the sharing of losses could be criticized for its failure to develop some technique to encourage and evaluate efficiency within the housing authorities. The different Commissions may have different levels of efficiency in maintenance and general administration, all of which reflect on costs and hence the level of economic rents.

This book argues that the key test of the efficiency of Australian public housing is whether or not the Commissions cater for the poor. But there is another question: do they produce and manage the housing in the most efficient manner possible? This is very difficult to measure. The level of losses is no real guide since a high level of loss may mean that the Commissions are catering for those in most need. Moreover, low-cost housing often means low-quality housing. Still, there are criteria for judging efficiency. The VHC ranks the lowest on the scale of cost consciousness, its fascination with engineering overcoming cost considerations. The THC and the QHC have day labour organizations, traditionally a source of inefficiency in public housing authorities, but there are no accurate surveys to test whether this applies to them; the Commissions were not anxious to investigate it as any attempt to dissolve the day labour organizations would meet opposition from the unions. The NSWHC's efficiency is marred by the large payments it makes to the Rural Bank for the administration of its house sales programme. The NSWHC could do this more cheaply and more efficiently itself.

It is, of course, a political decision. The Rural Bank needs captive lucrative business from government departments even though the absurd result is that in every NSWHC estate every second house—the one being sold—is administered by the Rural Bank, and bankers have never been known for any appreciation of the social problems behind the balance sheet. The NSWHC realizes this, of course, but cannot change the position.

In any ranking of cost consciousness the SAHT and the WAHC would take equal first place. Unique amongst Australian Housing Commissions, the Trust is a statutory corporation rather than a government department directly responsible to a minister. This means that the Trust has been loath to try to recoup any losses from the South Australian Treasury and its non-participation for most of the first CSHA meant that there were very strong incentives to avoid losses. The SAHT double-unit programme is a good example of its cost consciousness. The WAHC's cost consciousness is probably connected with constant examination by the Commonwealth Grants Commissions—Australia's most competent and probing economic sleuths—because of its status as a claimant state in the federal system. WAHC costs may rise with the move towards high-rise developments.

The arrangement whereby the Commissions generally rely on surpluses from house sales to make up the losses on rental operations has many disadvantages. The amount of the surplus is always a matter of considerable uncertainty, depending on such vague possibilities as a rental adjustment or the level of house sales. This uncertainty probably makes the Commissions reluctant to increase the supply of rental housing to those unable to pay 'economic' rents. The figures for 1968–9 suggest that the Commissions can supply significantly more dwellings to those unable to pay 'economic' rents if they use internal surpluses. In 1968–9 all Commissions except the THC made 'profits', and for the moment no account will be taken of the different accounting procedures used in the Commissions although these may make the following figures not exactly comparable. In 1968 the NSWHC had a surplus of $1,654,573 (enough for approximately 165 dwellings, allowing $10,000 per unit), the VHC surplus was $422,120 (approximately 42 dwellings), the SAHT produced a surplus of $1,066,202 (about 106 dwellings), the QHC surplus was $541, 696 (about 54 units) and the WAHC had the largest profit of all—$5,070,496 (about 507 dwellings).

Instead of using their surpluses completely to pay for new dwellings the Commissions could use their CSHA advances for this purpose and use the surpluses to cover the difference between the rebated rent paid by the tenant and the 'economic' rent on the unit under the standard CSHA formula. On a general calculation that the tenant unable to pay an economic rent needs, on average, a subsidy of $300 per year to bridge the gap between his rental payment and the economic rent, the 1968–9 surpluses would have enabled the following approximate numbers of needy households to be housed: NSWHC 5,500; VHC 1,400; SAHT 3,500; QHC 1,800; WAHC 16,900. Of course, this would mean that the Commissions would have to curtail the supply of public housing to other—presumably more affluent—groups such as married couples without children. But, as stated above, the Commissions would be in serious financial difficulties if large surpluses did not continue.

Conclusion

This chapter has shown that rent policy has been an attempt to relate the rent paid to the household's capacity to pay and to ensure that no household should be denied access to public housing because it can afford only a low rent. In terms of equity comparisons among public housing renters, current policies do not rate very highly. Since a majority of the Commissions operate a basic historic cost system the main determinant of what level rent a household pays is the period of time it has spent in the dwelling. This directs the benefits of inflation at the older households, the effects of which were discussed in the home ownership chapter. A market rental system would attain the highest level of equity between public housing tenants, but since it would encourage the more affluent tenants to leave public housing it could make the estates become ghettos. On the other hand, market rents could encourage the more affluent tenants to purchase their dwellings, with all the effects discussed in the last chapter.

How much can a household afford to pay for its housing? The usual claim is that a family cannot spend more than 20 to 25 per cent of its income on housing costs. Attempts to set fixed proportions must necessarily be arbitrary since they involve subjective judgments on what is a 'reasonable' standard of living and they do not take into account the different demands or the efficiency with which different households budget their incomes. Moreover, there is also the problem of defining housing costs and incomes. The problem of defining economic welfare was discussed in chapter 3 and, with qualifications, it was argued that assets and the size of family are important factors in determining a measure of comparative welfare. Because housing in different areas will involve different levels of travel costs, these costs should be included in calculations of how much a family can afford to pay for housing. Equity comparisons can be made between the rents charged in public housing and the costs of home ownership of either government or privately built housing. The progression principle suggests that the poorer the household the smaller the proportion of its income it can afford to spend on rent, but those on rebates—the poorest group in public housing—pay the highest proportion of their incomes in rent.

It is difficult to discuss rebate policy and the minimum and maximum rent payable in public housing without referring to the idea of minimum standards of living. The Henderson poverty study and other research has shown that the main groups in receipt of rebates are the poverty groups in Australian society. With these low income households having to pay 20–25 per cent of their incomes on housing a type of inverse progression operates with housing costs, the proportion of income spent on housing decreasing as income increases. The rebate system assumes that the basic wage is a reasonable guide to minimum living standards and that the child endowment payments cover the costs of children and hence takes no account of the number of children in a family when assessing the capacity to pay. Halladay has shown in his study of large families in Sydney (*Poverty Among Large Families in Sydney 1968–9*) that the basic wage or even 20 per cent above it and child endowment are insufficient to prevent a substantial proportion of large families from falling into poverty.

Since the financial conflict between the Commonwealth and state governments is a basic reason for the diversion of public housing away from some needy groups, some reform is necessary. There are some alternative policies available. The Commonwealth could reintroduce the loss-sharing arrangement of the 1945 Agreement which has close controls over Commission costs. The Commonwealth is unlikely to do this given the sensitive nature of Commonwealth-state relations. Without these detailed controls over state costs, the Commonwealth is unlikely to introduce a loss-sharing arrangement that would reimburse the states for the difference between incomes from rents and outgoings on rental properties. Such an arrangement would involve large Commonwealth subsidies for such projects as the VHC urban renewal programme where these funds would help to cover the high cost of the VHC high-rise flats, discussed above.

The Commonwealth could continue tying the CSHA interest rate to the long-term bond rate, and provide repayable grant money to the states for the housing of those with a very low capacity to pay, as was done in 1969 with the aged. With such relatively small schemes (for the aged and aborigines) the Commonwealth can supervise standards, especially costs, and withhold funds where the units are excessively expensive. This type of aid could be extended to female households with dependent children, the physically handicapped and other groups unable to pay economic rents under the CSHA formula (or preferably under a revised rebate formula that took account of the size of the family). As with the 1969 Commonwealth Act for the Aged, the money could be advanced to the states on the condition that it was spent for housing specific groups—in the case of the 1969 legislation it was the single aged pensioners in the inner areas of capital cities—and thus overcome the tendency for CSHA funds to go to groups other than those on the lowest incomes.

Lastly, the Commonwealth could insist that the states reform their rent structures so that they spread the benefits of inflation over a wide group and thus avoid charging the new tenants the total cost of the dwelling under the CSHA economic rent formula. Together with a reform of the rebate system, application of market rents to 'rich' tenants, and the increase in the price of houses sold, the Commissions could probably generate additional finance that would cover the losses from supplying houses to those on the lowest incomes.

9 SOCIAL EFFECTS

Most of the analysis so far has been concerned with determining the socio-economic status of those who gain admission to public housing under the various schemes. A considerable amount of space has been devoted to detailing some of the characteristics of the public housing units offered, especially whether they are houses or flats, for rental or ownership, and at what cost. This chapter deals with some of the other characteristics of public housing developments. It is concerned partly with the dwelling itself, but primarily with the amenities supplied and especially with the social environments in different developments. The first section develops some criteria for appraising the dwelling, the amenities and the social environment, and the second looks at some developments and appraises them according to these criteria.

The dwelling itself

A number of researchers have recently stressed the importance of the dwelling itself, since many households appear to spend most of their leisure hours in the home. This family-centred existence was illustrated in Scott and U'Ren's survey of a Melbourne public housing estate (*Leisure*, Melbourne, 1962). This depreciates the importance of the social environment, but the degree of family centredness varies between different social groups. The Commissions build a wide variety of dwellings, and since it is extremely difficult to evaluate 'standards', there is no discussion of this matter here.

Amenities

In its 1944 Report, the Commonwealth Housing Commission developed criteria for the supply of amenities to public housing areas. It recommended that these areas should be supplied with shops, playing areas, infant health centres, meeting halls, schools and conveniently located workplaces and transport networks. It also assumed that these estates would obtain the required services such as water, roads and sewerage. Public housing areas are sometimes attacked by critics for not having many of these facilities. Although the Commissions have overcome the lag in the supply of basic services such as roads and sewerage that was widespread in the late 1940s and early 1950s, they often have not been able to supply the desired quantity of the other services. The Commissions are concerned with supplying housing, and in most cases the supply of all other services (education, etc.) rests with other government authorities, which may be state, local or federal, and private organizations. The CSHAs do not allow the states to use funds provided under the agreement for shops, community centres and other important facilities.

Mr J. Bourke, the secretary of the NSWHC, claimed that only financial assistance from the Commonwealth in addition to the CSHA would enable the Australian housing authorities to provide balanced communities in appropriately planned neighbourhoods with open space and adequate recreational facilities and in areas well placed with regard to education, employment, worship, entertainment and commercial and shopping centres. It is difficult to argue that additional funds for these activities could be obtained from the present sources of finance. Some of the profits generated by the Commissions could be used for these purposes but this would mean a reduction in the number of dwellings built, particularly for certain groups such as the aged. The Commissions usually finance the construction of shops, using state funds or profits, and generally set aside land for all other purposes, attempting to induce other organizations to supply them. Some of the results of these policies are discussed below, but one point can be raised here: the standards of amenity in Commission areas should be compared not with the absolute standards referred to above but rather with the standards in comparable low and middle income private housing areas. Such comparisons usually show that there is a general shortage of these amenities in almost all parts of the urban area, particularly the urban fringe (see below). There is little agreement on the actual level of amenity needed in public housing areas. Demands for numerous shopping centres and leisure centres may conflict with the findings that, because of increasing incomes and automobile ownership, low income families no longer spend their leisure hours in the immediate neighbourhood of their dwellings (see Peter Willmott, 'Developing Patterns of Urbanization', *Urban Studies*, 1969).

Social environment—homogeneity or heterogeneity

At various times those concerned with public housing in Australia have expressed the opinion that public housing programmes should concern themselves with more than improving the physical standard of the housing alone. The 1944 report of the Commonwealth Housing Commission said that the public housing programme should '. . . form a background for satisfactory mental and physical development for a full social life'. In 1959 the SAHT said that in adequate public housing developments 'As well as homes there must be a sense of community, a feeling of solidarity with one's fellow citizens, a spirit of which like the air a man breathes he is scarcely conscious except in its absence'. Public housing areas are sometimes criticized because they tend to 'segregate' large numbers of low income households in one area. Ideally, in order to discuss the effects of 'homogeneity' on an area one would require extensive data on the socio-economic status (occupation, income, assets, ethnicity, state of life cycle, etc.) and information on styles of life. The data available for this book were limited to the information from the 1966 CD areas used extensively in the earlier chapters.

This section examines the arguments for and against the view that residential areas should be made as heterogeneous in their socio-economic composition as possible. The available evidence is not clear but supports the view that people are segregated by income, stage of life cycle, life styles and social class. There are two general interpretations of the reasons for this large degree of segregation. The first stresses economic forces. People live in a particular area because the operation of the urban property market groups the available dwellings in accordance with the particular price ranges so that segregation occurs as a by-product of economic forces. Although research shows that most areas are, in fact, highly segregated in socio-economic terms, this is not necessarily an argument for segregating areas in the future. If the economic arguments described above are correct much segregation occurs because of the operation of the urban property market rather than by people's free choices.

A key concept in this area is 'social integration'. Writers generally agree that some forms of social environment are 'better' than others. Most argue that in addition to physical shelter people need environments where they can interact with other people. For the sake of simplicity this book refers to the desired levels of sociability and so on as 'social integration'. In his book *The Social Integration of the Aged* (New York, 1967), Irving Rosow says

> The integration of individuals into their society results from forces which place them within the system and govern their participation and patterned association with others. This network of bonds has three basic dimensions: (1) social values, (2) formal and informal group memberships, and (3) social roles. Thus, people are tied into their society essentially through their beliefs, the groups that they belong to, and the positions that they occupy.
>
> Without exception, stratification studies show that friendships and inclusive association develop among people of comparable social position and basically similar status characteristics: social class, race, occupational level, ethnicity, education, marital status, stage in the family cycle, values and beliefs, aspirations, life styles, deviance. Not only is this apparent in stratification research, but also in a diverse range of possible friendship contexts. The general principle is that friendships develop among socially homogeneous persons who are comparably situated in the social structure and share the same relationship to the system.

For some groups, residential proximity to similar households is a necessary ingredient in social integration. Keller sums up the research on the patterns in working class life in her book *The Urban Neighborhood* (Random House, 1968):

> In solid working class areas of skilled and semiskilled workers, need and limited opportunity, isolation and relative poverty, insecurity and fear of outsiders, all combine to make neighbouring an essential part of the close web of family, kin and work relationships. Often this neighbouring is neither selective nor personal but rather a generalized expression of attachment to the local area—its shops and taverns, its streets and residents—promoted by common problems of economic uncertainty and often in conjunction with particular ethnic and cultured traditions . . .

In contrast to the working class, the middle class generally desires less involvement with neighbours. Keller claims that

> In middle class milieus neighbouring takes on a different form. Above all, it is more selective, more personal. And personal compatibility comes to matter as much as occupational and cultural compatibility. Greater economic well-being decreases the need for mutual aid and increases the use of critical, selective faculties. At the same time the pursuit of competitive success accentuates the importance of social status and makes selectivity more necessary.

Social heterogeneity may lead to conflict between social groups. For the analysis in this section it is assumed that population 'heterogeneity' means that households of significantly different socio-economic status are interspersed throughout a residential area. A study by Collison relates how a group of residents in Oxford, England, attempted to segregate themselves from the working class residents of an adjacent council estate by building walls across two roads (*The Cuttleslowe Walls*, London, 1963). Willmott's study of a low status council housing estate in Dagenham (England) found that people on the estate did not see their neighbours as adversaries but as allies in a collective advance: social comparison did not lead to status competition, and concern and anxiety over differences in consumption patterns were far less marked than in the middle class suburb that he had studied earlier (*The Evolution of a Community*, London, 1963).

Perhaps the most thorough study of the effects of dispersing working class people in middle class areas was that by Goldthorpe *et al.*, *The Affluent Worker in the Class Structure* (London, 1969). In this study, a sample of highly-paid workers living in mixed residential areas was studied over a period and the results showed that there was very little mixing between the working class groups and the middle classes (blue-collar and white-collar respectively), and the working class group did not try to emulate middle class life styles, despite rising affluence. Rosow found that the aged much preferred to live with other aged people than mix with younger groups.

One argument sometimes advanced for population heterogeneity is that it affects the education of children, presumably inducing working class children to aspire to middle class life styles. This may happen both through the child's observation of middle class life styles and through interaction in the local schools which presumably have a cross-section of pupils from different socio-economic levels. The Coleman Report on education in the

United States (*Equality of Educational Opportunity*, Washington, 1966)—based on extensive empirical research—concluded that

> . . . it appears that a pupil's achievement is strongly related to the educational backgrounds and aspirations of the other students in the school . . . Analysis indicates, however, that children from a given family background, when put in schools of different social composition, will achieve at quite different levels . . . Thus, if a white pupil from a home that is strongly and effectively supportive of education is put in a school where most pupils do not come from such homes, his achievement will be little different than if he were in a school composed of others like himself. But if a minority pupil from a home without much educational strength is put with school mates with strong educational backgrounds, his achievement is likely to increase.

If one attaches considerable importance to educational advancement as a means of upward mobility for low income groups then planned heterogeneity in public housing areas—the intermingling of public housing with private housing—may be justified.

Some political scientists argue that extreme socio-economic segregation makes democratic government very difficult, especially at the local level, and the spectre of extreme distributional inequalities presents an intolerable threat to social stability, cohesion, and the peaceful, parliamentary settlement of problems. Little research has been done on the effects of grouping particular socio-economic affinity groups in small clusters (say 20 dwellings) while at the same time maintaining general population heterogeneity for the suburb as a whole. This may combine some of the benefits of both homogeneity and heterogeneity.

There is evidence that the concentration of very low income, 'problem' people in public housing areas does not produce satisfactory environments. While it is argued below that some mild form of concentration of the 'problem tenant' (e.g. ten houses) would assist in his rehabilitation, the large-scale congregation of these families on an estate produces areas commonly known as low income ghettos. This type of public housing development is most common in the United States, where strict income limits ensure that only the poor gain entry into public housing. In addition, the developments are typically high-rise, very large, and situated in low-status neighbourhoods.

Rainwater has described the characteristics of the Pruitt-Igoe public housing development in the U.S.A. ('The Lessons of Pruitt-Igoe', *The Public Interest*, No. 8, 1967). The project had a total of 2,800 dwelling units in the one estate—all of them high-rise flats. Allocation policy—especially the stipulation that only the very poor could gain entry into the public housing and that if they increased their economic level they would have to leave—meant that the project became a congregation of households with social problems. Female-headed households accounted for a large proportion of the residents who depended on welfare and did not form any cohesive social group in the same way as, say, certain migrants do. The high turnover of tenants discouraged friendship formation. Added to this, the settlement became a centre for vice, especially drug addiction and alcoholism. Such an environment is probably not conducive to social integration. It does not refute the argument below—that deviants form generally beneficial concentrations. While deviants such as 'Skid Row' men form reasonably clear deviant subcultures, the households in an area such as Pruitt-Igoe referred to above probably represent no single deviant culture and hence the social environment in the project will not be supportive in the way the 'Skid Row' one may be.

Suttles's study of the effect of an American housing project on the Negro residents provides a valuable illustration (*The Social Order of the Slum*, Chicago, 1968). The project consisted of flats in a large estate limited to those on very low incomes, those who improved their socio-economic status having to leave. Suttles notes that, unlike the other ethnic groups nearby, the residents of the public housing project could not alter the interior or exterior of their dwellings in any significant manner, a source of deprivation in areas where such adornments and alterations were an important activity in residents' lives. Project residents were also unable to carry on small, technically illegal businesses in their dwellings and were thus denied a form of economic advancement utilized by many other migrant groups. Suttles claimed that this latter state of affairs forced project residents to turn to other forms of income generation, especially prostitution, shoplifting and drug peddling. The homogeneity in the project meant that indigenous leaders and spokesmen were difficult to produce, any possible leadership being discouraged because of the widespread fears of the housing authority. Various other aspects of project living created problems: the inability of settling affinity groups in close proximity to one another; and rather strict rules on noise.

Stigma

In *The Dimensions of Urban Social Structure* (Canberra, 1969) Lancaster Jones says that

> . . . each area in the city tends to acquire a social evaluation reflecting the social characteristics of its inhabitants and residential areas become in time socially important symbols. Where a person lives reflects not only the level of his income but also his values and his preferences. Especially in Australian cities, where the overwhelming majority of residents own the houses in which they live—in Melbourne in 1961, eight out of ten private householders owned or were purchasing their residences—the choice of a residential area conspicuously displays for most householders their economic position, the amount of their disposable income, their life style, and their pattern of expenditure.

Attached to almost all social services is the idea of stigma—that the recipient is in some way unworthy, deviant and unable to succeed without assistance.

Because of the role of stigma, the degree of observability of public housing may be an important factor in evaluating the advantages of different developments. The degree of stigma attached to the public housing development is largely determined by site planning characteristics in the design of the dwelling itself, and particularly its diversity of external design and the degree of concentration of public housing units. The more such an area departs from the 'norm' in terms of design and also partly social behaviour, the more likely it is to be stigmatized.

The social environment of an area may also be a major source of stigma, and Huttman's study of American public housing found that it was highly stigmatized, primarily because of the very low socio-economic status of the residents. The stigma attached to public housing—the admission of 'failure' implicit in seeking aid outwardly visible to all—may induce households in 'need' of housing assistance not to seek admission to public housing. The poor avoid social services, especially highly 'stigmatized' ones, in an attempt to avoid increasing their 'dependent' status.

Inner area flats

Tables 84 to 89 show the characteristics of the VHC and NSWHC inner area flats. These inner area flats have a slightly lower socio-economic status than either the NSWHC or VHC CD averages, or Green Valley in Sydney or Elizabeth in South Australia. A comparatively high proportion of the households in these flats are either widows, deserted wives, married but permanently separated or divorced. Table 38 in chapter 4 showed that about 43 per cent of all VHC and NSWHC flats were occupied by female householders. There are marked differences in the numbers of young children in VHC and NSWHC inner area flats, reflecting the Commissions' different approaches towards housing young families in flats (given in chapter 4). Some 40 per cent of the population in VHC flats are under 15 years of age, while in the

TABLE 84 *Occupations of the workforce in inner metropolitan public housing flats (per cent of total), 1966 census*

	NSWHC	NSWHC total metro.	VHC	VHC total metro.
	%	%	%	%
Professional	2	4	2	4
Managerial, self-employed	6	8	6	9
Clerical workers	21	19	18	20
Armed forces	3	2	8	1
Craftsmen, foremen	13	18	13	18
Shop assistants, process workers	28	30	28	29
Personal, domestic, service workers and labourers	26	17	24	17
Not stated	2	2	2	2

Source: Compiled from summary data supplied by the Commonwealth Statistician (Collectors' District data for the total population).

TABLE 85 Education of the population (excluding children not at school and full-time students) in inner metropolitan public housing flats (per cent of total), 1966 census

	NSWHC	NSWHC total metro.	VHC	VHC total metro.
	%	%	%	%
University qualifications	—	—	—	—
Other tertiary qualifications	—	1	—	1
Matriculation passed	7	5	8	8
Intermediate passed	26	29	18	16
Attended high school	35	39	33	35
Attended primary school	26	23	35	37
No education	1	1	1	1
Not stated	5	2	5	2

Source: Compiled from summary data supplied by the Commonwealth Statistician (Collectors' District data for the total population).

TABLE 86 Motor vehicle ownership in inner metropolitan public housing flats, number of vehicles per occupied private dwelling (per cent of total), 1966 census

No. of vehicles per dwelling	NSWHC inner flats	NSW total metro.	VHC inner flats	VHC total metro.
	%	%	%	%
None	63	61	59	57
One	29	32	33	34
Two	2	3	2	3
Three +	—	—	—	—
Not stated	6	5	6	6

Source: Compiled from summary data supplied by the Commonwealth Statistician (Collectors' District data for the total population).

TABLE 87 Age structure in inner metropolitan public housing flats (per cent of total), 1966 census

Age group	NSWHC	NSWHC total metro.	VHC	VHC total metro.
	%	%	%	%
0–4	8	14	16	10
5–9	5	17	14	13
10–14	4	12	10	14
15–19	6	8	8	13
20–29	14	12	15	11
30–39	13	16	14	12
40–49	15	10	10	14
50–59	17	6	6	8
60 +	19	5	9	6

Source: Compiled from summary data supplied by the Commonwealth Statistician (Collectors' District data for the total population).

NSWHC only 17 per cent are in this category. Occupants of inner area flats are more likely to have an over-representation of the overseas born (mainly British), are less likely to possess a motor vehicle and are of slightly lower education than public housing tenants as a whole.

There is no clear evidence on whether the comparatively high proportion of female-headed households in inner area public housing flats has any harmful effects. Female-headed households with children need specialized compensatory education to overcome the lack of a father and the financial difficulties that generally accompany the lack of a male. The concentration of female households in the inner area flats would enable the Commissions to implement special services for this group although no Commission has taken advantage of this opportunity to date.

As shown in the rest of the book, three broad influences work towards making Australian public housing areas of comparatively high socio-economic status: the vagueness of the 'means tests' used to determine eligibility; the lack of any means test once the client has been admitted to public housing; and the widespread incidence of home purchase among those allo-

TABLE 88 Birthplace of the population in inner metropolitan public housing flats (per cent of total), 1966 census

Birthplace	NSWHC	NSWHC total metro.	VHC	VHC total metro.
	%	%	%	%
Australia	82	88	76	83
New Zealand, England, Wales, Ireland, Scotland	11	8	14	9
Austria, Czechoslovakia, Germany, Hungary, Yugoslavia	2	1	2	1
Greece, Italy, Malta	1	1	4	3
Other	4	2	5	3

Source: Compiled from summary data supplied by the Commonwealth Statistician (Collectors' District data for the total population).

TABLE 89 Marital status of the population (excluding the never married) in inner metropolitan public housing flats (per cent of total), 1966 census

Marital status	NSWHC	NSWHC total metro.	VHC	VHC total metro.
	%	%	%	%
Married	76	88	79	86
Married, but permanently separated	6	4	8	3
Divorced	5	—	2	2
Widowed	14	7	11	10

Source: Compiled from summary data supplied by the Commonwealth Statistician (Collectors' District data for the total population).

cated public housing. Only the first two of these influences operate in the inner area flats. Tables 84 to 89 are based on 1,644 NSWHC flats containing 4,039 people and 1,629 VHC flats containing 5,862 people. Both NSWHC and VHC flats are in inner suburbs built on sites cleared of 'slum housing'.

It was shown in chapter 4 that the VHC concentrates on the construction of flats in the Melbourne metropolitan area. Generally, its flat estates are large and of distinctive architecture. The rationale for this policy is to be found in the economics of slum reclamation. Land resumed for slum clearance purposes costs an average of $120,000 per acre, and this fact forces the VHC to increase the density of dwellings built on the site to reduce the land cost per dwelling. The Commission has decided that it must build a density of around 50 dwellings or 200 persons per acre. This can be achieved by building walk-up flats, and this was the only kind of flat built by the VHC up to 1959. The VHC claims that the design of the walk-up flats was criticized because the lack of lifts created a burden for pregnant mothers and also because the location of laundries and garbage disposal—on the roof and ground floor respectively—increased the amount of stair-climbing. As a result of these criticisms and also to increase the amount of open space in flat developments the VHC began to build high-rise flats in 1959, and by 1964 they had replaced walk-up flats. These flats vary in height. Most are 20 storeys, but a recent block was 30 storeys high. The VHC also says that the high-rise flats offer many advantages—community laundries and drying areas on each floor, refuse disposal by way of a chute with access on every floor, and maximum open space. Furthermore, central heating and hot-water systems are economically feasible.

The study of the social effects of living in flats has centred on the physical aspects. In order to assess the wider costs of the policy it is necessary to consider other, more intangible effects. For example, an important proposition of social welfare theory is that groups receiving a subsidized service should do so without 'stigma'. Much of Australian public housing policy has attempted to minimize or eliminate this stigma attached to occupancy of a public housing unit. The NSWHC does not standardize the architectural styles of its flat developments. Its programme of scattered flat construction in middle suburbs means that apart from about 1,500 units in Redfern, Waterloo and Surry Hills, the NSWHC avoids the creation of large concentrations of flat developments. In contrast, the VHC has produced large flat developments in areas cleared in slum clearance schemes that have distinctive design and are prominent in the urban scene. They may suggest a certain style of life—a group set apart from the rest of the population—and the developments are subject to frequent, often sensationalist attacks in the press. Although no adequate research has been done on the results of this, it is clear that these factors may help to make these large VHC estates a highly distinctive form of public housing. Hence it is heard so often that these estates are the new 'slums'. Mr Meagher, the Minister for Housing in Victoria, complained in parliament in 1969 that the new VHC flats were being called 'prisons in the sky', 'slums of the future' and 'high-rise monsters'.

About 26 per cent (June 1969) of the flats have three bedrooms, and although the VHC would prefer to be able to allocate cottage or row houses to all families with young children, it claims that it is inevitable that high-rise flats will become the homes for families with young children. Hence the more recent high-rise blocks provide for a utility room in each flat and a community play room on each floor so that mothers can watch young children whilst doing the laundry. The flats are usually grouped in comparatively large estates. The Hotham estate built in 1964 consists of 712 dwelling units, the Carlton estate completed in 1966 contains 532 flats, and future projects planned include 1,000 flats in one estate in Richmond. Whereas in single-family houses (cottages) privacy exists by virtue of the separation of units, privacy in all its forms, both visual and auditory, indoor and outdoor, is difficult to achieve in multi-family developments when units are close together. Generally, the higher the density the less the privacy.

In 1966 the Brotherhood of St Laurence conducted a study of the effects of VHC flats on tenants and claimed that they did not meet the needs of family life, particularly for families with children (*High Living*, Melbourne, 1967). In comparison with a cottage, a flat cannot be altered as family structure changes. The lack of storage space was also a problem, as was the difficulty of controlling children once they got into the no-man's-land outside the flat. In a study of high-rise flats in Britain, Maizels found that living above the fifth floor is associated with a high incidence of concern with the safety of young children and a lower incidence in the use of playgrounds (*Two to Five in High Flats*, London, 1961). He also shows that, generally, the higher the flat the less the tendency for children to play outside their homes. Holme and Massie point out that high-rise flats may have additional effects (*Children's Play*, London, 1970):

> So much play is spontaneous and this spontaneity is bound to be inhibited if a major effort is needed to reach a suitable and permissible place. This implies that, ideally, for children the immediate home environment should be planned so as to ensure maximum opportunity for what we may describe as 'doorstep play'—play within sight and sound of home. Various attempts to achieve this in the tower block have been made—play decks, wide balconies, closed circuit television—but with comparatively little success. So many things operate against success, particularly for the young child—danger from stairways and lift, icy draughts (a perennial problem for housing estates), unco-operative caretakers and, for the closed circuit television idea, the sheer inappropriateness of a mother being able to see her child in trouble and not being able to do anything about it.

Although it was argued in chapter 1 that poor housing—referring to old, dilapidated dwellings—was not a significant cause of social problems, flats, particularly high-rise flats, seem to be a major cause of poor health. The main evidence for this is in a study by Fanning of 558 families in Germany in 1965 ('Families in Flats', *British Medical Journal*, 1967). Two groups of families, one living in cottages and the other in high-rise flats, were matched on socio-economic status. Most had young children. Fanning found that the families who lived in flats had a much higher rate of respiratory disorders which he attributed to the lower exposure of flat dwellers to open air than the cottage occupants. He also found a higher rate of psychoneurotic disorders in the flats than in the cottages, which he links with the cramped conditions of flat living, especially the necessity to confine young children to the flat, and the lower degree of sociability among flat dwellers than among households in cottages. These results are surprising in view of the negative findings of the studies of poor housing reviewed in chapter 1. But the Fanning study does appear methodologically sound. It used properly chosen control groups and was generally similar in design to the Wilner *et al.* study referred to in that chapter (*The Housing Environment and Family Life*, Baltimore, 1962).

The comparatively high cost of services in inner areas was discussed in chapter 5. In 1970, the Victorian Minister for Education, Lindsay Thompson, expressed concern over the effect that the VHC redevelopment was having on inner suburban schools. While admitting the need to construct new schools in these areas he sought special federal grants to cover the high cost of construction due to the necessity for high-rise construction on expensive slum clearance land.

Large estates on the fringe

This section examines a common type of public housing estate: large developments (around 6,000 dwellings) built on the outer fringe of the capital cities, without any attempt to develop a satellite city by the decentralization of industry or by other means. Large tracts of land on the outer fringes of the city are economical, and the Commissions build large estates which may become enclosed in the general expansion of the city. This section concentrates on the development of Green Valley, the estate developed by the NSWHC 22 miles from the centre of Sydney during 1961–6. While generalizations to other developments are not possible, the study of Green Valley may illustrate some of the typical characteristics of these types of developments.

Tables 90 to 95 present the CD data for Green Valley and show that the occupants of Green Valley are overwhelmingly married couples with young children. As many as 53 per cent of the population were under 15 years of age and 74 per cent were under 30, much higher proportions than for either the NSWHC CD total or the whole Sydney metropolitan area. The overseas born, especially British migrants, are well represented. Motor vehicle ownership is comparatively high, possibly reflecting the geographical isolation of Green Valley from employment centres. The population of Green Valley are predominantly blue-collar workers (71 per cent), although 11 per cent of the residents are in the professional and managerial and self-employed categories. Another 15 per cent of the workforce are engaged in white-collar occupations, bringing the total white-collar content to about 26 per cent. These figures suggest that it may be inaccurate to term Green Valley an 'income ghetto', since only about 17 per cent of the population are in the 'personal, domestic and service worker' category although 33 per cent are in the largely unskilled category of shop assistants and process workers. The socio-economic status of Green Valley is midway between the level of the inner flats and the 'new towns' discussed below. It is about the same as the NSWHC metropolitan average. Tables 90 to 95 are based on the analysis of Green Valley CDs containing 4,419 dwellings and 22,084 people; 92 per cent of the dwellings were cottages and 8 per cent flats. Of the cottages, 53 per cent were sold.

TABLE 90 Occupations of the workforce in Green Valley, Sydney (per cent of total), 1966 census

	Green Valley	NSWHC total metro.	Sydney metro. area total
	%	%	%
Professional	3	4	11
Managerial, self-employed	8	8	13
Clerical workers	14	19	23
Armed forces	1	2	1
Craftsmen, foremen	21	18	16
Shop assistants, process workers	33	30	21
Personal, domestic, service workers and labourers	17	17	14
Not stated	3	2	1

Source: Compiled from summary data supplied by the Commonwealth Statistician (Collectors' District data for the total population).

TABLE 91 Education of the population (excluding children not at school and full-time students) in Green Valley, Sydney (per cent of total), 1966 census

	Green Valley	NSWHC total metro.	Sydney metro. area total
	%	%	%
University qualifications	—	—	2
Other tertiary qualifications	—	1	3
Matriculation passed	4	5	11
Intermediate passed	28	29	33
Attended high school	39	39	26
Attended primary school	24	23	20
No education	2	1	1
Not stated	3	2	4

Source: Compiled from summary data supplied by the Commonwealth Statistician (Collectors' District data for the total population).

By 1966 Green Valley contained a population of about 24,000 in about 6,000 dwellings, mostly cottages. In addition to providing the cottages the NSWHC provided the required roads and made contributions for the provision of water and sewerage and provided land for the supply of schools, parks, community and other facilities. The provision of other facilities such as baby health centres and community facilities is the function of local government authorities, as is the construction of playing fields. The NSWHC supplies land free of charge to the local authorities for these facilities but has been criticized for delays in providing them. The Department of Social

TABLE 92 Motor vehicle ownership in Green Valley, Sydney, number of vehicles per occupied private dwelling (per cent of total), 1966 census

No. of vehicles per dwelling	Green Valley	NSWHC total metro.	Sydney metro. area total
	%	%	%
HOUSES			
None	31	31	26
One	60	57	51
Two	6	10	17
Three +	1	—	4
Not stated	2	2	2
FLATS			
None	69	61	42
One	24	32	44
Two	1	3	7
Three +	—	—	3
Not stated	6	5	4

Source: Compiled from summary data supplied by the Commonwealth Statistician (Collectors' District data for the total population).

TABLE 93 Age structure in Green Valley, Sydney (per cent of total), 1966 census

Age group	Green Valley	NSWHC total metro.	Sydney metro. area total
	%	%	%
0–4	20	14	9
5–9	23	17	9
10–14	10	12	8
15–19	6	8	9
20–29	15	12	15
30–39	16	16	13
40–49	6	10	14
50–59	2	6	11
60 +	2	5	12

Source: Compiled from summary data supplied by the Commonwealth Statistician (Collectors' District data for the total population).

Work at the University of Sydney surveyed Green Valley in 1966 and again in 1969, and showed that many facilities were added to Green Valley between 1966 and 1969. The development has been planned on the neighbourhood principle, each neighbourhood having its own primary school, local shopping centre and recreation areas. A central shopping centre for the area is adjacent to an hotel, professional offices, community hall, library and baby health centre, and land for the erection of churches has been provided.

The NSWHC is building another development similar to Green Valley at Mt Druitt, 32 miles west of Sydney. It will consist of 12,000 homes for an estimated population of 40,000 people. The first NSWHC house was occupied there in 1965, and in 1971 (30 June) there were 4,258 dwellings completed. Like Green Valley, the population of Mt Druitt consists largely of young families on low incomes.

Frequent mass media publicity may help stigmatize large Housing Commission developments. An example of this was a report in *The Australian* on 10 August 1968 by Moffit. The report—a feature article in the Saturday

TABLE 94 Birthplace of the population in Green Valley, Sydney (per cent of total), 1966 census

Birthplace	Green Valley	NSWHC total metro.	Sydney metro. area total
	%	%	%
Australia	86	88	78
New Zealand, England, Wales, Ireland. Scotland	9	8	9
Austria, Czechoslovakia, Germany, Hungary, Yugoslavia	2	1	3
Greece, Italy, Malta	1	1	5
Other	3	2	5

Source: Compiled from summary data supplied by the Commonwealth Statistician (Collectors' District data for the total population).

TABLE 95 Marital status of the population (excluding the never married) in Green Valley, Sydney (per cent of total), 1966 census

Marital status	Green Valley	NSWHC total metro.	Sydney metro. area total
	%	%	%
Married	93	88	84
Married, but permanently separated	3	4	3
Divorced	1	—	2
Widowed	4	7	11

Source: Compiled from summary data supplied by the Commonwealth Statistician (Collectors' District data for the total population).

Review section of the paper—describes various forms of deviant behaviour by residents of Green Valley. These deviations range from pack rapes, dodging the debt collector (the informal title was 'Dodge City' and 'Sioux City' because people were 'always shooting through on hire purchase debts') to general family fragmentation. Moffit does not blame the innate characteristics of the people but rather the incompetence of the planners responsible for Green Valley.

The NSWHC does not attempt to provide industrial sites close to developments such as Green Valley to give the residents work close to their homes. Since little industry locates nearby, at least in the early stages of development, one of the criticisms that researchers have made of Green Valley is that it involved low income households in long and expensive journeys to work. While this appears to be true in the early stages of development of Housing Commission estates on the fringes of the city, there is some evidence that industrial decentralization follows the development of these suburbs so that the number of job opportunities increases rapidly with the passage of time. The comparative isolation of Green Valley may be lessened by the high rate of car ownership in the area. In 1970 the NSWHC completed a survey on car ownership in Mt Druitt and found that about 65 per cent of all families owned a car. One possible method of alleviating the financial burdens on long journeys to work is in the area of rent policy. Those in the outer suburbs could be required to pay less rent than those in more favourably situated suburbs.

A number of writers have investigated the society of Green Valley and found that the most frequent problems result from low incomes, money mismanagement, and disturbed family relationships, involving desertion and juvenile delinquency. A sample of the cases examined by McLelland showed that financial and medical problems involving heavy expenditures were the prime features of the problem cases in the area ('Needs and Services in an Outer Suburb', *Australian Journal of Social Issues*, 1968). The residents interviewed claimed that, after financial problems, the most important need was the provision of physical facilities for recreation, especially for children.

A later stage of the McLelland survey found that there were significantly fewer social problem cases in Green Valley in 1969 than in 1966. Summing up this part of the study, Shtein says that 'The period of social transition studied in 1966 is over. Green Valley is in the process of becoming culturally structured. Social problems can be said to have stabilized and can be viewed against a background of ordinary family life and social aspiration'. The survey measured the incidence of social problems by the calls made on social agencies near Green Valley. One unknown factor in this method is the large number of families who were evicted from public housing in Green Valley between 1966 and 1969 and the unknown nature of those who left voluntarily. No exact figures are available but in 1968–9 about 248 dwellings were vacated, about 5 per cent of the total units in the area. In a survey undertaken in 1968 34 per cent of families vacating units at Green Valley were evicted. If the vacancy rate for this sample period is typical of the 1966–9 period it appears that Green Valley could have 'improved' because the 'problem tenants' were removed. Taking account of the removal of the 'problem tenants', Shtein's figures on the number of social problem cases in Green Valley in 1966 and 1969 do not appear so optimistic: he found 233 cases in 1966 out of a total population of 24,900 and 216 in 1969 out of a population of 29,000.

The McLelland study found that there was little local leadership to develop and sustain the voluntary agencies such as the Boy Scouts and a Progress Association, normally part of the Australian suburban scene, and it suggested that this is due to the '. . . lack of talent necessary to take initiative'. McLelland claims that

> It would be naïve not to ascribe a large part of the general problem to the lack of indigenous leadership and the preponderance of individual problems or financial difficulties to the rapid putting together of a large working class population with big families in an area distant from sources of employment for the unskilled and semi-skilled . . . they are young, have large families, not very much education, and have enjoyed only a fairly narrow experience in the kinds of social participation which we know are necessary to develop or initiate both the facilities and the processes which are part of suburban community life.

These conclusions, which are probably shared by large numbers of professionals, are open to some debate. The first and probably the most fundamental point is the set of assumptions on which the above statements are based. It is assumed that a strong set of voluntary organizations is an essential and vital part of social life. Gans argues that many working class groups are not interested in voluntary associations because they involve a different set of values from those of the working class. Many of the problems of the area were caused by chronically low incomes, and reforms in the social service system, in NSWHC rent policy, and in other aspects of social welfare could be much more important than the growth of voluntary associations. Thirdly, and this is admitted by McLelland, most of the generalizations about the effects of various aspects of Green Valley could be proved only by comparative studies which isolate the influence of certain variables such as the journey to work or the type of physical planning. Such studies have never been undertaken in Australia.

The passage of time affects the supply of amenities to these areas. The initial few years are typically periods of shortage in transport and other facilities. The following list of shortages was supplied by the NSWHC and refers to the experience with the Mt Druitt development: (a) lack of transport facilities; (b) overcrowding in the schools and the lack of any high school (evidence of poor co-ordination with the Education Department); (c) shortage of doctors in the area; (d) few shopping facilities because the state planning authority and the local council could not agree on either neighbourhood shopping centres or a central large-scale shopping centre;

(e) no other government department has offices in Mt Druitt (e.g. Commonwealth Employment Service, Department of Social Welfare)—this is closely connected with the failure to develop shopping centres; (f) lack of developed parks and playgrounds as the council claims that it has not got the funds to develop the raw land set aside by the Commission; (g) no halls, meeting rooms, cultural or recreational facilities, although the NSWHC has set aside sites for this purpose; (h) no local industry.

The passage of time is important also in determining the level of sociability in housing developments. Willmott notes that many of the studies of housing areas that claim that various aspects of housing developments cause social problems have been carried out in the early stages of these projects. Later studies have found that these problems were largely temporary. As time passed the friendship networks developed providing that the rate of population mobility was relatively low, since this is also an important determinant of sociability amongst lower class residents. In addition the attempt to define a set of rigid 'needs' in an area, with claims that there is '. . . very slender provision in the social and recreational amenities for a population of over 25,000 . . .', is open to question. There is little agreement on these needs. Since there are many competing claims on public resources, these demands have to be weighed against other goods and services. For example, would it be better to spend money on community facilities in Green Valley or allocate this money to help lower the rents in the area? There are no simple answers to such questions because they involve value judgments about the importance of different objectives.

New towns

New towns have been seen by some as the panacea to all the ills of the large city. The older industrial cities are condemned for being poorly planned, suffering from traffic congestion, air pollution, social disorganization and a variety of other ills. The new town movement was fed by such anti-metropolis feelings and by the promised advantages of short journeys to work, 'balanced' communities, a high level of general amenity and other benefits. The only large-scale 'new town' planned by the public housing authority in Australia is Elizabeth in South Australia, built by the SAHT.

The first dwelling was occupied at Elizabeth, 19 miles north of Adelaide, in 1955. By 1969 the population was almost 49,000, the Trust having completed almost 12,000 houses and flats. More than 250 commercial and professional premises were occupied at Elizabeth by 1969, 11 of these in Trust-built and rented factories. (This has been discussed above in chapter 6.) Elizabeth cannot be considered a self-contained area with most of the residents working within the city. The 1966 Census figures show that 27 per cent of the male workforce and 44 per cent of the female workforce resident in Elizabeth actually worked in Elizabeth (an overall average of 32 per cent). If Salisbury, an adjacent town, is included then a total of 49 per cent of the workforce of Elizabeth actually worked in either Elizabeth or Salisbury. This means that about 50 per cent of the residents of Elizabeth travel about 20 miles to Adelaide, the only other nearby employment centre. A survey of large employers at Elizabeth by the SAHT in 1969 found that only about half of their employees were residents of Elizabeth. Hence a sizeable proportion of the workforce coming to Elizabeth travels considerable distances, probably from Adelaide. These figures are similar to research findings on British new towns. In British new towns 7.3 workers enter and leave the town in their daily work trip for every ten who live and work in the same new town. The space between the new town and the metropolitan area lengthens travel and makes it more costly. Many question the so-called advantages of new towns, including those quoted above from the SAHT: the costly extension of services in the haphazard urban sprawl is avoided; and all the anti-city feelings summed up in the phrase 'Undue centralization of urban life is an evil . . .'. Many of the economies of new towns are

TABLE 96 Occupations of the workforce in Elizabeth (per cent of total), 1966 census

	Elizabeth	SAHT total metro.	Adelaide metro. area total
	%	%	%
Professional	9	9	12
Managerial, self-employed	10	11	14
Clerical workers	16	18	21
Armed forces	3	2	1
Craftsmen, foremen	26	24	19
Shop assistants, process workers	21	21	17
Personal, domestic, other service workers and labourers	14	14	15

Source: Compiled from summary data supplied by the Commonwealth Statistician (Collectors' District data for the total population).

TABLE 97 Education of the population (excluding children not at school and full-time students) in Elizabeth (per cent of total), 1966 census

	Elizabeth	SAHT total metro.	Adelaide metro. area total
	%	%	%
University qualifications	1	1	2
Other tertiary qualifications	2	2	3
Matriculation passed	12	11	12
Intermediate passed	25	24	21
Attended high school	34	32	23
Attended primary school	26	29	35
No education	1	1	1
Not stated	1	1	3

Source: Compiled from summary data supplied by the Commonwealth Statistician (Collectors' District data for the total population).

really the economies of large-scale tract development—the maximum and rapid use of services—and could be gained by large-scale fringe developments such as the NSWHC's Green Valley project.

One of the fundamental claims for new towns is that, unlike fringe suburbs such as Green Valley, the new town will have a balanced population in terms of socio-economic status and stage in the life cycle. Tables 96 to 101 show that there is some validity in this claim for 'balance'. Elizabeth contains a wider socio-economic range than does Green Valley—19 per cent of the population of Elizabeth are in the professional or managerial

TABLE 98 Motor vehicle ownership in Elizabeth, number of vehicles per occupied private dwelling (per cent of total), 1966 census

No. of vehicles per dwelling	Elizabeth	SAHT total metro.	Adelaide metro. area total
	%	%	%
HOUSES			
None	17	16	20
One	66	65	55
Two	13	16	19
Three +	3	3	5
Not stated	1	1	1
FLATS			
None	50	56	40
One	43	31	48
Two	7	6	7
Three +	—	—	—
Not stated	—	6	5

Source: Compiled from summary data supplied by the Commonwealth Statistician (Collectors' District data for the total population).

TABLE 99 Age structure in Elizabeth (per cent of total), 1966 census

Age group	Elizabeth	SAHT total metro.	Adelaide metro. area total
	%	%	%
0–4	15	13	9
5–9	17	15	10
10–14	12	13	10
15–19	9	9	10
20–29	13	12	13
30–39	16	16	12
40–49	11	12	13
50–59	5	6	10
60 +	3	4	13

Source: Compiled from summary data supplied by the Commonwealth Statistician (Collectors' District data for the total population).

and self-employed categories, compared with 11 per cent in Green Valley; 38 per cent of the workforce in Elizabeth are in the white-collar group, compared with 26 per cent in Green Valley; the population of Elizabeth is both better educated and more likely to own a motor vehicle than the residents of Green Valley. There is little evidence of 'balance' in terms of a significant mixture of married couples, the aged, the never married and so on. Most householders in Elizabeth are married (95 per cent) and although information on the 'never married' households is not available there are likely to be few of them. Only 44 per cent of the population of Elizabeth are under 15 years of age (compared with 53 per cent in Green Valley) and 66 per cent are under 30 (compared with 74 per cent in Green Valley). A very large proportion of residents of Elizabeth were born in the United Kingdom (47 per cent compared with only 14 per cent of the total Adelaide population). Other overseas born groups also form a significant number.

Some of the socio-economic differences between Elizabeth and Green Valley could be due to the timing of their respective development: Green

TABLE 100 Birthplace of the population in Elizabeth (per cent of total), 1966 census

Birthplace	Elizabeth	SAHT total metro.	Adelaide metro. area total
	%	%	%
Australia	45	58	73
New Zealand, England, Wales, Ireland, Scotland	47	35	14
Austria, Czechoslovakia, Germany, Hungary, Yugoslavia	2	2	3
Greece, Italy, Malta	1	1	6
Other	4	5	4

Source: Compiled from summary data supplied by the Commonwealth Statistician (Collectors' District data for the total population).

TABLE 101 Marital status of the population (excluding the never married) in Elizabeth (per cent of total), 1966 census

Marital status	Elizabeth	SAHT total metro.	Adelaide metro. area total
	%	%	%
Married	95	93	86
Married, but permanently separated	1	1	2
Divorced	1	1	2
Widowed	3	4	10

Source: Compiled from summary data supplied by the Commonwealth Statistician (Collectors' District data for the total population).

Valley was developed almost entirely between 1962 and 1966 while Elizabeth's growth has been from about 1955. But the earlier development of Elizabeth would probably account only for the differences in age structure. The differences in socio-economic status (occupation, education, motor vehicle ownership) are mainly due to the SAHT's provision of subsidized housing to much higher income groups than the NSWHC's.

Tables 96 to 101 are based on the analysis of 8,105 dwellings at Elizabeth, containing 34,907 people; 99 per cent of the dwellings were cottages and 1 per cent flats. Of the cottages, 42 per cent were sold.

What are the main differences between new towns such as Elizabeth in South Australia and fringe developments such as Green Valley or Mt Druitt in Sydney? In the new town a great deal of attention is paid to industrial location. Hence Elizabeth contains a far greater number of jobs than Green Valley or Mt Druitt, even though the latter do attract industry although with a considerable time-lag and often some distance from the residential areas since industrial estates are not provided as part of the settlement as they are in a new town. The other main difference is in population composition: Elizabeth is more heterogeneous than Green Valley or Mt Druitt. This is the result of the different allocation policies of the NSWHC and the SAHT. The population heterogeneity in Elizabeth is a result of the SAHT subsidy plan for middle income households while the low socio-economic status (comparative to Elizabeth) reflects the NSWHC policy to supply public housing only to the low income group. Lastly, Elizabeth has developed at a much more leisurely pace than either Green Valley or Mt Druitt, with all the social dislocation and serious shortage of services in the latter. Perhaps the most important argument about the relative advantages of new towns and fringe developments is that new towns could obtain the advantage of fringe developments by locating as close as possible to the main city. This would remove the expensive cross-commuting that occurs between the new town and the large mother city. New towns would continue to have advantages over fringe developments if they helped to rapidly decentralize a sizeable number of jobs away from the crowded metropolis and they produced a more heterogeneous environment. Of course, if they located nearer the mother cities they would cease much of their traditional justification to be called new towns but would still be far different from normal Australian public housing fringe developments.

Scattered site developments

Some of the housing authorities have, at various times and to varying degrees, attempted to build dwellings so that they were scattered amongst private housing developments. This practice was common early in the 1950s in most states when delays in servicing new areas provided an inducement to develop scattered allotments to take advantage of available services. The NSWHC now limits scattered site developments to country areas and to walk-up flats in the Sydney metropolitan area. The Commission purchases land in the middle Sydney suburbs and constructs fairly small flat developments (usually from 50 to 150 flats). In addition to being economical (this is discussed in chapter 5), these flats are also deliberately made architecturally diverse. These developments do not involve a great degree of homogeneity. It is likely that the people living near these flat developments are slightly above the socio-economic level of NSWHC tenants but this gap is unlikely to be very great since the land prices in higher status areas are likely to deter Commission development. To the extent that these developments are architecturally diverse and relatively small, they probably decrease and possibly almost eliminate the stigma attached to public housing. Since they cater for the Commission client who desires a walk-up flat in a middle suburb rather than an inner area flat or an outer area cottage, these flats do provide choice.

In 1969 the NSWHC began to develop a large mainly cottage estate at Campbelltown about 30 miles south-east of Sydney. Partly out of dissatisfaction with the experience at Green Valley and Mt Druitt, the Commission is to build the neighbourhoods of about 5,000–6,000 people one to two miles apart from one another, with private developments interspersed between them. This policy creates difficulties in the supply of amenities since the private areas take much longer to develop than the Commission estates.

The VHC claims that its policy of selling land in its fringe estates creates a mixture of these estates by allowing private home builders to construct homes in these areas. The sale of slum clearance land to private developers at a subsidized price has also been justified on the grounds that it creates some social mixing in the estates.

The SAHT scatters its low income developments to some degree because its middle income programme enables it to mix its own estates. However, the prime form of low income housing available is the double unit, a semi-detached form of housing which may be somewhat stigmatized. The SAHT scatters its flat developments in a manner similar to the NSWHC. When developing Elizabeth the SAHT left about 10 per cent of available building sites vacant in the expectation that private builders would construct dwellings for those desiring a higher standard. However, few of these sites were used in this manner and most of them were eventually used for the construction of Trust dwellings. Private builders have difficulty in competing with the Trust's favourable finance rates, and the higher income residents in Elizabeth are catered for with higher-priced, higher-quality houses offered under the Trust's middle income scheme.

The QHC has scattered its developments since about 1959. Since the QHC builds few flats and those it does build are in small developments, this analysis is limited to cottage construction. The sites for the QHC dwellings are scattered primarily because many of them are for sale and, generally, it is easier to sell Housing Commission dwellings, particularly to those who can afford the substantial deposits required by the QHC, when the dwellings are not concentrated in one area. In addition, the QHC completes a relatively small number of dwellings in Brisbane during each year so that economic-organizational incentives for large estates are not as strong. Thirdly, there is the belief that large concentrations of public housing units are undesirable.

The WAHC attempted to diversify its estates in the 1950s by interspersing war service homes amongst WAHC estates and by setting aside a certain proportion of land in each estate for private development. The intermingling of war service homes dwellings—often as much as 30 per cent of all dwellings—was possible because the WAHC was in charge of allocating and administering war service homes legislation in the state. Since there is no means test on war service homes this probably raised the average socio-economic status of WAHC areas. The second policy—the selling of a proportion of blocks in WAHC estates to private builders—was not successful, probably for the same reasons as are mentioned above for South Australia. From 1969 onwards the WAHC has implemented a plan whereby about 70 per cent of sites in Commission estates are offered to private builders at below private market prices. The WAHC attempts to ensure that the low cost of land is passed on to the private home buyer. This scheme has proved popular, and means that Commission estates are mixtures of private and WAHC units. Up to 1969 the THC generally built its metropolitan cottage estates in fairly large estate form.

The argument against scattering is basically an economic one. It is more economical to develop large estates on the fringe of the capital cities for a number of reasons. The Housing Commissions operate as developers, and make substantial profits from the sale of land for commercial development. Because of economies of scale they are probably able to lower the cost of services such as roads, water and sewerage. It is also claimed that construction of large numbers of dwellings in one spot can be managed more economically. There is only one set of building approvals to process and so on, compared with the multitude of decisions involving state and local government agencies if many scattered sites were being developed. Moreover the Commissions would probably have to pay more per block for land not purchased in large tracts. It is also claimed that large estates are easier to maintain once they are built than smaller estates.

There is a very strong belief both inside and outside the Housing Commissions that public housing in Australia simply has to be built in large-scale estates. The advantages of estate development over scattered sites are thought to be obvious. Many of these arguments are doubtful. What appears to be low per unit costs in estate development in a place like Green Valley in Sydney are in fact just part of the public housing subsidy. The Commissions often do not have to pay any rates on vacant land and they use their normal very low-interest funds for holding land, often for many years. Sometimes they pay the interest charges on such landholding from their own profits and then do not include them in their estimation of the costs of land development. With the opportunity cost of money around 10 per cent per year this could underestimate the real cost of estate development by at least 100 per cent. While these costs may not be directly charged to the Housing Commissions, they are still very important and cannot be overlooked. Another factor is the use of services. As a result of poor urban planning in most Australian cities there are many unused building blocks scattered around the middle suburbs often much closer to the city than tract developments like Mt Druitt in Sydney. These blocks could usually be built on without great expenditure on roads, schools, sewerage and other important services which must usually be provided in new large Commission estates. One reason often cited for not removing the affluent from older Commission dwellings is that this would create an income ghetto. If dwellings were scattered the resultant heterogeneity would obviate the need for this and also for such huge subsidies as are used in Elizabeth in South Australia to ensure income mixing. The public housing subsidy could then be allocated far more effectively than at present. These issues require much more investigation but the advantages of estate development should not be assumed without a wider perspective than simply the Commissions' direct construction costs.

The segregation of social groups

It was argued above that people of similar socio-economic status generally like to live close to one another. Mainly because families with children are the Commissions' main clients, and because of the tract developments such as those described in the section on fringe suburbs above, there is a large amount of segregation of families with children. There are groups where the evidence suggests that some concentration would be beneficial. The aged, the migrants from Europe and the 'problem tenants' are all used as specific examples of the wider principle discussed above: similar socio-economic groups want to live together.

Although there are no Australian data available, American studies suggest that the aged have a very strong desire to live together. After surveying the results of a number of studies on the effects of scattering the aged throughout the community, Rosow says that the aged are largely isolated from the wider society and most of their friends are also aged. Hence residential areas heavily weighted with old people multiply the chances of the aged making friends, probably the basic reason for the success of so many American retirement villages.

The Housing Commissions generally build aged units in small numbers scattered throughout the community. This trend is somewhat changing with the VHC's tendency to include groups of around 200 aged units (high-rise) in slum clearance redevelopments. In addition the 1969 Commonwealth legislation discussed in chapter 4 almost inevitably involves some concentration of the aged because it requests that some units be built in inner areas and there the high land costs necessitate high-rise construction, which to be economic means building in groups of around 200 units.

In his study of Melbourne's social structure Lancaster Jones has found evidence that ethnic groupings, especially of Greeks and Italians, are widespread. The Housing Commissions do not provide for such ethnic concentrations in their developments and this may be a partial explanation for the comparatively low representation of continental European migrants in public housing, also discussed in chapter 4.

As sociology gradually turned away from a condemnation of deviant life styles, it was realized that many apparently irrational and disorganized aspects of deviant society fulfilled important functions in the residents' lives. Residential segregation was an important part of this system. Research has found that the problem tenants referred to in chapter 4 frequently want to live in adjacent dwellings. This is most likely to be the case where the groups share a common set of values (especially deviant values). In the SAHT a previously troublesome group of twelve problem families responded to a programme that allowed them to live in adjacent dwellings. Such 'groupings' of problem tenants were possible in the emergency housing settlements of the 1950s and early 1960s. The Report of the Bristol project in the United Kingdom claimed that some segregation of problem families was unavoidable and desirable and it gave the opportunity for planned services for these groups that probably would not be available if they were dispersed. The dispersal of problem families may involve their extreme isolation because of the hostility they may arouse in other residents. After the closure of the emergency housing settlement (by 1965) the Housing Commissions' general philosophy was similar to that expressed by the NSWHC in 1968:

> It has generally been found that overall management is facilitated . . . if 'problem' or 'borderline' cases are not allowed to be grouped into one area. The interaction between the different types has the tendency to lift the level of achievement of the 'weaker' members of the community without detracting from the efforts of the stronger. It is important, of course, that the 'weaker' families should not be in the majority in any neighbourhood or their influence may unduly affect and weaken the structure of the neighbourhood community.

Conclusion

It is difficult to come to any definite conclusions on the matters raised in this chapter. It is not clear, for example, what relative importance should be given respectively to the dwelling itself, the amenities and the nature of the social environment. Ultimately most of the answers given come down to value judgments and only widespread consumer research can ascertain how the residents who actually live in the areas evaluate the various types of development.

There is a tentative recommendation for some degree of heterogeneity in public housing areas, and ironically, mainly because Australian public housing is comparatively inefficient in allocating the available units to those who could be classed as the really poor, it has produced fairly heterogeneous residential areas. Inner area flats are the one case where public housing in Australia appears to approach the American form of the 'income ghetto' although even these areas do not constitute 'income ghettos' in the American sense. The Commissions could experiment with scattered site developments in order to avoid the stigma of large-scale developments and also to promote population heterogeneity. There is also a need for the Commissions to recognize the peculiar problems of new estates, especially the shortage of services and the distance to work, and make allowances for families who appear to be acting irresponsibly in the new estates. Lastly, the Commissions should allow social groups to concentrate more than is allowed under current policy.

10 POLICY CONCLUSIONS

The material presented in this book shows that there are many things wrong with public housing in Australia. Chapter 1 established a theoretical framework for evaluation based mainly on the authorities' stated objectives: public housing as a social service, and, less importantly, as a means of regional development. Also important in evaluation—and a constant theme—were the assumptions of causal links implicit in public housing: that poor housing causes social problems; and that the housing market is imperfect and public housing is therefore necessary if everyone is to have an adequate dwelling. The discussion of these causal assumptions was limited by the comparatively small amount of reliable research done on them and the fact that what has been done has been based mostly on overseas experience which may not be true of Australia. However, from the limited data available, it was concluded that poor housing as defined on traditional criteria listed in chapter 5 does not cause social problems; and that the housing market is generally competitive. What imperfections do exist are due mainly to the peculiarities of low income markets in general: poor education, supply malpractices, and compensatory consumption. It was also concluded that poor housing is really a symptom of low income, and that any policy that increases income will usually improve the housing situation of low income households.

The discussion of the differences in the aggregate supply of public housing between the states showed that, as a result of the financial arrangements of Australian federalism, the more sparsely populated states (South Australia, Queensland, Tasmania and Western Australia) are able to devote a much larger amount per capita to public housing than the states with larger populations (Victoria and New South Wales), and all but Queensland do so. An examination of the very broad means tests applied by the Commissions showed that the poor are not given high priority in the allocation of public housing. This was borne out by the data from the 1966 Census which showed public housing tenants to be of relatively high socio-economic status.

Three categories emerged in the study of which social groups are given access to public housing. The first, the 'deserving' poor able to pay economic rents, fares well except in recent flat-building projects in Melbourne and Perth. Australian public housing authorities are overwhelmingly concerned with housing families with children although they have gradually assumed responsibility for non-husband-wife households. In the next group, the deserving poor unable to pay economic rents and in need of specialized services, female-headed households with dependent children have gained the most favourable treatment. Possibly because their 'deservingness' is so apparent and because of their comparatively small numbers they have not been discriminated against as have the aged. This group is a major poverty group in Australian society, but has been treated relatively badly in access to public housing, although the situation has been eased somewhat by Commonwealth legislation in 1969. Because of their very low capacity to pay, the aged, and other groups such as the physically handicapped, have suffered from the continual arguments between the Commonwealth and state governments over who should be responsible for the losses resulting from housing them. The last social group, the problem tenants, 'undeserving' poor unable to pay economic rents and in need of specialized services, are a most important group in need. This very group often formed the basis of the original public housing movement but because they refuse to adjust to the requirements of public housing residence—regular rent payments and certain stable life styles—little has been done to help them. The aborigines form a very important subgroup among the problem tenants.

It was argued in chapter 5 that although originally concerned with helping the slum dweller, 'slum clearance', especially in the VHC, has become increasingly occupied with other aims, particularly the revival of the central city. The VHC has failed to develop efficient methods for measuring the extent of poor housing, and its policy may not help the slum dweller since many of those displaced in slum clearance schemes do not desire to relocate in public housing and compensation practice does not ensure that they can obtain adequate alternative private housing. The high cost of VHC flats appears to outweigh the advantages of utilizing some surplus capacity in inner area services through redevelopment policies. Moreover, many expensive services, especially schools, may be so much more expensive in inner areas as to compensate for costs of developing the suburban fringe. Not only is the VHC's emphasis on reviving the central city of doubtful effectiveness but the private redevelopment plan—potentially of great magnitude—does little to assist those on low incomes, and may even harm them by diverting part of the subsidy to the middle groups.

The role of the SAHT in area development is the most important of its kind in Australia. The occupants of SAHT dwellings are of a much higher socio-economic status than those of other Commissions' dwellings, reflecting the Trust's middle income housing programme, aimed at promoting the growth of South Australia's economy. It is likely that, in addition to assisting those connected with industrial development, the Trust's programme assists many low income households, mainly because such a large overall amount is allocated to public housing in South Australia.

Home ownership is deeply ingrained in Australian public housing policy and, with the possible exception of the QHC and to a less extent the SAHT, most states offer very attractive opportunities for low income home purchase. Selling such a large proportion of dwellings has affected the supply of public housing—houses sold are rarely available for reallocation—although the profits generated by house sales provide vital funds for housing those in need and unable to pay economic rents. This is made particularly important by the lack of an efficient loss-recoupment arrangement between the Commonwealth and the states.

Rent policy is generally such that the longer the householder has occupied a public housing dwelling the lower will be his rent compared with that of new tenants. With the rebated rent plan and the lack of any attempt to charge those with higher incomes higher rents up to the market rent, public housing rent policy ensures that those with a very low capacity to pay (those on rebated rentals) pay a relatively high proportion of their income in rent, while those on higher incomes (the 'rich' tenants) pay comparatively small proportions.

In contrast to the generally critical findings of chapters 2 to 8, chapter 9 argued that Australian public housing provides comparatively good social environments. The very forces which direct public housing away from the poor promote social heterogeneity: the loose means tests; the home ownership and rent policies which encourage those who improve their socio-economic status to remain in public housing; and the area development schemes, particularly in the SAHT, which supply public housing to those on middle incomes.

In this final chapter some alternatives to public housing are presented—housing subsidies, income supplements—and rent control—and the relationship between general urban planning and housing problems is discussed. But we must face the sad fact that policy changes move slowly and that our real course of action is confined to patching up existing public housing within its present framework, so the last sections of this chapter deal with some of the ways in which this could be done.

Housing subsidies

If the government paid a housing subsidy to cover the difference between the capacity of the household to pay and the market rent of an adequate house, the household could obtain adequate housing without the government entering into the direct provision of dwellings as it does in a public housing programme. The effects of a housing subsidy on the supply of housing are largely dependent on whether or not the housing market operates in a manner close to the competitive model. Assuming that the market is competitive and supply is elastic, a housing subsidy will, in the long run, provide units of housing service at the same price per unit as before the subsidy is applied. The subsidy could be adjusted frequently so that it was always equivalent to the margin between the capacity to pay and the level of the market rental for adequate accommodation. However, this process would depend on the production of large amounts of information about the household's capacity to pay, the collection of which may be both expensive and an invasion of privacy. However, a housing subsidy has been introduced recently in West Germany and the problem of information collection does not appear to be a serious difficulty. The collection of such information would probably be similar to that in a public housing scheme, especially if rent policy in the latter involved frequent review of a household's capacity to pay.

Housing subsidies, either for rental or ownership, would give households much greater flexibility in the geographic location of the housing than is the case with existing public housing policies. Since the Commissions make no attempt to force their more affluent tenants to vacate public housing units and since they sell so many of their metropolitan dwellings, houses on the fringe form the main supply of housing for applicants. In the case of the NSWHC this now means Mt Druitt more than 30 miles from the centre of Sydney. The Commissions do have flats available in inner and outer suburbs but these are generally only two bedrooms in size except for the VHC units. The fact remains that there are many families who do not want to live in the fringe areas. Many larger low income families who live in inner suburbs have to live close to their workplace and would be able to purchase or rent reasonably cheap inner suburban accommodation if they could obtain a subsidy, probably less than the public housing subsidy now available to those prepared to live in the fringe areas. These points are well documented in the doctoral thesis by Halladay, completed at the Australian National University in 1971 ('Poverty Among Large Families in Sydney 1968–9'). Halladay interviewed many poor large families in inner suburbs and found that many of them had poor housing because of the inability of the NSWHC to supply family accommodation in these areas.

Because they rely on the complex information-generating processes in the private market, housing subsidies should cater for consumers' preferences much more than public housing. The scheme would avoid the problems of stigma associated with most public housing because those obtaining housing subsidies would not be concentrated in any one settlement. It would most likely lead to considerable population heterogeneity. By increasing the demand for housing, housing subsidies would improve the quality of older housing although they might not solve the wider problems of so-called 'slum' areas: mixed land uses and a poor general environment.

Perhaps the biggest advantage of a housing subsidy plan is that it does not tie a subsidy to a particular dwelling as does the allocation of the public housing subsidy where, if it is an old dwelling and the tenant has been in occupation for a long period, the rent is likely to be very low. A housing subsidy plan should be more flexible in allocating the subsidy: if the subsidy is stopped the tenant can continue in residence paying a higher rental. On the other hand, the same political forces that are mainly responsible for the inflexibility of the public housing subsidy may prevent housing subsidies from being allocated to those in need. They would probably become more like social services payments such as the aged pension which are based on a means test, and, if anything, tend to lag slightly behind inflation.

Many of the supporters of public housing are suspicious of housing subsidies. This is mainly because of the imperfections they see in the private housing market. They no doubt can quote case after case where people were swindled or where landlords obtained 'excessive' returns on their investments. They point to spiralling property values and so on. The most important factor in low income markets is information to the consumer about alternative products, their prices, quality, location and conditions of acquisition. This is quite clear in the inner urban areas where university students obtain good housing at economical rates. At the same time, the disadvantaged groups such as the aged find that no such housing is available. What seems to be needed in the housing field as well as in other markets is a government information and organizing service. Like the housing offices in the universities, the government agency could inspect accommodation, guarantee the rent, and be an important protector of tenancy rights as well as a source of information on available accommodation. The Commonwealth already does some of this in the employment field through the Commonwealth Employment Service. Such an organization in the housing market would be an excellent basis for administering a housing subsidy. There are malpractices in the private housing market, and, as in all markets, it is mainly the lower income households who suffer. The New South Wales government investigated these malpractices in 1969 and their report and the minutes of evidence is a catalogue of how shady builders and land sharks swindle people. But, like the information process, these faults could be overcome with effective yet cheap licensing systems and more severe penalties. The hire-purchase laws, for example, should be much fairer on the consumer, especially with regard to faulty workmanship.

People advocating rent control should realize that when investors can easily get around 10 per cent annual return in very safe investments, and probably more in land, factories or office buildings, landlords are not going to invest in rental housing if they are allowed only around a 6 per cent net return. They can get capital gains on many other investments as well as rental housing. The British have realized this so that they are attempting to reform the complicated network of government controls that has all but destroyed the private housing market. Moreover, things such as spiralling land values are a symptom of poor urban planning in general, something that public housing is not going to improve. Another common argument against the use of rental subsidies is that they would result in dramatic private rent increases in the short term, before the private housing market had a chance to adapt to the rise in demand caused by their introduction. This could be avoided by staggering the introduction of housing subsidies so that the increase in demand in any one year is within the housing market's capacity. After all, the housing market is continually making adjustments to changes in demand without price increases relative to general price inflation, which is reflected in the cost of public housing anyway. Another important feature is that the demand for housing that would result from a housing subsidy plan would be a reallocation of housing demand from the public to the private sector, since the public housing programme would be cut back. It should not be an increase in the total demand for housing. Those interested in social reform should constantly ask themselves not whether a private market is imperfect compared with an abstract theoretical model of a perfectly competitive market, but whether it is less perfect than the public sector substitute, with its inbuilt imperfections. It is often much easier to control a private firm than a government agency. If a private firm in a fairly competitive market is inefficient it will soon go out of business. No such rule applies to a government agency.

A housing subsidy plan could be applied to home ownership. It could take a number of forms. The government could grant low income families a sum that allowed them to place a deposit on a house obtained in the private market. This would undoubtedly help the substantial proportion of people now provided with public housing who could afford unsubsidized repayments but not the normal private market deposits. Another form of assistance may not involve any subsidy. At the moment, the repayments on house purchase are a constant amount per week over the duration of the loan. This has a number of unfortunate effects: the household is asked to pay the highest proportion of its income on housing costs at the time when normally the family is burdened with young children and the wife is not in the labour force; and, as the capacity to pay normally increases through increases in real income with the stage in the life cycle, general economic changes and inflation, the level of housing costs becomes a smaller proportion of income. A government could either persuade or force private institutions to take this into account when allocating housing finance or could manage the repayments for individuals. The resulting repayment pattern would mean that the household would increase its money payments for housing in accordance with inflation and changes in the household's capacity to pay. The aim would be to maintain expenditure on housing as a constant proportion of income, say around 10 per cent, until the loan is repaid instead of the current system where the proportion probably ranges from 25 per cent in the early period of the loan to 5 per cent in the later period. Under this scheme there would be no necessity for a subsidy to most households, and for the small proportion of families who needed a subsidy the amount would probably be much smaller than under existing housing programmes.

The latter system would be even more attractive if coupled with another policy change: the taxation of the imputed income from owner-occupied houses. Under the present system, the occupants of owner-occupied public housing dwellings get the benefits of these latter concessions, making them the lucky recipients of a double subsidy: the subsidized CSHA interest rate and the non-taxable imputed income from the owner-occupied dwelling. Take, for example, a householder who purchased a private dwelling in Australia in 1950. Assume that he paid $4,000 cash for a dwelling then. With inflation and capital gains on property the dwelling would probably be worth at least $10,000 in 1971. In 1971 the dwelling is returning the occupant around $1,000 a year in accommodation, an amount that he would have to pay if he was renting the dwelling. In effect, then, he has invested his $4,000 in an investment that has returned him tax-free capital gains and tax-free income in the form of accommodation. He would have had to pay income tax on this income if it has been invested in shares, or real estate that was rented.

Given that the tax rate is progressive, that is, increases in proportion as income increases, the gain in tax savings is highly regressive: it helps the rich far more than the poor and discriminates against the substantial proportion of the low income group who cannot afford home purchase. The amount of this tax saving is difficult to measure but some estimates can be made. In 1971 there were about two and a half million owner-occupied houses and flats in Australia. Assuming that the average equity in these dwellings was around $7,000, probably an underestimate, then the imputed income from this equity (at 6 per cent per annum) is $420 a year. In 1971 average weekly earnings were around $80, making the average tax saving per household around $100 per year, or a total of about $250 million per year. This is a crude estimate but is an indication of the importance of the subsidy. It is a major form of regressive income redistribution. In chapter 1 it was pointed out that in 1970 the dwellings completed by governments in Australia had a market value of at least $8,500 million. If one assumes that the subsidy on these dwellings is the difference between what the occupants pay and the market rate for the housing, then the subsidy comes to around $255 million a year (3 per cent of $8,500 million). Thus the value of the non-taxation of owner-occupied dwellings is about equal to the value of all direct government subsidies through the public housing programme in its various forms.

If there were taxes charged on the imputed rent of owner-occupied dwellings, then, probably, more people would require assistance in obtaining housing but the cost should be much lower than at present allowing for the massive disguised subsidies to home owners. It would be far more efficient in allocating the subsidy to those in need. Since the taxation of imputed rental income would only be on net equity—excluding interest charges—it would be very small during the early period of the loan and would increase in accordance with inflation. The taxation of imputed rent from owner-occupied dwellings is current policy in many countries and is not unduly difficult to administer.

Income supplements

This book has argued that poor housing is mainly the result of low incomes and that poor physical housing does not cause any obvious social problems. Given these facts, the housing market may not be the best means of income redistribution from the more affluent to the poor. Recent research into the problem of poverty strongly favours income supplements. Under this scheme the poor would be given cash grants to raise their incomes to some agreed minimum level.

Perhaps the most important advantage of income supplements is that they give the maximum freedom to the poor. They can decide whether they need additional care or education or more food rather than additional housing. And they can obtain these goods through the normal private markets, more attuned to diverse consumer preferences than are government agencies. Critics of the income supplement system—and many of them are probably supporters of public housing—claim that the poor are just as likely to spend the cash grant on alcohol or other 'luxuries'. Children, important beneficiaries from public housing, are not likely to have much say in how the cash grants are spent; nor may wives. Even those who wish to give the maximum discretion to the poor argue that they are incapable of spending efficiently in the private market partly because of their poor education and partly because of the imperfections in the supply of goods in low income markets, discussed in chapter 1. The remedy to this latter problem, of course, may be consumer education and closer controls over the supply of goods to low income markets; hire-purchase law reform is one example.

There are other objections to income supplements. Unless they have a work incentive incorporated, they may encourage households to cease working, especially if they are doing the 'dirty jobs' in our society. This may vastly increase the cost of welfare. To be efficient, an income supplement plan should take account of the differing level of housing costs between households which, superficially, have the same income. The solution would be to include the imputed rent from owner-occupied dwellings in the occupant's income. If the income supplement is spent on additional housing, the effects will be identical to the effects of housing subsidies.

In many ways the Housing Commissions bear the brunt of the general failings in the Australian social welfare system. Cash social service payments to those unable to participate meaningfully in the labour market are pitifully inadequate. It was not an accident that those existing on cash social service benefits formed the major poverty groups that were found in the 1966 Melbourne poverty survey. Most important amongst these groups were aged pensioners, especially those paying rent, invalids, widows and deserted wives on pensions, and, to a lesser extent, those on unemployment benefits. These inadequate social services are coupled with the regressive nature of the educational, medical and general amenities—in general the poor are unable to obtain sufficient quantities of these services within their capacity to pay. The subsidies that do exist usually work on the principle that the government should assist those who also help themselves, hence the reliance on voluntary health insurance and matching grants in education. There is little doubt that the burden on the Housing Commissions from the really needy would be greatly reduced if these latter problems were solved. For those optimists who believe that human beings can be influenced to change their ways then general rehabilitation services—especially employment training—could be expanded to help to attack the basic causes of some poverty for which the payment of cash social services only relieves the symptoms.

Rent control

A government can subsidize low income households unable to afford free market rents for housing by controlling the rents in privately-owned dwellings so that they are below the free market level. The amount of the subsidy is the difference between the free market rental and the rent charged in the controlled dwelling. Hence there is a redistribution of income from the landlords who own the controlled premises to the tenants who occupy the premises and this may not be a redistribution from high income groups to low income groups. In theory, rent control could allocate subsidies to the groups in need, that is, according to the tenants' ability to pay. The practice in Australia is to place a blanket set of controls on rented dwellings at a particular point, such as in war-time. The rents of these dwellings are controlled, and very little, if anything, is done to ensure that the dwellings are occupied by those in need of subsidy. In addition, many difficult problems of tenancy accompany rent control and many types of complex litigation often result.

If rent control were applied to all rented dwellings, then it would discourage investment in rental housing by reducing the rate of return. This would apply to both new rented dwellings and conversions from dwellings in the existing stock. Since rent control reduces the rate of return on the controlled dwelling unit it removes all incentive for the proper maintenance of the dwellings. It thus may tend to produce deterioration of the stock of housing.

Areas for policy reform within public housing

On the assumption that completely scrapping the public housing authorities is not politically feasible—bureaucracies rarely commit suicide singly, let alone collectively—there are many areas in which the existing public housing programme could be improved. The result would not be perfect, since there are ineradicable deficiencies inherent in public housing, but it is better to accept marginal changes than none at all.

Identifying the reasons for the wide dispersal of the public housing subsidy is the key to policy changes that will assist the poor. The following analysis suggests possible policy changes and generally consists of five main themes. First there is the doubtful validity of the theories of causality underlying public housing: that poor housing is caused by imperfections in the private market and that poor housing causes social problems that improved housing will alleviate; second is the role of the values of the middle class decision-maker, especially the belief in the distinction between the deserving and the undeserving poor, conceptions of a household's capacity to pay (i.e. minimum standards of living) and of general ideas of the good life, especially on what constitutes a 'good' environment; third is the failure to obtain information on what consumers are in need, on consumers' preferences and on other key aspects of the client groups; fourth is the diversion of resources from pursuit of the central aim of assisting those on low incomes to other aims such as urban renewal and area development in general; fifth, the perpetual disagreements over who is responsible for paying for housing those in most need, usually arguments between the Commonwealth and state governments.

Within the states the means tests applied by the various Commissions do not ensure that the poorest have easiest access to public housing. The Commissions could remedy these problems to some extent by making means tests less general: they should take into account more aspects of economic welfare, such as number of children and income of spouse, instead of relying on a maximum income level for the breadwinner. The other Commissions should also allocate on the basis of need for housing, like the QHC and WAHC, rather than working by waiting times alone.

Ideally, the Commissions require information on all Australian households cross-classified by size of family, income, assets and housing costs. This would enable the Commissions to work out priorities for specific groups on a much more systematic basis than at present. It is unlikely that comprehensive socio-economic information will be available in Australia in the foreseeable future. The 1971 Census of population did not contain questions on income or housing costs. Because the Commissions cannot discover the size of the groups in most need they must adopt a second-best method. They can supply housing to those in most need by using the comparative waiting times as a reasonable guide, supposing that the Commissions produce a range of dwellings that matched the preferences of the groups mentioned in chapter 4 as being in greatest need: the aged, single men and women, aborigines, the physically handicapped, and so on.

It is possible that even with rationalization of the allocation policies such as making the means tests more effective, public housing might not go strictly to the poor, because the distinction between the deserving and the undeserving poor is so deeply ingrained in social welfare thought. Likely reforms in this area are not so obvious. The one most frequently suggested —specialized social work services to the problem tenant—would probably be very expensive and is by no means guaranteed success since the problem tenant may not wish to reform, that is, he may not wish to exchange his values for western middle class ones. It seems doubtful from studies of other bureaucracies that the problem tenant will be given assistance. Welfare organizations of all sorts tend to help those who will respond most readily to the service—in this case the deserving poor—and neglect those who require disproportionately great resources and who may never respond with any obvious improvement. Besides, such a reversal of one of the basic tenets of the social welfare system is highly unlikely. An appeal system for 'problem' tenants in American public housing resulted in fewer evictions than under the previous system with no appeal (currently operating in Australian public housing). The appeal board included heavy representation from citizen volunteers and professionals.

A useful reorganization could be to administer welfare schemes along client group rather than function lines. At present the total supply of services to a particular group such as the aged involves a complex patchwork of Commonwealth, state, and local governments and numerous private agencies. Like most patchworks, such a system has gaps and anomalies such as the inability of a specialized but 'deserving' group of the poor, the physically handicapped, to make use of public housing for lack of modifications to cater for them. (The SAHT has done most for this particular group but even its efforts are inadequate.)

In many ways, the slum clearance activities of the Commissions, especially of the VHC, reflect some of the main faults in Australian public housing. While the consensus on the need for public housing in all states in the 1930s was remarkable, there seems never to have been any examination of the fundamental assumptions on which these programmes were based. The first principle was that poor housing causes social problems such as juvenile delinquency, poor health and crime. The almost unvarying coincidence of the two factors in the cities of the thirties does not justify the unquestioning assumption of causality, an assumption which has been proved false by recent research. It has become clear that the physical environment of old housing has very little, and social environment has a great deal, to do with general welfare, including even health. A second assumption was that, given the imperfections of the private housing market, the poor would never be adequately cared for; but again, this is questionable.

Emphasis on the physical environment at the expense of the social is one of the reasons for the VHC's concentration on inner area high-rise flats as a means of reviving the city centre. There is evidence that the communities in these flats are not as heterogeneous, at least in socio-economic terms, as in other types of development; they may be stigmatized, because of the size of the public housing concentration and the distinctive architecture; and they may be unsuitable for families with young children. On the other hand, since the proportion of housing in planned clearance areas which by the VHC's own definition are fit only for demolition is rapidly decreasing, much of the 'slum' housing destroyed in block clearance activities may be quite adequate physically, better suited to the occupant's taste, and provide a more satisfying social environment. The probability of this is increased by the VHC's failure to develop adequate criteria for classifying even the physical quality of housing. The ineffectiveness of slum clearance in improving the slum dwellers' housing is even more problematical if most of those removed in clearance areas are Greeks and Italians who have a strong desire to live with their countrymen and for whom the older inner suburban housing may provide adequate housing when compared with the public housing alternative. Combined with the inadequacies of the compensation system, these factors imply that the slum dweller may not get even marginally better housing—particularly if his preferences are considered—after clearance of an area.

There is apparent incompatibility between the VHC's main objective of assisting those on low incomes and the secondary aim of increasing inner city densities implicit in urban renewal policies. The limited evidence available indicates that redevelopment of inner areas is more expensive than new cottage developments or middle suburban flat construction—in some cases up to twice as expensive per dwelling provided. The replacement of 'slum' areas with middle income housing, aimed at producing a heterogeneous environment and increasing inner city rate revenues, also reduces the supply of finance for those on low incomes since the middle income redeveloped housing is highly subsidized, and reduces the supply of older housing available. Another aspect of the high-rise policy is that the concentration on high-rise flats not only provides a poor social environment but also, because of their expense and the necessary demolition of older houses for their erection, seriously reduces the amount of low income housing available if the areas were left alone or perhaps rehabilitated and other, cheaper forms of public housing constructed.

Emphasis on area development also often diverts resources from achieving the objective of housing the poor. Proportionately more housing is built in towns other than the metropolitan areas even though the latter are the major growth areas. Although the general aim of this policy is to encourage industrial decentralization, results in this direction are probably not significant since the housing is not concentrated in a few towns with 'growth' potential and is not allied systematically with other efforts to achieve decentralized development. Even where the policy is effective and industry is attracted to particular states, as in South Australia, this may not be in the interests of national welfare. Meanwhile, these policies result in the allocation of housing to a wide range of income groups, and eventually may redistribute income to the manufacturers who locate in areas with plentiful public housing. Such policies are most widespread in South Australia, but there the large amounts of money devoted to public housing (outside the CSHA) reduce the conflict between the aims of development and housing the poor.

Home ownership policies, though partly an expression of a strong preference for owning one's own home in all sectors of Australian society, also reflect the emphasis on helping those who attempt to help themselves. They also help the Commissions to avoid the losses involved in renting, and since the houses are sold at a profit they generate funds for the construction of more houses for the needy. Such policies generally aid social integration by encouraging population heterogeneity and stability, but, when intending purchasers are given preference, they mean that the more affluent are allocated housing before the poor who cannot afford to buy, and effectively take the dwelling off the lower income market. Further, such capital gains as there may be accrue to the initial occupant, which gives him equity with home owners outside public housing but advantages over the poor who cannot afford to buy.

The decision in 1956 to channel 30 per cent of all CSHA advances into co-operative societies is probably the greatest single factor diverting public housing funds away from the poor. The justifications for this step were various but in general were based on the theory that the co-operatives, by catering to the same group, would relieve the Commissions of some of their customers and at the same time, by operating through the private market, would allow more freedom of choice and avoid the bad points such as stigma that had been criticized in Housing Commission developments. The evidence presented above suggests that this has not happened: the market of the co-operative societies is of a substantially higher socio-economic status than any group in public housing except perhaps the clients in the QHC Workers' Dwellings scheme and the SAHT's middle income programme.

In 1971 Bob Hawke, the president of the powerful Australian Council of Trade Unions, said that the trade union movement intended to move into the housing finance field. Perhaps the unions can direct the co-operative society funds to those in greatest need of housing assistance. This may seem more realistic than arguing for the abandonment of the co-operative housing subsidy scheme. The co-operatives were still very well treated in the new CSHA in 1971. About 95 per cent of the $68 million a year that currently flows to co-operative housing societies in Australia is subsidized: about two-thirds comes from the CSHA and most of the rest is from banks, especially government banks and insurance companies, complying with federal government persuasion to invest in the co-operative societies as a community service. Very little of these scarce, subsidized funds is reaching those on low incomes. Firstly, as has been argued above, the allocation system for the money is heavily weighted against the poor and, secondly, compared with western Europe, very few of the co-operatives are formed by 'working class' organizations such as unions. If the unions in Australia decided to set up housing co-operatives they would have a very strong moral case for receiving much of the current funds from banks and insurance companies, particularly if they established administrative machinery to ensure that the funds allocated went to the poor. And since the co-operatives receive about $2 from the CSHA (at a low interest rate) for every $1 they raise from other sources there is no reason why they cannot obtain the bulk of CSHA finance. The unions' strongest weapon is the co-operatives' own rhetoric: that the societies cater to those on low incomes. In any event the publicity resulting from the union activities in this area might make the societies more socially responsive.

The failure to relate rents charged effectively to capacity to pay also leads to great inequities in the public housing system. The usual system of basing rents on historic costs not only favours those who have been public housing tenants for a long time (since it is based on the rent charged when the tenant first occupied the dwelling) but also by doing this tends to help older families who are generally past the stage of their life cycle where children are young and expenses highest. Further, although there is a rebate system it makes little allowance for the classic poverty groups of Australian society, such as the aged, female-headed households with dependent children, and aborigines, in which some households may have zero capacity to pay rent. Nor does it take into consideration the size of the family, although, since the Commissions cater largely to families with children, this is a crucial factor in determining equitable rents and the capacity of a household to pay. The so-called 'problem tenant' is usually detected after failure to pay rent, and it may be that to some groups such as aborigines failure to pay even a small rent is due to lack of capacity rather than unwillingness or irresponsibility. Reform of rent policy by relating it more effectively to capacity to pay would at least enable the two groups to be distinguished. Probably the most worthwhile change would be to introduce an averaging system based on the market value of the dwelling but incorporating a far more effective rebate system. A system of market rents, too, could be worth while if it induced more affluent tenants to buy their dwellings, thus generating profits. But rent reform policies will face the political difficulties of raising some rents and the general strong feeling that those who improve themselves—the obviously deserving poor—should not be penalized.

The next inequity in the supply of public housing in Australia is due to the federal system which favours the less populous states, allowing them to build proportionately more housing. The pattern of vacancies reinforces this bias so that the poor household in New South Wales or Victoria is less likely to obtain public housing than its exact counterpart in the states with smaller populations.

Disagreement between Commonwealth and states as to responsiblity for losses involved in housing those on the lowest incomes means that Australian public housing does not give maximum assistance to the poor. Desire to avoid and offset losses was a main cause of the emphasis placed on house sales, and therefore of the effects of these policies in reducing the supply of housing to the very poor. There is no easy solution to this problem. On the one hand, the states are reluctant for political reasons to raise rents, especially since the 'rich tenants' in public housing feel they have as much right to the benefits of inflation as home owners outside public housing and that they should not have to subsidize the poorer tenant through increased rents; on the other hand, the Commonwealth is naturally unwilling to join in loss-sharing arrangements when the states, for their own reasons, are not doing all possible to cut these losses. There is also little doubt that when public housing benefits such a wide range of income groups many taxpayers will begrudge paying for such a haphazardly administered subsidy. A possible model for the future is in the 1969 Aged Persons' Homes Act, which provides non-repayable grants from the Commonwealth for a specific group of the poor (single aged pensioners in the inner areas of capital cities). This system of finance could be broadened to include other groups unable to pay normal CSHA economic rents, like female householders with dependent children, and the physically handicapped.

In 1971 the states made the reduction of the CSHA interest rate—6 per cent—the main platform in their submissions on the new CSHA made necessary by the expiry of the 1966–71 Agreement. The Commonwealth Housing Department supported the claim for a reduction in the interest rate but the federal Treasury was not in favour: a high interest rate is anti-inflationary in a small way. Consequently, when the agreement was renewed in August 1971 (with only minor changes otherwise), instead of tying the CSHA interest rate to 1 per cent below the long-term bond rate, the Commonwealth raised it to the equivalent of the long-term bond level (currently 7 per cent). In place of the concessional interest rate, the Commonwealth offered a cash, non-repayable grant that more than equalled the previous concession. In addition, the Commonwealth offered another non-repayable cash grant to help the states to cover the losses on housing those unable to pay economic rents. This amounted to $2¾ million a year to be shared between all the states.

There is a good case for keeping the CSHA interest rate at a high level. Firstly, it makes the Commissions very cost conscious by forcing up the economic rent on new dwellings so that many of the tenants are unable to pay the economic rent and have to be allowed rebates. Secondly, it could help to force the states to reform their rental policies, especially the raising of older rents, an action that would easily allow them to pay the CSHA interest rate while still charging low rents overall. Lastly, it means that the subsidy for tenants who improve their economic position after entry into public housing is not as great as it has been. In addition, those who purchase Commission dwellings would not get as great a subsidy as they have enjoyed through low interest rates and the benefits of inflation. Only a high initial interest rate on CSHA funds can prevent those who no longer really need the subsidy from obtaining it. Those in need can be assisted through the rental rebate system, preferably in a revised form. As usual, however, the Commonwealth plans to do very little to ensure that the grants under the new CSHA actually mean more public housing for the really poor. The states still have complete control over their allocation policies. The VHC could continue using Commonwealth funds for wasteful block clearance. There is no guarantee that the Commonwealth grants will not be used as a substitute for the rental increases that, although justified by inflation, the state politicians are loath to execute.

The inefficiency of rent, home ownership, and general allocation policies in subsidizing the poor has, ironically, had a good effect on the social integration of public housing developments by allowing a wide range of socio-economic groups into public housing, continuing the subsidy to encourage the upwardly mobile to remain in public housing, and excluding such tenants as are likely to create problems and stigmatize Housing Commission areas. Another factor which helps to ward off stigma is that most of the dwellings provided are cottages, the type of dwelling that the vast majority of the population at all economic levels occupies. The only exceptions to this are the NSWHC and especially the VHC emphasis on large inner area flat developments which may be highly stigmatized. Cottage developments in outer areas may also lose attractiveness by the delays in providing services, especially to new developments. This is sometimes due to poor co-ordination but is more often a function of simple overall lack of resources in the public sector. Similar integration effects might be achieved, however, without the inefficiencies of the rent and home ownership policies, by scattering the dwellings built among private housing in the middle and outer suburbs. The social benefits of this and the economies of efficient allocation would probably balance the loss of the economies of scale, particularly in land development, achieved through the present policies. Another worthwhile adjustment would be to allow groups who wished to live together to do so in public housing. This is already done to some extent for the aged, but other groups like non-western migrants, aborigines, and 'Skid Row' men would also benefit from such a policy.

It is difficult to see how there can be any major reforms in Australian public housing without much more control by the Commonwealth over the funds it allocates. The 1969 aged persons' home scheme was a good model for future policy. It makes sure that the homes are allocated to those pensioners in need. This may seem strange at a time when all the popular feeling is against centralization. A dependence on state discretion will only perpetuate the tremendous wastage of funds that is currently the hallmark of the public housing programme. The Commonwealth should extend the same close controls to the money it gives to the co-operative societies and under the Aged Persons' Homes Act (which involves voluntary associations). It can use its conditional grants powers as it did under the 1969 aged legislation and widen this to specific groups such as homeless men, large families, the handicapped and other groups neglected under present policy. It would involve more detailed administration than at present but the sort of close controls envisaged operate successfully in many areas of Commonwealth-state policy, for example in the Commonwealth Bureau of Roads. The existing CSHA should be scrapped for it is too general and therefore highly ineffective in reaching the poor. With more controls over state expenditure the Commonwealth would be much more willing to pay for the losses involved in housing those in most need of housing assistance. A loss-sharing arrangement without detailed federal controls over state expenditure would be economic madness. From federal Labor Party policy statements it seems that a Labor government would be likely to place very detailed controls on all federal housing funds.

Public housing and urban planning

Quite often, what appears at first glance to be a housing problem is really a failure in general urban planning. The basic argument for urban planning is that the urban economy is highly interdependent. The demand for housing, for example, is very closely linked with the demand for land, water, sewerage, telephones, transport, schools and numerous other amenities. Unless the planning of these services is properly co-ordinated, and a sufficient volume of resources devoted to them to start with, the supply of land for urban housing will be restricted, forcing up land prices for newly released land and raising prices for houses in the existing stock. There is general agreement that poor planning practices in Australian capital cities have something to do with the problem of spiralling land costs. The case for urban planning using the principles developed in Canberra and in Elizabeth, South Australia, is eloquently presented by Hugh Stretton in his 1970 book, *Ideas for Australian Cities*, and need not be expanded here. G. M. Neutze, of the Urban Research Unit at the Australian National University, argues for the establishment of a government land corporation to make the release and development of the metropolitan fringe areas a more economical process than it is now ('The Price of Land for Urban Development', *Economic Record*, 1970). General urban planning reforms could make housing costs lower, but, of course, not help substantial numbers of families who still could not afford to pay market prices.

Urban planning is a glamorous profession. Decisions made by a bureaucrat today may well affect the welfare of thousands of families both now and in the future. Moulding the environment is part of the progress fixation basic to western thought. Hence it is no surprise that many of the top administrators in the Housing Commissions want to broaden the Commissions' role in general urban planning. This is so particularly in Sydney and Melbourne. The VHC's attempt to become the Melbourne urban renewal authority was a good example of this trend. One important reason why the Commissions should not be given any further planning function—and possibly be stripped of their existing ones—is that they already have more than enough on their plate. This book has illustrated many faults in current policy, the problem tenant dilemma, for example, which could keep the Commission occupied for many years to come. Moreover, despite the hopes of the original founders, Australian public housing authorities now have a generally very small role in the metropolitan housing market. In 1969–70, the Housing Commissions completed an average of about 8 per cent of the total metropolitan completions of houses and flats, ranging from 5 per cent in Sydney and Brisbane, 7 per cent in Melbourne, 11 per cent in Adelaide and Perth, to a high of 20 per cent in Hobart. With such a small and generally falling percentage of new metropolitan dwelling construction, it is difficult to see how the Commissions can influence urban development to any great extent under present organization. As in the NSWHC estate at Mt

Druitt in Sydney, the Commissions may appear to extend the city in certain directions but it could be argued that, at best, this simply precedes normal metropolitan extension in that direction and cities often extend on the authorization of the general planning bodies such as the state planning authority in New South Wales.

It is difficult to see that the Commissions have any special competence as general urban planners. As Stretton argues, the SAHT is the one state housing authority that has distinguished itself in the quality of its planning. He claims that the two largest Commissions—the NSWHC and the VHC—have distinguished themselves by their blunders over urban renewal in Melbourne and Green Valley in Sydney. Even so, this book has argued that the SAHT achievements have not been gained without costs, especially the massive costs of subsidizing middle income groups to live in SAHT houses. The Commissions are not at all suited to coping with the demands for participation and consultation that will be the main characteristic of planning in the future. Like old-style urban planners, they have become used to government by decree. With very few detailed controls over their activities, the Commissions can build an extraordinary variety of dwellings, from VHC 30-storey flats to the SAHT middle income cottages. Australian public housing is so heavily subsidized and the waiting lists are so long that the Commissions can fill virtually any type of housing they build. Low income clients, and gift recipients generally, are not normally complainers. This is far distant from the sort of sensitive understanding of consumers' preferences that will be the most important single feature of future urban planning.

There is the possibility that reducing housing costs by improved productivity will help to provide adequate housing to those unable to afford it under present cost structures. There seems little hope of this. For many years architects have argued the case for prefabrication in housing construction but almost all Housing Commissions have experimented at some time. None has been able to provide housing cheaper than using normal methods. The VHC concrete housing factory is one example of a prefabrication scheme. Apart from stressing prefabrication in the construction of individual houses, architects have vehemently argued that the higher the density of housing development, the cheaper the overall costs. Hence, according to them, middle density flats are cheaper than cottages and high-rise flats are cheaper still. This has continued to be part of the conventional wisdom in much town planning despite all the evidence to the contrary. In a brilliant article Peter Harrison of the Urban Research Unit at the Australian National University points out that the single cottage is still the cheapest form of accommodation, even allowing for the overall service costs (N. Clark (ed.), *The Analysis of Urban Development*, Melbourne, 1970). Harrison points out that residential land accounts for only about one-third of the land use in most cities and that any attempt to increase residential densities calls for increases in many of the non-housing facilities: schools, hospitals, and so on. The savings in services are non-existent, and indeed, as is shown in chapter 5, they are more expensive in higher densities. Even taking the residential land alone, multi-unit dwellings require much more open space than do cottage developments with their private space. Finally, multi-unit dwellings with load bearing walls and other costly building forms are more expensive than the single cottage, costs rising with the density.

Coupled with the cost disadvantages of high-density living are the social effects: the loss of privacy; the inflexibility of the dwelling unit to changes in the life cycle; the difficulty of controlling children where there is no secure open space; and the many other features of higher density accommodation that make it unsuitable for families with young children, the major public housing clients. It is ironic that for all the professional talk about high-density accommodation, very few private flats or home units are used by families with young children. It is most unjust that poor families with children should be forced to bear the costs of an ideology which is not only false but is not followed by other sections of the community. The Commissions can do it only because they are dealing with many people in desperate situations. The lower the income, the less the choice.

Participation, local governments and welfare

As in practically all Australian social welfare organizations, there is virtually no client participation in Australian public housing. Participation is not regarded as the panacea that it has become overseas. In 1970 a new Urban Renewal Act was passed by the Victorian government giving a semblance of participation in future VHC urban renewal. But twelve months after it has been passed things are no different from before. Like the United States participation programmes, the administrators see it as a public relations tool that gets over their message accurately. It is based on the assumption that the only problem in urban renewal is a communication blockage: the people affected have not understood the nobility of the policy and how it will help them. This assumption is wrong. Residents interviewed in areas affected gave the impression that they did fully understand the message but they did not like it. With all the rhetoric about participation the VHC still has unlimited power to do what it likes, all the participation 'safeguards' being advisory only. Critics argue that if the VHC was really interested in participation it would drop the incredible powers that allow it to clear any area it wishes, without justification. Instead it would prepare a case on a given area, and after much thorough research and careful consideration of the costs of all alternatives it would contest the plan in the courts, allowing other people—and there are many professionals who have prepared fully costed alternatives to VHC plans—to voice their views. In 1971 people in one area to be cleared in Fitzroy succeeded in bringing a case against the VHC but it is unlikely to succeed, given the VHC powers.

As in most cases of so-called participation, most of those representing the people in slum clearance areas are professionals who do their best to consult the residents on their actual opinions, but there are obvious problems of imposing professional values on low income people. The VHC used this argument as a reason for stating that what the organizations say is not what the people think. Then, like so many organizations, it uses the lack of knowledge as a policy instrument. It says that it simply doesn't know and therefore cannot debate. Survey research is a highly refined technique and there is no reason why properly administered it could not give a very accurate picture of what the residents really feel. But the VHC has never done this and argues that it does not have the money, even though the main result of the new Urban Renewal Act in 1970 was the creation of two new jobs as Urban Renewal Commissioners on salaries of over $14,000 per annum each. In one year that money would cover quite a lot of surveys.

The fear of centralization has become so great that many professionals, especially social workers, are placing their hopes in local government to solve many welfare problems. In many influential areas this is also looked upon as a panacea, but this is too optimistic a view to be acceptable. The history of social welfare planning in Australia is full of instances where local government was given the opportunity to do constructive things but failed to do so. The creation of the State Housing Commissions was largely the response of the failure of local government to improve housing conditions. Local councils were allowed to participate in the Commonwealth aged persons' homes schemes but their response to date has been very poor indeed. Britain is perhaps the best example of the results of placing such important services as housing and education under local government jurisdiction. The quality of services differs among local government areas and is dependent on the quality and administrative competence of the leaders. Even in Britain where the local councils have much more responsibility than in Australia local government politics is noted for its short-term opportunist approach to problems, with 'jobs for the boys', and it is not an accident that the British welfare services are studied as an example of a bureaucratic nightmare, a fragmented jungle.

There is another problem. In general, the quality of services in a local government area is dependent on the wealth in that area. If the area is rich then the area will have very good facilities, and if it is poor then it will have poor services. This can be overcome by some form of redistribution between rich and poor but this is not an easy task. But perhaps the most important case against local government is the limitation of all attempts to redistribute income in the form of goods and services rather than simply as cash grants. This is argued in the section of income supplements and is a very powerful argument indeed. Yet many professionals want to compound past errors by vastly increasing the number of relevant government departments, making the co-ordination problem even more difficult, creating a diversity of confusion rather than being constructive. It is difficult to understand the support for the local government idea. It is probably partly a response to the cry for participation. But the problem that was discussed in chapter 5 arises: participation usually becomes either a public relations exercise or a situation where middle class professionals decide for those on lower incomes. And professional groups are not entirely altruistic about this. Local governments could become major employers of social workers. It is no substitute for broadly based research with a good theoretical foundation that looks at objectives, costs and benefits of alternatives and uses survey research to find out consumer preferences but does not artificially limit the scope of the surveys to preconceived professional ideas. Another important factor is the nostalgia many people have for the small community, making its own decisions, heavily involved with its own problems.

Even where there is a community there is little evidence that many of its problems could be solved by voluntary action or advice from social workers. The problems of Green Valley in Sydney, for example, are overwhelmingly problems of income distribution, a conflict problem rarely solved by mutual co-operation. Nor are local governments a particularly efficient means of advertising social services. The private market is fully aware of the effectiveness of radio, television and newspapers to sell its products. The argument for local social workers as a humanizing force is also rather weak. Obtaining a service, or even an income, through a welfare worker is much more stigmatizing than the anonymity of a cash supplement through the post.

Research and planning

Perhaps the greatest failure of Australian public housing is the unwillingness to do research into crucial issues, especially the size and characteristics of the subgroups of those in need and other aspects of the Commission–client relationship discussed in this book. The Commissions do not systematically advertise their services except to the sought-after skilled workers for area development schemes discussed in chapter 6.

There is evidence to show that the poor know less about the workings of the bureaucracy and the benefits to be gained from it, and that in general their consumer practices are less efficient. No Commission advertises effectively to the poor, in contrast to suppliers on the private housing market, and admission to a waiting list is dependent on completely unsolicited application. It would therefore be expected that the wealthier, better educated groups would know more about the Commissions' operations and therefore stand to gain more than the lowest income groups. The obverse of providing information to potential customers, gathering information about them—the extent of the lower income groups, their distribution, and their preferences in housing—is equally neglected. What research is done by the Commissions is usually concerned with improvements in technical aspects such as the dwellings themselves and the site planning rather than with the people involved—a preoccupation revealed very clearly by the annual reports of the Commissions; with cutting the losses involved in existing programmes;

and with detecting better ways of implementing already decided policies without any attempt to question fundamental assumptions and decisions. These limitations are an effect (as well as a cause) of the tendency of the Commissions to assess their progress in terms of the amount of housing produced rather than whether or not they are housing those in most need most effectively.

Finally, professionals probably overemphasize the importance of research. There is no doubt that even if research were to produce an excellent plan of action there would be enormous barriers to its implementation. But at least there would be a plan of action, a direction, a clarification of ends and means that might have some chance of implementation at least in the long run. To fail to look ahead and transcend immediate political and bureaucratic constraints is to ossify the public housing programme. The reformers who fought for the introduction of public housing expected policy to be altered in the light of experience; it was an experiment rather than a memorial.

1972 Developments

In May 1972 it seemed likely that the federal Liberal government would adopt a scheme for the capitalization of child endowment to help young families pay for a house. The amount payable would vary according to family size, press reports indicating that it could be as much as $3,000 for a six child family. This scheme is open to a number of objections. Firstly, by capitalizing child endowment in one sum the family foregoes the regular monthly income that could be vital in helping low income families to care for their children. This suggests that only those affluent enough to do without longer-term child endowment could take advantage of the scheme. Secondly, for the scheme to be of any real use, a family would have to have a considerable number of children. Public housing authorities' experience shows that low income families with children desperately need housing assistance just after the birth of the first child when the wife usually leaves the work-force and more housing space is needed. As more children arrive the situation worsens so that only the fairly affluent can raise the thousands of dollars necessary to bridge the gap between the amount of capitalized child endowment and the deposit required. As with other Liberal Party housing programmes, it is likely that the means test, if there is one, will be very loose. Therefore the plan continues the general pattern of housing policy criticized in this book: policy too often helps those who could already help themselves. Ironically, the scheme is copied from a New Zealand plan which has been severely criticized in the 1972 Report of the Royal Commission of Inquiry into Social Security in New Zealand.

BIBLIOGRAPHIC ESSAY

A major source of information is the unpublished records of the State Housing Commissions as well as interviews with the Commissions' officers. Another very important source was the mainly unpublished data from the Commonwealth Bureau of Census and Statistics. Other general sources, used very extensively, are the Housing Commissions' Annual Reports, the state and federal *Parliamentary Debates*, and the mainly unpublished proceedings of the Commonwealth and State Housing Ministers' Conferences from 1945 to 1970. The latter were particularly valuable.

INTRODUCTION

Any reader new to the field of Australian urban planning and public housing should read Hugh Stretton, *Ideas for Australian Cities*, Adelaide, 1970. The other important Australian research works in the field are Alan Hall and Malcolm Hill, 'Housing Demand in Australia 1959-74', *Economic Record*, Vol. 36, No. 76, December 1960, pp. 550-67; Malcolm Hill, *Housing Finance in Australia 1945-1965*, Melbourne, 1959; Malcolm Hill, 'Housing Finance Institutions' in R. R. Hirst and R. H. Wallace, *Studies in the Australian Capital Market*, Melbourne, 1967, pp. 98-129; Mary McLelland, 'Needs and Services in an Outer Suburb', *Australian Journal of Social Issues*, Vol. 3, No. 1, April 1968, pp. 44-62; David Scott and Robert U'Ren, *Leisure: A Social Enquiry into Leisure Activities and Needs in an Australian Housing Estate*, Melbourne, 1962; Anne Stevenson, Elaine Martin and Judith O'Neill, *High Living—A Study of Family Life in Flats*, Melbourne, 1967. In the past five years there has been a veritable flood of American research on public housing, most of it theoretical. This literature was very helpful as a background for empirical research on policy. A selection is James Russell Prescott, 'The Economics of Public Housing—A Normative Analysis', Ph.D. thesis, Harvard University, Cambridge, 1966, microfilmed; Richard Edward Wagner, 'The Incidence of Public Expenditure—Public Housing as an Illustrative Example', Ph.D. thesis, University of Virginia, 1966, microfilmed; Edgar Oliver Olsen, 'A Welfare Economic Evaluation of Public Housing', Ph.D. thesis, Rice University, 1968, microfilmed; Robert L. Bish, 'Public Housing: the magnitude and distribution of direct benefits and effects on housing consumption', *Journal of Regional Science*, Vol. 9, No. 3, December 1969, pp. 425-38 (this article is a summary of a doctoral thesis which is unavailable); Edgar O. Olsen, 'A Normative Theory of Transfers', *Public Choice*, Vol. 6, spring 1969, pp. 39-58; Edgar O. Olsen, *Should Government Transfers be adjusted for geographic cost differences*, Rand Corporation Staff Papers, P 4105, January 1969; Joseph S. De Salvo, *A Methodology for Evaluating Housing Programmes*, Rand Corporation Staff Papers, P 4364, April 1970; Jerome Rothenberg, *Economic Evaluation of Urban Renewal: Conceptual Foundations of Benefit Cost Analysis,* Washington, 1967; Charles Wade Clifton, 'Toward a Model of the Housing Market', Ph.D. thesis, University of Michigan, 1970, microfilmed; C. B. Weisman, 'The Study of a Conditional Benefit: subsidized public housing', Ph.D. thesis, Columbia University, 1970, microfilmed.

For a general discussion on the growth of social services in Australia see T. H. Kewley, *Social Security in Australia—the Development of Social Security and Health Benefits from 1900 to the Present,* Sydney University Press, Sydney, 1965. There is a large literature on the growth of the social welfare view of housing. The first notable government document was in 1860. See Henry Parkes, Chairman, *Report of the Select Committee on the Condition of the Working Classes of the Metropolis, 18 April 1860,* Sydney, 1860. The necessity to improve the housing conditions of the metropolis was the major recommendation of the Committee. This tradition was continued in a report in 1913, by Professor R. F. Irvine, *Investigations into the Housing of Workmen in England and America,* Sydney, 1913. The last major report on housing conditions in Sydney was in 1937, *Interim Report of the Housing Conditions Investigation Commission,* Sydney, 1937. In Melbourne the first major report was in 1913, *Progress Report of the Joint Select Committee on the housing of the people in the Metropolis together with minutes of evidence and appendices,* Melbourne, 1913. The most detailed and sophisticated publication was the report of the Victorian Commission in 1937, Housing Investigation and Slum Abolition Board, *First (Progress) Report with Appendices and Supplements, Slum Reclamation and Housing the Lower Paid Worker,* Melbourne, 1937. In Adelaide the main study is the *Report of the Building Act's Enquiry Committee,* Adelaide, 1940. On the Commonwealth level the main document was a reflection of the literature developed in the states, especially Victoria. See *4th Interim Report from the Joint Committee on Social Security,* 20 May 1941, Canberra, 1944. Also *Final Report of the Commonwealth Housing Commission, 1944,* Canberra, 1944. A good indicator of post-war opinion favouring the short-term view of public housing is Walter Bunning, W. H. Ifould, C. R. McKerihan and Sidney J. Luker, *The Housing Situation in Australia—Papers Read to the Winter Forum of the Australian Institute of Political Science,* Sydney, 1947. A testimonial to Oswald Barnett's influence on Australian public housing is Oswald Barnett, 'The Economics of the Slums', M.Comm. thesis, University of Melbourne, 1931. For evidence of the religious backing for the anti-slum movement see E. W. Russell, 'Ideology and Social Orders—Some Movements in Victorian Politics 1930-50', B.A.(Hons) thesis in Political Science, University of Melbourne, 1967.

An excellent general account of society's attitude to social problems is David Matza, *Becoming Deviant,* New Jersey, 1969. Matza stresses the distinction between the deserving and the undeserving poor. McLoughlin notes that aesthetic goals are the oldest and possibly the most important aim in urban planning in J. Brian McLoughlin, *Urban and Regional Planning—a systems approach,* New York, 1969. This is also stressed by Wallace F. Smith, *Housing—The Social and Economic Elements,* Berkeley, 1970. The basic reference work which comprises a report of a large-scale research project as well as an extensive review of other work is Daniel M. Wilner, Rosabelle Price Walkley, Thomas C. Pinkerton and Matthew Tayback, *The Housing Environment and Family Life—A Longitudinal Study of the Effects of Housing on Morbidity and Mental Health,*

Baltimore, 1962. Other studies on the effects of improved housing were carried out at Korea, Monterey, Mexico, Venezuela, the Pine Ridge Indian Reservation in South Dakota, central California, and central Puerto Rico—Leland S. Burns *et al.* (eds), International Housing Productivity Study, 'Housing in Regional Economic Development and Planning', *The Annals of Regional Science,* Vol. 11, No. 2, December 1969, pp. 100-10. Studies of delinquency that are sceptical of blaming housing are Bernard Lander, *Towards an Understanding of Juvenile Delinquency*, New York, 1954; Richard A. Cloward and Lloyd E. Ohlin, *Delinquency and Opportunity—a Theory of Delinquent Gangs*, New York, 1960. On whether the housing market is competitive see William G. Grigsby, *Housing Markets and Public Policy*, Philadelphia, 1966; Richard F. Muth, *Cities and Housing—The Spatial Patterns of Urban Residential Land Use*, Chicago, 1969; George Sternleib, *The Tenement Landlord*, New Jersey, 1966; D. V. Donnison, Christine Cockburn and T. Corlett, *Housing Since the Rent Act*, London, 1961; Adela Adam Nevitt, *Housing, Taxation and Subsidies*, London, 1966; J. B. Cullingworth, *Housing in Transition—a Case Study of the City of Lancaster 1958-62*, London, 1963. For a review of these studies see D. V. Donnison, 'Research and Policy in Housing: Current Developments in Britain', *JOAIP*, Vol. 33, No. 2, March 1967, pp. 123-6; Edgar O. Olsen, 'A Competitive Theory of the Housing Market', *American Economic Review*, Vol. 59, No. 4, Pt. 1, September 1969, pp. 612-22. For an extensive review of studies on low income consumer behaviour see Louise G. Richards, 'Consumer Practices of the Poor', *Welfare in Review*, Vol. 13, No. 11, November 1965, pp. 1-13. The basic work on consumer protection is David Caplovitz, *The Poor Pay More: Consumer Practices of Low Income Families*, New York, 1963. Externalities are clearly discussed in Otto Davis and Andrew B. Whinston, 'The Economics of Urban Renewal', *Law and Contemporary Problems*, Vol. 26, winter 1961, pp. 105-17; Jerome Rothenberg, *Economic Evaluation of Urban Renewal—Conceptual Foundations of Benefit Cost Analysis*, Washington, 1967. The theory on industrial location—and it gives little causal role to housing—is reviewed in William Alonso, 'Location Theory' in J. Friedmann and William Alonso, *Regional Development and Planning*, Cambridge, 1965, pp. 78-106. Some Australian material is Tom McKnight, 'Industrial Location in South Australia', *Australian Geographical Studies*, Vol. 5, No. 1, April 1967, pp. 50-72; Arnold Kan, 'Some Aspects of Local Forces in the Establishment of Secondary Industries in Victorian Country Districts 1947-66', *Economic Activity—Studies in Economics and Business*, Vol. 12, No. 2, April 1969, pp. 8-17. An academic supporter of the use of slum clearance policy for countercyclical purposes is Alan R. Hall, *Housing Trends and Economic Growth*, Melbourne, 1961, pp. 15-16. The role of housing policy in economic stabilization in the United States is discussed in Leo Grebler, *Housing Issues in Economic Stabilzation Policy*, New York, 1960.

STATE DIFFERENCES

A useful reference work on the complicated nature of Australian federalism is James A. Maxwell, *Commonwealth-State Financial Relations in Australia*, Melbourne, 1967. The Commonwealth Treasury annual publication, *Commonwealth Payments to or for the States*, gives a wealth of information on how the states fare from Commonwealth hand-outs. The *Reports of the Commonwealth*

Grants Commission are also very valuable. The Commonwealth Bureau of Census and Statistics produces a yearly bulletin that contains historical series on completions and much other information—*Building and Construction.* The Commonwealth Department of Housing produces, among other things, an annual review of housing policy, the latest called *Housing 1969-70.* The Department, however, is mainly concerned with the stability of the building industry and with ensuring that a sufficient volume of resources go into housing. It does not keep very close controls or information on the state housing authorities.

MEANS TESTS

An example of an extremely simplistic federal attempt to measure the level of housing 'needs' is the Department of National Development, *The Housing Situation,* Canberra, 1956. J. B. Cullingworth discusses general methods of measuring housing needs in 'The Measurement of Housing Need', *British Journal of Sociology,* Vol. 9, 1958, pp. 341-58. There is a vast literature on measuring poverty. A good argument for looking at expenditure as well as income is Martin David, 'Welfare, Income and Budget Needs', *Review of Economics and Statistics,* Vol. 41, No. 4, November 1959, p. 395. The application of different poverty lines—based on a variety of value judgments—is used extensively in Allan Halladay, 'Poverty among Large Families in Sydney 1968-9', Ph.D. thesis, A.N.U., 1971. See also, Samuel Mencher, 'The Problem of Measuring Poverty', *British Journal of Sociology,* Vol. 18, No. 1, 1967, pp. 1-12; R. J. A. Harper, 'Survey of Living Conditions in Melbourne 1966', *The Economic Record,* Vol. 43, No. 2, June 1967, pp. 262-88; S. M. Miller, Martin Rein, Pamela Roby and Bertram M. Gross, 'Poverty, Inequality and Conflict', *The Annals of the American Academy of Political and Social Science,* Vol. 373, September 1967, pp. 16-52. The socio-economic status code is discussed and listed in detail in Leonard Broom, F. Lancaster Jones, Jerzy Zubrzycki, 'An Occupational Classification of the Australian Workforce', *The Australian and New Zealand Journal of Sociology,* Vol. 1, No. 2, October 1965 (Supplement). See also Leonard Broom, F. Lancaster Jones and Jerzy Zubrzycki, 'Social Stratification in Australia' in J. A. Jackson (ed.), *Social Stratification,* Sociological Studies, No. 1, Cambridge, 1968. No attempt is made to reduce the Census data to a single numerical indicator comprising weighted elements from the occupational, educational, birthplace, motor vehicle ownership and marital status data. Such a technique has been used by F. Lancaster Jones, *The Dimensions of Urban Social Structure The Social Areas of Melbourne, Australia,* Canberra, 1969. For the present study, it was felt that the data on socio-economic status were an imperfect indicator and that extreme reduction in the available classifications was undesirable.

POVERTY GROUPS

The connection between poverty and the number of children in a family has been discussed by Margaret Wynn, *Family Policy,* London, 1970; Alvin V. Schorr, 'The Family Cycle and Income Development', *Social Security Bulletin,* Vol. 29, No. 2, February 1966. pp. 14-25; James C. Vadakin, *Children, Poverty and Family Allowances,* New York, 1968, pp. 7-17; Allan Halladay, 'Poverty among Large Families in Sydney 1968-9', Ph.D. thesis, A.N.U., 1971. Halladay argues that Australian social services do not go very far in covering the costs of having children; hence the widespread poverty amongst large low income families. For the VHC emphasis on high-rise flats see VHC, *Housing Commission Victoria—First 25 Years*, Melbourne, 1963. For the surveys on what the residents think of flat living see Lindsay Thompson, *Victorian Housing—Today and Tomorrow*, Melbourne, 1965; also Anne Stevenson, Elaine Martin and Judith O'Neill, *High Living—a Study of Family Life in Flats*, Melbourne, 1967. The WAHC change to high-rise construction is described in the WAHC *Annual Report for 1966-7*. The Commissions' treatment of migrants was documented partly from their own records and partly from Department of National Development Circular, 'Eligibility of Migrants for State Housing Authority Houses', mimeographed, 18 September 1963. The high incidence of poverty amongst Greek and Italian migrants can be seen from J. McCaughey, 'Migrant Study', Institute of Applied Economic Research, Melbourne Poverty Survey, mimeographed, Melbourne, 1968. About the only systematic Australian research on aged poverty is R. F. Henderson, Alison Harcourt and R. J. A. Harper, *People in Poverty—A Melbourne Survey*, Melbourne, 1970. Irving Rosow, *The Social Integration of the Aged*, New York, 1967, is an excellent work on the things that aged people think important. An historical account of the Commonwealth Aged Persons' Homes scheme is in T. Kewley, *Social Security in Australia*, Sydney, 1964, and in the *Annual Reports of the Director-General of Social Services*, Canberra, 1955. An illuminating Commonwealth survey of the Aged Persons' Homes scheme is in Commonwealth Department of Social Services, 'Survey of Aged Persons' Homes', June 1967, mimeographed, August 1968. Most Housing Ministers' Conferences and Premiers' Conferences include some material on the long disputes on aged housing between the Commonwealth and the states. Some of these conference proceedings are published. Evidence of relatively poor domiciliary services to the aged in Australia is in R. F. Henderson *et al.*, *People in Poverty*, Melbourne, 1970. This is also a useful source on female households and poverty, as are Mollie Orshansky, 'Counting the Poor—Another Look at the Poverty Profile', *Social Security Bulletin*, Vol. 28, No. 1, January 1965, pp. 3-24; and Alison Harcourt, 'Poverty and the Widow', *The Australian Journal of Social Issues*, Vol. 4, No. 2, July 1969, pp. 49-59. There is little information on the physically handicapped in Australia. Probably the best source—and very critical of existing services—is the Australian Senate Standing Committee on Health and Welfare, *Report on Mentally and Physically Handicapped Persons in Australia*, Canberra, 1971. The details of SAHT houses for the handicapped are in the SAHT *Annual Report for 1966-7*. For details of the specialized design requirements of housing for the disabled see U.S. Department of Housing and Urban Development, *Housing for the Physically Impaired—a Guide for Planning and Design*, U.S. Government Printer, Washington, 1967. Details of the Commonwealth assistance to the handicapped are in *Annual Report of the Commonwealth Department of Social Services 1968-9*, Canberra, 1970.

Methods of classifying 'problem families' are given in S. M. Miller, 'The American Lower Class; A Typological Approach', *Social Research*, Vol. 31, No. 1, 1964, pp. 1-22; John Spencer, 'The Multi-Problem Family', in Benjamin Schlesinger (ed.), *The Multi-Problem Family—A Review and Annotated Bibliography*, Toronto, 1965; Roger Wilson, 'Difficult Housing Estates', *Human Relations*, Vol. 16, No. 1, February 1963, pp. 3-43. For an extensive review of the literature see Abner D. Silverman, *Selected Aspects of Administration of Publicly Owned Housing—Great Britain, Netherlands and Sweden*, Washington, 1961. Rossi argues that five factors characterize the 'culture of poverty': (i) low level of labour force participation; (ii) low level of skills when employed; (iii) high rates of marital instability (desertion, divorce, separation) high proportion of households headed by women—unstable interpersonal relations; (iv) low status residential areas—low level of participation in community agencies; (v) a sense of helplessness and low need achievement in Peter Rossi and Z. Blum, 'Social Class Research and Images of the Poor: A Bibliographical Review', in D. Moynihan (ed.), *Understanding Poverty—Perspectives from the Social Sciences*, New York, 1969. A study that showed how poor rent payment was a symptom of general instability is W. B. Herbert, 'Who Owes Rent', *Sociological Review*, New Series, Vol. 13, No. 2, July 1965, pp. 149-56. Alan Jordan's work on 'Skid Row' men in Melbourne is largely unpublished. Most of my references to him are from personal communications. A brief note is Alan Jordan, 'Rehabilitation Hostels for Homeless Alcoholic Men', a paper delivered at A.N.Z.-A.A.S. Conference, Adelaide, August 1969, mimeographed. See also N. Linsell, 'Detached—A Study of Homeless Men in the City of Melbourne', *Australian Journal of Social Work*, Vol. 15, No. 2, December 1962, pp. 8-11. A basic reference on aboriginal population trends is F. Lancaster Jones, *The Structure and Growth of Australia's Aboriginal Population*, A.N.U. Press, Canberra, 1970. Jones estimates that the aboriginal population will reach half a million by the year 2000. In 1970 the Australian National University began publication of an excellent series on Australian aborigines. The most important of them are C. D. Rowley's *The Destruction of Aboriginal Society*, Canberra, 1971 and Ronald Taft, John L. M. Dawson and Pamela Beasley, *Attitudes and Social Conditions (The Australian Aborigines)*, Canberra, 1970. Also interesting are Ian G. Sharp and Colin M. Tatz, *Aborigines in the Economy—Employment Wages and Training*, Brisbane, 1966; Leonard Broom, 'Educational Status of Aborigines', *The Australian and New Zealand Journal of Sociology*, Vol. 6, No. 2, October 1970, pp. 150-6; C. D. Rowley, 'Aboriginals in Australian Society' in H.R.H. Duke of Edinburgh's Third Commonwealth Study Conference, Commonwealth Department of Housing, 'Housing Aborigines in Australia', Minute Paper, 9 February 1968, mimeographed; Ian McKay, 'Housing for Aborigines in New South Wales', *Architecture in Australia*, June 1968, pp. 486-94; F. J. Schonell, L. G. Middleton and B. H. Watts, *School Attainments and Home Backgrounds of Aboriginal Children*, Brisbane, 1960. Some fascinating material on the emergency housing camps is in E. Hamilton-Smith, 'Community Development Among Socially Inadequate Families', *Australian Journal of Social Work*, Vol. 13, No. 1, June 1960, pp. 1-6. The Brotherhood of St Laurence described the emergency housing settlement at Camp Pell as '... one of the most serious aspects of our whole housing programme in Victoria. Originally an emergency measure it now threatens to become a permanent feature of the housing picture of this State—a government sponsored slum where through lack of official appreciation of the human problems of housing, the Government is gradually allowing many of Melbourne's problem families to congregate to the detriment of other families forced to live there' in Brotherhood of St Laurence, *What's Wrong with Victoria's Housing Programme?*, Melbourne, 1954. See also Brotherhood of St Laurence, 'Report on Family Service Project 1955-6', mimeographed, Melbourne 1956. The general inadequacies of the voluntary social welfare networks are discussed in R. J. Lawrence, *Community Service, Citizens and Social Welfare Organizations*, Melbourne, 1966. On the necessity to organize services along social group, client lines the basic source is F. Seebohm (ed.), *Report of the Committee on Local Authority and Allied Personal Social Services*, Cmd 3703, H.M.S.O., London, 1968. A good discussion of the tendency for bureaucracy to neglect difficult cases is in Jack Levin and G. Taube, 'Bureaucracy and the Socially Handicapped—A Study of Lower Status Tenants in Public Housing', *Sociology and Social Research,* Vol. 54, No. 2, January 1970, pp. 209-19. On the effectiveness of intensive counselling, see Henry Meyer, *Girls at Vocational High,* New York, 1965, and Gordon Brown (ed.), *The Multi-Problem Dilemma,* New Jersey, 1968, both of which come to pessimistic conclusions as to its worth and appear methodologically sound.

SLUM CLEARANCE

Two architect supporters of urban renewal are Robin Boyd, *The Australian Ugliness*, F. W. Cheshire, Melbourne, 1960, and Leslie M. Perrott, 'Report on Comprehensive Development Area—Carlton', three volumes, mimeographed, Melbourne, 1965. R. Jensen, a town planner, provides strong support in *High Density Living*, London, 1966. For a good summary of general support from most of the above groups see H. R. Petty, Minister for Housing, 'Slum Reclamation and Urban Redevelopment Conference', Melbourne Town Hall, Friday, 2 December 1960, mimeographed; also Brotherhood of St Laurence, 'What's Wrong with Victoria's Housing Programme: An Analysis of Some of Victoria's Housing Problems', Melbourne, mimeographed, 1954. There is fascinating reading on early VHC policy in Housing Investigation and Slum Abolition Board 1936-7, *First (Progress) Report with Appendices and Supplements, Slum Reclamation—Housing and the Lower Paid Worker*, Melbourne, 1937, and in the Annual Reports of the VHC from 1938 onwards. If the reader wants to get an understanding of how strongly the VHC is convinced that the slums and urban sprawl are spreading through Melbourne like a plague he should read *Report on Slum Reclamation and Urban Redevelopment of Melbourne Inner Suburban Areas*, H. R. Petty, Minister for Housing, Melbourne, 1960 (the Shaw-Davey Report was affixed to this report and was the basis of the policy outlined by Petty); also *The Enemy Within Our Gates—Report by the Victorian Housing Commission*, Melbourne, 1966. All of the figures on numbers of houses in need of demolition came from unpublished VHC statistics. John Roseth, 'The Extent, Progress and Location of Rehabilitation Activity in Paddington, Sydney', unpublished Ph.D. thesis, University of Sydney, 1968, is about the only important Australian study of the rehabilitation process in Australian cities. The British policy is outlined in *Old Houses into New Homes*, Cmd 3602, H.M.S.O., April 1968. A comparison of British and U.S. policy has been made by Joan Ash, 'Residential Rehabilitation in the U.S.A.', *Urban Studies*, Vol. 4, No. 1, 1967, pp. 22-40. For the VHC policy see *Annual Report of the* VHC *1956-7*. W. G. Grigsby makes the case for the necessity for some form of subsidy in his review of Martin Anderson, *The Federal Bulldozer*, Cambridge, 1964, in *Journal of Regional Science*, Vol. 6, No. 1, 1965, pp. 81-5. Rent control—the pegging of rents below free market levels—is recognized as a major cause of inadequate dwelling maintenance, see Richard F. Muth, *Cities and Housing—The Spatial Pattern of Urban Residential Land Use*, Chicago, 1969; Frank S.

Kristof, 'The Uses of Housing Quality Data in Public Policy Formation', *Proceedings of the American Statistics Association—Social Statistics Section*, Washington, 1968. Sternleib found that, in Newark, home ownership was associated with a high level of rehabilitation—see George Sternleib, *The Tenement Landlord*, New Jersey, 1966, p. 13; Michael A. Stegman, 'Slumlords and Public Policy', *Journal of the American Institute of Planners*, Vol. 33, No. 5, November 1967, pp. 419-23.

For a discussion of the complexity and high cost of relocating households when the power of eminent domain is not used see K. R. McInnes, 'Sydney University Expansion: Site Acquisition' in P. N. Troy (ed.), *Urban Redevelopment in Australia*, Canberra, 1967; D. R. Mandelker, 'Housing Codes, Building Demolition and Just Compensation: A Rationale for the Exercise of Public Powers over Slum Housing', *Michigan Law Review*, Vol. 67, No. 4, February 1969, pp. 635-78. There is an excellent review of the literature on the positive aspects of slum life in Marc Fried and Joan Levin, 'Some Social Functions of the Urban Slum', in B. J. Frieden and R. Morris, *Urban Planning and Social Policy*, New York, 1968. The high cost of VHC flats was determined from internal sources. There are other somewhat controversial statements by VHC leaders in the minutes of Executive Officers' Meetings (mimeographed). Stone has shown, based on extensive British data, that building costs for flats increase sharply with increases in the height of the building, particularly above 12 storeys —P. A. Stone, *Housing, Town Development Land and Costs*, London, 1963. The surplus in inner suburban water and sewerage systems is shown in N. M. Dunlop, 'Effects on Sydney's Water, Sewerage and Drainage Systems', in P. N. Troy (ed.), *Urban Redevelopment in Australia*, Canberra, 1967. The catastrophic effect of VHC redevelopment on Fitzroy is predicted, correctly it turned out, in *Report on the Community and Welfare Facilities in Fitzroy*, Victorian Council of Social Services, Melbourne, 1969. An example of the American attempt to alleviate poverty through economic and social methods is in U.S. Department of Housing and Urban Development, *Improving the Quality of Urban Life—A Program Guide to Model Neighbourhoods in Demonstration Cities*, Washington, 1967. For a discussion of the importance of comprehensiveness see J. Brian McLoughlin, *Urban and Regional Planning—A Systems Approach*, Praeger, New York, 1969.

AREA DEVELOPMENT

The early history of area development policies can be found in the Annual Reports of the Housing Commissions. The Royal Commission examining the WAHC criticized the granting of houses to 'key personnel', including government employees, in *Report of the Royal Commission on the State Housing Commission*, Perth, 1948. Nelson Lemmon, *Homes for Australia*, Canberra, 1949, is a useful summary of the Commonwealth policy, as is A. G. Warner, *Housing in Victoria*, Melbourne, 1949, of Victorian attitudes. Commonwealth and state parliamentary debates have much material on the imported housing programme, a sad story overall and probably an important reason why the Commonwealth did not want to have close controls over state policy. The early history of the SAHT is described in an article by H. C. Hogben, innovator in the establishment of the SAHT in 1936, and a key figure in the Trust until recent times—'Housing in South Australia', *The Australian Quarterly*, Vol. 19, December 1947, pp. 33-41; see also T. J. Mitchell and J. W. Wainwright, 'The Industrialisation of South Australia 1935-40', *Australian Journal of Politics and History*, Vol. 8, No. 1, January 1962, pp. 27-40. A very useful guide to the complexities of state politics is Colin A. Hughes and B. D. Graham, *A Handbook of Australian Government and Politics 1890-1964*, Canberra, 1968, pp. 127-37. K. W. Knight, *The Literature of State Budgeting in Australia, Canada and the United States—A Survey and Select Bibliography*, Brisbane, 1970, surveys basic budgeting methods.

HOME OWNERSHIP

An attempt to develop a set of criteria for public finance generally is Carl Shoup, *Public Finance*, New York, 1969. The Urban Research Unit's survey on Sydney's housing costs is in Max Neutze and Pat Troy, 'Household Composition in the Major Types of Dwellings', mimeographed, Urban Research Unit, A.N.U., 1969. Similar findings are in R. F. Henderson *People in Poverty*, Melbourne, 1970. The best source on 1909-45 public housing schemes for home ownership is the reports of the state banks. Commonwealth and state attitudes to home ownership are in the Premiers' Conferences and state and federal parliamentary debates. Spooner's views are summarized in his article called 'Why the Commonwealth Revised its Housing Policy' in the *Sydney Morning Herald*, 13 October 1955. For a more recent statement of the Spooner tradition see the four articles by Senator Dame Annabelle Rankin, Commonwealth Minister for Housing, 'Private Housing Finance', *Tasmanian Trade Protective Institute Trade Gazette*, Vol. 162, Nos 10, 11, 12, 13, March-April 1969. A good review of the literature on whether it is cheaper to rent or buy is John P. Shelton, 'The Cost of Renting Versus Owning a Home', *Land Economics*, Vol. 44, No. 1, February 1968, pp. 59-72. There are substantial indirect income tax gains from home ownership because of the failure to tax the imputed rent of owner-occupied dwellings, see Richard Goode, 'Imputed Rent of Owner-Occupied Dwellings Under the Income Tax', *Journal of Finance*, Vol. 15, No. 4, December 1960, pp. 504-30. A broad study of the home purchase decision is Irving Rosow, 'Home Ownership Motives', *American Sociological Review*, Vol. 13, No. 6, December 1948, pp. 751-6. State Housing Commission lending terms—and those for most other lending institutions—are in the Commonwealth Department of Housing, *Housing Finance—Terms and Conditions* (biennially). The literature on the effects of income changes on household consumption is reviewed in Martin Paldam, 'What is Known about the Housing Demand', *The Swedish Journal of Economics*, Vol. 72, No. 2, June 1970, pp. 130-48; James N. Morgan, 'Housing and Ability to Pay', *Econometrica*, Vol. 33, No. 2, April 1965, pp. 289-306. The connection betwen the life cycle, housing costs and income is discussed in David Donnison, *The Government of Housing*, London, 1967, and in Margaret Wynn, *Family Policy*, London, 1970. Useful sources on co-operatives are Commonwealth Department of Housing, *Housing Quarterly*, December 1969, Canberra, 1969; Malcolm Hill, 'Housing Finance Institutions', in R. R. Hirst and R. H. Wallace, *Studies in the Australian Capital Market*, Melbourne, 1967; E. T. Ebbels, R. F. Henderson and G. E. Knox, 'Report of the Co-operative Housing Committee of Review', mimeographed, Melbourne, 1968. Also Spooner, 'Why the Commonwealth Revised its Housing Policy', op. cit., and Dame Annabelle Rankin, 'Private Housing Finance', op. cit. The case for 'ballooning' mortgages is well presented in A. J. Merrett and Allen Sykes, *Housing Finance and Development*, London, 1965.

RENT POLICY

For details of the Dacey Gardens scheme see *Report of the Commonwealth Housing Commission, 1944*, Canberra, 1944. The quotes from Dacey, Stevens and Dedman are from the parliamentary debates of the time. A discussion of the market value of estimating the public housing subsidy is in Eugene Smolensky *et al.*, 'The Economics of Anti-Poverty Programs Involving Income in Kind; Phase 1: The Public Housing Case', Chicago, 1967, mimeographed. Edgar O. Olsen discusses the need to incorporate the costs of information collection into appraisals of public policy, in 'A Normative Theory of Transfers', *Public Choice*, Vol. VI, spring 1969, pp. 39-58. Details of rent systems in the Housing Commissions can be found in their Annual Reports, Housing Ministers' Conferences' minutes, the *Royal Commission into the* VHC *1956*, Melbourne, 1956, and the *Reports of the Commonwealth Grants Commission*, Canberra, 1945-68. R. L. Wettenhall, 'The Recoupment Concept in Public Enterprise', *Public Administration* (London), Vol. 44, No. 4, winter 1966, pp. 391-413, is a good survey of recoupment problems. An example of the SAHT's cost-consciousness is the emphasis placed on double-unit dwellings referred to in A. M. Ramsay, 'Housing Problems', *The Australian Quarterly*, Vol. 17, No. 4, December 1945, pp. 87-94; H. C. Hogben, 'Housing in South Australia', *The Australian Quarterly*, Vol. 19, No. 4, 1947, pp. 34-41. Peres discusses the idea of autonomy versus dependence in L. Peres, 'The Resurrection of Autonomy: Organization Theory and the Statutory Corporation', *Public Administration* (Sydney), Vol. 17, No. 4, December 1968, pp. 360-70. For a general discussion of the problems of achieving efficiency in non-profit institutions see Joseph P. Newhouse, 'Towards a Theory of Non-profit Institutions: An Economic Model of a Hospital', *American Economic Review*, Vol. 60, No. 1, March 1970, pp. 64-74. The assumption that day labour organizations are generally less efficient than other forms of construction is supported in Hamish Gray, *The Cost of Council Housing*, London, 1968. Gray produces extensive evidence to show that the day labour system in English public housing is inefficient, producing housing at a cost higher that could be achieved by private enterprise. The Commissions' experiments with prefabricated housing are listed in the minutes of the 1967 Executive Officers' Meeting, mimeographed. The necessity to include travelling costs in computing capacity to pay is stressed in F. G. Pennance and Hamish Gray, *Choice in Housing*, London, 1968, p. 44. A study that argues that as income increases a progressively smaller proportion of income is spent on housing costs is reported by Tong Hun Lee, 'Housing and Permanent Income: Tests based on a three-year re-interview study', *The Review of Economics and Statistics*, Vol. 50, No. 4, November 1968, pp. 480-90. The debate on this subject is summarized in Martin Paldam, 'What is Known about the Housing Demand', *The Swedish Journal of Economics*, Vol. 72, No. 2, June 1970, pp. 130-48.

SOCIAL EFFECTS

The importance of family centredness is shown in F. Stuart Chapin and Henry C. Hightower, 'Household Activity Patterns and Land Use', *JOAIP*, Vol. 31, No. 3, August 1965, pp. 222-31; John H. Goldthorpe, David Lockwood, Frank Beckhofer and Jennifer Platt, *The Affluent Worker in the Class Structure*, London, 1969 (they state that 'The majority of the manual and white collar couples do have in common a propensity to devote their spare time overwhelmingly to home and family and to limit their wider social contacts even to the point at which the family is in a state of near isolation'); Herbert J. Gans, *The Levittowners: Ways of Life and Politics in a New Suburban Community*, New York, 1967; David Scott and Robert U'Ren, *Leisure: a Social Enquiry into Leisure Activities and Needs in an Australian Housing Estate*, Melbourne, 1962. A good discussion of leisure patterns is Peter Willmott, 'Developing Patterns of Urbanization—Some Social Trends', *Urban Studies*, Vol. 6, No. 3, November 1969, pp. 298-9. A typical criticism of public housing in Australia is John Stubb's claim that the NSWHC large-scale development at Green Valley in Sydney is an 'income ghetto' into which the Commission has imported the 'culture of poverty', see *The Hidden People—Poverty in Australia*, Melbourne, 1966, pp. 128-30. An example of social area analysis in the Australian context is F. Lancaster Jones, *The Dimensions of Urban Social Structure—The Social Areas of Melbourne, Australia*, Canberra, 1969. Some general references on the homogeneity question are Susanne Keller, *The Urban Neighbourhood—A Sociological Perspective*, New York, 1968; Elizabeth Bott, *Family and Social Network*, London, 1957; Marc Fried and Peggy Gleicher, 'Some Sources of Residential Satisfaction in an Urban Slum', *JOAIP*, Vol. 27, No. 4, November 1961, pp. 305-15; Herbert J. Gans, *The Urban Villagers*, New York, 1962; Leonard Duhl (ed.), *The Urban Condition*, New York, 1963; Marc Fried, 'Functions of the Working Class Community in Modern Urban Society—Implications for Forced Relocation', *JOAIP*, Vol. 33, No. 2, March 1967, pp. 90-103; Melvin Webber, 'Order in Diversity: Community Without Propinquity', in L. Wingo (ed.), *Cities and Space*, Baltimore, 1963, pp. 25-56; Richard Meier, *A Communications Theory of Urban Growth*, Cambridge, 1962; Melvin Webber, 'Culture, Territoriality and the Elastic Mile', in H. Wentworth Eldredge, *Taming Megapolis*, Vol. 1, New York, 1967, pp. 35-53 (these studies are reviewed in Robert Gutman, 'Site Planning and Social Behavior', *Journal of Social Issues*, Vol. 2, No. 4, 1966, pp. 103-15); P. Collison, *The Cuttleslowe Walls—a Study in Social Class*, London, 1963; Peter Willmott, *The Evolution of a Community—a Study of Dagenham after 40 years*, London, 1963; Herbert J. Gans, 'The Balanced Community: Homogeneity and Heterogeneity in Residential Areas', *JOAIP*, Vol. 27, No. 3, August 1961, pp. 176-84; Peter Willmott, *Family and Class in a London Suburb*, London, 1960, p. 122; J. S. Coleman *et al.*, *Equality of Educational Opportunity*, Vol. 1, Washington, 1966; K. W. Deutsch, 'The Price of Integration', in P. Jacob and J. Toscano (eds), *The Integration of Political Communities*, New York, 1964, pp. 143-78; Terence Lee, 'Urban Neighbourhoods as a Socio-Spatial Scheme', *Human Relations*, Vol. 21, No. 3, 1968, p. 264 (Lee's studies of English housewives found that considerable population heterogeneity did not discourage friendship formation because each household was able to find enough similar friends close by); Irving Rosow, *The Social Integration of the Aged*, New York, 1967.

The disastrous state of American public housing is discussed in Lee Rainwater, 'The Lessons of Pruitt-Igoe', *The Public Interest*, No. 8, 1967, pp. 116-26; Gerald D. Suttles, *The Social Order of the Slum—Ethnicity and Territoriality in the Inner City*, Chicago, 1968. For a theoretical discussion of the idea of stigma see Simon Dinitz, Russel R. Dynes and Alfred C. Clarke, *Deviance—Studies in the Process of Stigmatization and Social Reaction*, New York, 1969, especially pp. 3-22. Also Erving Goffman, *Stigma—Notes on the Management of Spoiled*

Identity, New Jersey, 1963; Robert D. Katz, 'Intensity of Development and Livability of Multi-Family Housing Projects', 'USFHA Technical Study', TS 7.14, January 1963, summary in *Ekistics*, Vol. 17, No. 98, January 1964, pp. 59-66; E. D. Huttman, 'Stigma and Public Housing', Ph.D. thesis, Berkeley, 1969. The thesis itself was not available but its arguments are summarized in E. D. Huttman and J. P. Huttman, 'The Effect of Public Expenditure in Providing Adequate Housing for Low Income Families: A Comparative Socio-Economic Analysis of Programmes in Five Countries', *The Annals of Regional Science*, Vol. 4, No. 1, June 1970, pp. 123-36. Some useful references on the effects of flats on family life are Anne Stevenson, Elaine Martin and Judith O'Neill, *High Living—A Study of Family Life in Flats*, Melbourne, 1967; J. Maizels, *Two to Five in High Flats*, The Housing Centre, London, 1961; Anthea Holme and Peter Massie, *Childrens Play—A Study of Needs and Opportunities*, London, 1970; J. and R. Darke, *Health and Environment: High Flats*, London, 1970; D. M. Fanning, 'Families in Flats', *British Medical Journal*, 18 November 1967, pp. 382-6. The Australian versions of the criticism of outer public housing developments are D. N. Jeans and M. I. Logan, 'The Problems of Growth in Sydney's New Suburbs', *The Australian Journal of Social Issues*, Vol. 1, No. 1, spring, 1961, pp. 29-48 (p. 43); Mary McLelland, 'Needs and Services in an Outer Suburb', *The Australian Journal of Social Issues*, Vol. 3, No. 1, April 1968, pp. 44-62; Department of Social Work, *New Town Forum*, 25-26 September 1970, various papers, mimeographed. The time variable has been found to account for the apparent low level of sociability in public housing estates soon after settlement. Once the time factor is taken into account there does not appear to be much difference between stable public housing areas and other suburbs of similar socio-economic status—Peter Willmott, 'Social Research in New Communities', *JOAIP*, Vol. 33, No. 5, 1967, pp. 387-98. An interesting, sceptical survey of the achievements of new towns is William Alonso, 'The Mirage of New Town', *The Public Interest*, No. 19, spring 1970, pp. 3-17. A good statement of the case for new towns is F. J. Osborn and A. Whittick, *The New Towns—The Answer to Megapolis*, London, 1963. The information on the journeys to work in Elizabeth was obtained from unpublished CBCS data from the 1966 Census. The importance and extent of ethnic concentration can be found in F. Lancaster Jones, 'The Growth of an Ethnic Concentration—Italians in the Carlton Area', *Australian Journal of Politics and History*, Vol. 10, No. 2, August 1964, pp. 83-95; Trevor R. Lee, 'The Role of the Ethnic Community as a Reception Area for Italian Immigrants in Melbourne, Australia', *International Migration*, Vol. 8, No. 30, 1970, pp. 50-63. The report of the Bristol project in the United Kingdom is in John C. Spencer, N. Dennis and Joy Tuxford, *Stress and Release in an Urban Estate*, London, 1963.

POLICY CONCLUSIONS

The United States eviction study is Richard Lempert, 'Evictions from Public Housing—Effects of Independent Review', *American Sociological Review*, Vol. 35, No. 5, October 1970, pp. 852-60. Rent control is discussed in Leo Grebler, 'Implications of Rent Control—Experience in the United States', *International Labour Review*, Vol. 45, No. 4, April 1952, pp. 462-85; S. A. Lindbeck, 'Rent Control as an Instrument of Housing Policy', in Adela Adam Nevitt, *The Economic Problems of Housing*, London, 1967; Edgar O. Olsen, 'The Effects of a

Simple Rent Control Scheme in a Competitive Housing Market', Rand Corporation Staff Papers, P 4257, December 1969, mimeographed. For evidence that rent control can redistribute income from the needy, particularly aged landlords, to those capable of paying free market rents see John Greve, *Private Landlords in England*, London, 1965. This is not to argue that all landlords are needy and all tenants wealthy, but rent control does tend to distribute the subsidy in a random fashion. Rent control in New South Wales, the state where it has been of the greatest importance, is summarized in *Report of the Royal Commission of Enquiry on the Landlord and Tenant Act 1948, as amended October 1961*, Sydney, 1961. See also John Barry Cullingworth, *Housing in Transition—A Case Study of the City of Lancaster, 1958-62*, London, 1963; Richard F. Muth, *Housing and Cities—The Spatial Pattern of Urban Residential Land Use*, Chicago, 1969, where Muth argues that rent-controlled areas possess the largest number of poorly maintained dwellings. The housing subsidy system has been used in West Germany and the United States. For the United States programmes see Edgar O. Olsen, 'A Competitive Theory of the Housing Market', *American Economic Review*, Vol. 59, No. 4, part 1, September 1969, pp. 612-22. For the West German scheme see F. G. Pennance and Hamish Gray, *Choice in Housing*, Institute of Economic Affairs, 1968, p. 77; Edgar O. Olsen, 'A Welfare Economic Evaluation of Public Housing—A Normative Analysis', Ph.D. thesis, Rice University, 1968. For a pessimistic viewpoint see John Bruce Lindeman, 'Economic Effects of Low Income Housing Subsidies upon the Housing Market', Ph.D. thesis, Duke University, Ann Arbor, 1968. An empirical, but indeterminate, study of the feasibility of housing allowances is Eugene Smolensky, 'Public Housing or Income Supplements—The Economics of Housing the Poor', *JOAIP*, Vol. 34, No. 2, March 1968, pp. 94-101. A discussion of the various types of income subsidies is in Robert Theobald, *The Guaranteed Minimum Income—Next Step in Socio-Economic Evolution*, New York, 1967; Gans argues that income supplements would lead to problems in work incentives for those doing the 'dirty' jobs in our society in Herbert J. Gans, 'Income Grants and "Dirty Work"', *The Public Interest*, No. 6, 1967, pp. 110-13; James C. Vadakin, 'A Critique of the Guaranteed Income', *The Public Interest*, No. 11, 1968, pp. 53-66. Michael Young, 'Distribution of Income Within the Family', *British Journal of Sociology*, Vol. 3, 1952, pp. 305-21, discusses the claim that the poor spend money on luxuries.

INDEX

This index includes the first-named author of each source included in the bibliographic essay.